The Pictorial History of
AUSTRALIAN
HORSE RACING

The Pictorial History of
AUSTRALIAN HORSE RACING

By Jack Pollard

PAUL HAMLYN
Sydney London New York Toronto

PUBLISHED BY PAUL HAMLYN PTY. LTD.
176 SOUTH CREEK ROAD, DEE WHY WEST,
NEW SOUTH WALES, 2099.

© COPYRIGHT PAUL HAMLYN PTY. LTD. 1971.

FIRST PUBLISHED 1971
PRINTED BY LEE FUNG, HONG KONG.
ISBN O 600 04142 5
EDITOR: JENNIFER ROWE
RESEARCH: WENDY LEHANE
DESIGN: IAN WOOD.

CONTENTS

ACKNOWLEDGEMENTS

Pictorial material for this book has come from many libraries, art galleries, newspapers and private collections. We are most grateful for help given by the following people and organizations.

Australian Jockey Club
Victoria Racing Club, Melbourne
Victoria Amateur Turf Club
South Australian Jockey Club
Tasmanian Racing Club
Mitchell Library, Library of New South Wales
La Trobe Collection, State Library of Victoria
National Library of Australia
Collection: The Art Gallery of South Australia
Ballarat Art Gallery
Swan Hill Folk Museum
Herald and Weekly Times Ltd.
The Age
The Mercury
West Australian Newspapers Ltd.
Windsor Photography Ltd., New Zealand
2GB Macquarie, Sydney
Tourist Development Authority of Victoria
Ministry of Tourism, Victoria
Racecourse Hotel, Flemington, Victoria
Ern McQuillan, Photographic Illustrators
The Honourable J. C. Maddison, B.A., LL.B., M.L.A., Minister of Justice for New South Wales
D. L. Bernstein
Douglas Barrie
Sir Daryl Lindsay
Dr Clifford Craig
Darby McCarthy
J. M. Royds
Pictorial material was also taken from:

The Australasian Sketcher	*The Sydney Sun*
The Australian Turf Register	*The Argus*
The Illustrated Australian News	*The Queensland Figaro*
The Leader	*Punch*
The Sydney Mail	

In particular the publishers would like to thank Mr D. Whitford of the A.J.C. and Mr C. Bennetts of the V.R.C. for their valuable assistance in the preparation of this book.

PREFACE

Horse racing is a universal sport conducted with varying degrees of decorum. Nowhere in the world has it been as colourful, down-to-earth, and demonstrative as in Australia. Fine horses and skilful riders have enjoyed special respect since Australia began. Committees have attempted to transplant the sophistication of the old world race meetings to Australia, but outside the race club rooms, fashion parades, and refined fraternization of the well-heeled, the Australian racegoer has always retained the right to vocal protest when the performance of horse or rider falls below past form.

After listening to an Australian race crowd demonstrate its discontent when a well-fancied horse and rider sadly disappoint, visits to overseas racecourses are almost eerie because of the silence when the same thing occurs. This does not mean that Australian race clubs do not exert proper control. Indeed, horse racing is conducted in Australia under tighter control than anywhere else in the world. Our racing administrators also have to deal with the smartest, most persistent cheats in racing.

The history of horse racing in Australia shows up an ingenious, repetitive flair for crookedness. It's the give-it-a-go sport when you are broke, the caper that contributes more than any other sport to charities, and pays out most generously to 'brokies'. Some claim it is dominated by Irish catholics, others that it is the refuge of those who refuse to work in legitimate vocations, and a few more that it is controlled by wealthy breeders and owners.

It is not the intention of this book to arbitrate on any of these issues. We seek simply to tell the exciting story of Australian horse racing since the early days, telling the story as it has happened and leaving the reader to make up his or her own mind.

JACK POLLARD

1. THE BEGINNINGS

There were no horses in Australia before the white man. The Aboriginal race, which since has become so skilled in horse handling, existed without them. Governor Phillip brought with him when he landed at Sydney in January 1788, a stallion, three mares and three yearlings which he obtained when the first fleet stopped for supplies at the Cape of Good Hope on the voyage from England. A convict herdsman allowed these horses to stray from the restricted confines of the settlement and it is doubtful if all were recovered. By 1793 only the stallion and one mare survived.

At this time the settlement was restricted to the narrow strip of land between the Pacific Ocean and the Blue Mountains, but the value of horses to the settlers as they struggled hard for existence became increasingly important. In 1794 more horses were brought in, and in 1795 a shipment of twenty-nine mares, three fillies and one stallion were imported from the Cape of Good Hope. They were not first-class stock but the good stallions and mares that did arrive were used to progressively improve each generation. By 1798 there were 117 horses in the colony, seventy-three of them mares.

In 1799 the first real step to improve the breed of horses in the colony was made, with the importation from Cape Colony of the English-bred Rockingham, later sometimes known as Young Rockingham. Dr W.H. Lang, who researched the subject for an early book, *The Racehorse in Australia,* considered it likely that Rockingham was by another Rockingham, a stallion which was covering in England about this period, but not the Rockingham mentioned in the pedigree of Doncaster.

Dr Lang recorded that a blood horse called Washington was imported from America in 1802, the same year that the ship *Buffalo* brought the first stallion to be imported direct from England to the colony. This was Northumberland, a superior quality stallion, who was accompanied by a splendid, but unnamed, mare. These arrivals enabled the 'breeding-

pages 8-9 : A lively illustration, showing the start of an early race, which appeared in the final New South Wales Sporting Magazine of 1848. The horses depicted are Slasher and Highflyer.

left : An explorer and his horse. Blaxland, Lawson and Wentworth, who crossed the Blue Mountains in 1813, were convinced of the value of well-bred horses and used the best they could find. This is considered to be an important reason for the success of their expedition. Mitchell

up' process to begin in earnest and today there are nineteen families with colonial taproots that are accepted by the *Australian Stud Book,* which are not traceable to a mare in the *English Stud Book.*

Some outstanding Arab horses were also imported from Persia by way of India, including Hector, Model and Satellite, all of which produced tough saddle horses that ideally suited the needs of the colony, if not the racetrack. Indeed by the time of the first official Australian race meeting in Sydney's Hyde Park in 1810, Arab horses predominated. Hector was probably the most popular of them and many horse-owners named their animals after him.

Officers of the 73rd Regiment organized that first three-day race meeting in Hyde Park, and although there had been earlier meetings at Parramatta and among Hawkesbury River settlers, it was the first to receive government approval. The *Sydney Gazette* in September 1810, announced the meeting: 'The Races commence on Monday the 15th October, and will continue until the Friday following with omission of the Tuesday and Thursday. The course has been completed at a very considerable expense and is esteemed a very fine one. Several handsome plates and other elegant presents, among which is a Silver Cup of 50 guineas value, given by the Ladies of the Colony, are to be contended for by the horses of Subscribers to the Race Course; and a Purse of 50 guineas will be given by the Magistrates of the Colony, free for all horses, to be run for on the last day.'

The historic first race at the Hyde Park meeting was run over three heats of two miles each, with the same field facing the starter each time. The winner was the horse with best results in the three heats. The Hyde Park course, and its immediate successor at Woollahra, were both fashioned for clockwise racing, and this had a major effect on the whole future of racing in Australia, where today horses run clockwise in Queensland and New South Wales, and anti-clockwise in the other states. According to the rules

right: 'The Portraiture of Sir Charles Sidley's Bay Gelding True Blew—Taken from the Life.' A.J.C.

of the meeting, horses which at the end of each race had not reached the distance pole, which signified the finishing straight and was placed just over a furlong from home, were judged to have been 'distanced' by the first horse home and could not start in subsequent heats. Another interesting condition of the first Hyde Park meeting was that under the rules framed by a committee of the 73rd Regiment, committee members' servants were not permitted to train their horses over the course beforehand.

The winner of the first race was Captain Ritchie's grey gelding Chase, offspring of an Arab sire and a Cape-bred mare. This first race meeting also produced perhaps the heaviest three days drinking in the colony's brief history, a tradition Australian racegoers have worked very hard to sustain ever since. Labourers, who were excused from work over the three days, found it difficult to carry out the Governor's wish that they conduct themselves in a sober and orderly manner. Two slap-up balls were staged during the carnival and another not so lavish affair for the nights of each racing day. Warnings that dogs found on the course would be shot were issued but this did not prevent D'Arcy Wentworth's grey Gig from being brought down by a dog on the last day.

The balls left all who attended delighted. Ticket-of-leave men and lackeys were left badly hung over by their sessions in the taverns, and altogether horse racing had a lusty launching in Australia. An aged black horse named Scratch rounded off a wholly successful meeting by winning the Magistrates' Purse, with the winning owner receiving the prize from the Governor's wife. The patterns of conduct associated with racing in England had been successfully transplanted in the colony, and the Hyde Park race meetings remained the highlight of the social year until 1813, the year of another highly significant event in the history of Australian horses.

For in 1813 Blaxland, Lawson and Wentworth crossed the Blue Mountains, opening up the vast land beyond the narrow strip of coastline on which the colony had struggled so precariously for survival. They did so partly because of the four horses and five dogs they took with them, all of which showed a

RACING KALENDAR.

SECOND DAY,

Wednefday. 14th of August, 1811.—To Start at One o'Clock.

A CUP, Value 50 Guineas, given by the LADIES of the Colony, will be run for by Horfes of ALL Ages belonging to the Subfcribers to the SYDNEY RACE COURSE, carrying Weight for Age, viz.

3 Yrs old to carry 7 st. 4lbs. 6 Yrs old to carry 9 st. 10lbs.
4 Yrs old .... 8 st. Aged .... 10st.
5 Yrs old .... 8 st. 10lbs.

Horses Entered	Colour	Age	Weight carried St. lbs.	Rider	Dress	Owners	Heats 1 2 3
Strawberry	Roan G.	6 yrs		Phil. Macdermot	White, blue facings, cap the same	Mr. Williams	
Tipsey	Bay G.	4 yrs		James Reynolds	Pink, blue facings, cap the same	Mr. Lord	
Flying Ben	Bay G.	4 yrs		....	....	Mr. Bayly	
Chace	Grey G.	aged		....	....	Captain Ritchie	
Scratch	Bl. H.	aged		Thomas Lucer	Pink jacket, white sleeves, black cap	Major Cleaveland	
Carlo	Bl. H.	3 yrs		John Fisher	All black	Colonal O'Connell	
Match'em	Ch. G.	6 yrs		Thomas Atkins	Sky blue jacket, yel. sleeves & cap	Mr. Bent	
Miss Bessy	Bay M.	3 yrs		Thomas Young	Orange jacket, purple sleeves and cap	Lieutenant Ovens	
Hawkesb'ry	B. H.	4 yrs		....	....	Captain Piper	
Gig	Bay G.	4 yrs		....	....	Dr. Wentworth	
Monmouth	Bay G.			....	....	Captain Cameron	

MATCHES.

A PONEY RACE (catch weight) for 10 Guineas each, will be run by the following Horses:

Lieutenant Ovens b. p. Fermagh—Rider, Young Reynolds—Dress, orange jacket, purple sleeves and cap
Lieutenant Maclean's b. p. Whiskey Mr. James Cox's ch Fidget.

A RACE for HACKS, open to all Horses, for a Saddle and Bridle, given by the Subscribers. The best of three one-mile Heats—The Horses to be entered at the Starting Post.

Defcription of Monday's Races.

FOR THE PLATE.

top left : A nineteenth century engraving of 'Herod: a famous running horse'. From the early 1830s there was a sharp increase in the number of English-bred horses imported into the colony—local owners were convinced of the superiority of English blood over Arab. A.J.C.

far left : Titled simply An Arab, this old engraving shows one of the horses imported from Persia in the early years of the colony.

left : Arthur Phillip, the first governor of New South Wales. He obtained the first horses to be brought to Australia at the Cape of Good Hope during the voyage from England.

above : The card for the second day of an early race meeting in the colony.

mastery of rough country. Lawson and Wentworth had a keen knowledge of horses and were ardent supporters of the first Sydney race meetings. They used the best horses they could find and in crossing the mountains with them they opened up important new uses for all Australian horses, which in turn benefited the sport of horse racing. Early crossings of the mountains by settlers located brumby herds, the progeny of strays from those early importations which had found their way through the mountains ahead of the white man.

The following year, 1814, the Reverend Samuel Marsden introduced horses for the first time into New Zealand when he sailed into the Bay of Islands from Sydney. White whaling crews had operated from New Zealand from 1769 when Captain Cook charted the country, but Marsden was the first to take horses there. Thus Australian horse racing had a big start on the sport in New Zealand. But from 1843 when Hercules, a champion stayer bred in Australia, was sent to New Zealand and started New Zealand importation of superior stallions, New Zealand horses have always had a big influence on Australian horse racing. It was Australian blood which gave New Zealand bloodstock breeding it first boost, but many of the most successful horses and horsemen in Australia since then have come from New Zealand.

The Maoris were very hard to convince concerning the merits of horses. When one of their leaders, Duaterra, visited Port Jackson and returned home with accounts of the horses he had seen his countrymen ridiculed him. J.L. Nicholas in his *Voyage To New Zealand*, tells the story: 'Having no name in his language for this animal, Duaterra thought that "corraddee", *(Kararehe)*, their term for a dog, would be the best designation he could adopt; but as they could not elevate their ideas of it to the same height as his description they believed not a single word he said. On telling them that he had seen large "corraddees" carry men and women about in land canoes (meaning carriages) they would put their fingers in their ears to prevent themselves from listening to him, and desire him very indignantly not to tell so many lies. A few of them, however, more curious

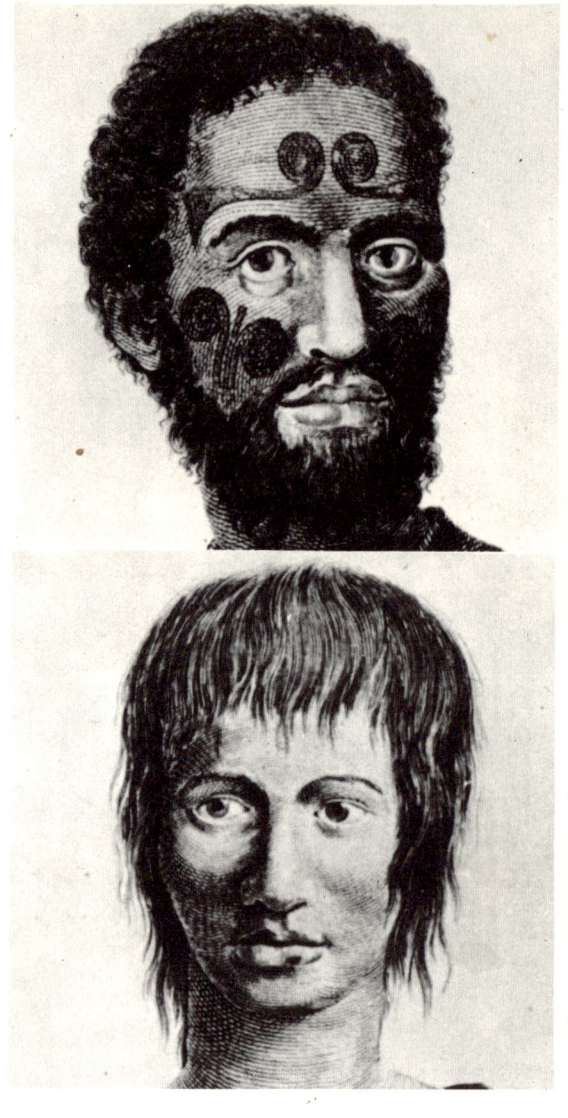

above : Late eighteenth century engravings of a man and woman of New Zealand. Horses were unknown by the Maoris until 1814. Mitchell

right : Victorious, another well-known English race horse of the nineteenth century. A strong appreciation of the value of good breeding was passed on from England to the colony of New South Wales. In 1799 the first step to improve the breed of horses in the colony was made with the importation of the English-bred stallion Rockingham. A.J.C.

top right : Forbury Park racecourse, Dunedin, New Zealand. Imported Australian horses gave New Zealand bloodstock breeding its first boost, but since then New Zealand horses have had a tremendous effect on Australian racing.

than the rest, to prove his veracity, would mount
upon the backs of their pigs, saying they must be more
fit for the purpose of riding than the "corraddees";
and, endeavouring to gallop them about in the style
of European horsemanship, they quickly tumbled into
the dirt, and became quite as incredulous as their
sceptical companions.'

Duaterra was vindicated when Marsden arrived in
the Bay of Islands. Marsden rode up and down the
beach; astonishing the Maoris. To quote Nicholas
again: 'To see a man seated on the back of such an
animal they thought the strangest thing in nature, and
following him with staring eyes they believed at the
moment that he was more than mortal.'

After four big annual race meetings in Hyde Park
the sport suffered a setback in March 1814, when the
73rd Regiment was transferred to Ceylon and took
with it the first race committee. For almost six years,
racing in the colony lapsed, and contests between
horses were confined to races out on the roads watched
by spectators who kept up with events by riding after
the contestants in carriages or on horseback. Side bets
were sometimes substantial, and for many of the
underprivileged, the desire to become a good rider,
breaker or groom came very stong.

That most diligent of researchers into Australian
horse racing history, Douglas M. Barrie, records that
many of these early unofficial tests between good
horses had colour which some might think today's
races lack. Horse races were interspersed with cock
fights ('a main of cocks') wheelbarrow races between
blindfolded competitors, three-card men, Aunt Sallys.
The idea, like that behind the Epsom Derby, was to
make the horse races the feature events of a fair.

Barrie has discovered that in 1816 a public subscription was taken up to re-establish Hyde Park,
which had been badly cut up by heavy wood carts, as
a racing surface. On 31 May 1819, a four-race programme was held in Hyde Park, and Mr Emmett's
four-year-old black Rob Roy won the main event, in
his first start. Speedy, who won an event for ponies,
won for his owner the rich prize of a London-made
saddle and bridle.

As an outcome of his first-up success Rob Roy ran

top left : The 73rd Regiment leaves New South Wales. The departure of the troops caused a break in the development of racing in the colony, because the officers of the regiment were responsible for most of the organization of early race meetings.

left : A settler strikes at a wild dog which has attacked his horse.

above : The racing trophy won by Mr Emmett's four-year-old Rob Roy at the first Australian race meeting to be organized by civilians. The meeting was held in 1819 in Hyde Park. This trophy is in the possession of Mr J.M. Royds, of Sydney.

in a series of match races against Mulberry, an 'old standard horse'. The conduct of these races aroused the ire of Governor Lachlan Macquarie who issued an edict banning unauthorised race meetings, because they had degenerated into outlets for low gambling and general misconduct. Macquarie relented to permit a re-run match between Mulberry and Rob Roy, both heats of which were won by Rob Roy, who went on to confirm that he was the best horse of the period by winning the 1820 Subscription Cup, and the 1821 Silver Cup.

In 1821, Sir Thomas Brisbane succeeded Macquarie as governor, briefed to carry out the reforms suggested by Commissioner Bigge. It could be argued that Brisbane's reforms made the colony a more attractive place for lawful young Britons, but Bigge objected to the social intercourse which went with horse racing and Brisbane banned the sport for a time, preferring not to be told of unauthorised meetings out at Hawkesbury. His attitude meant the end of racing in Sydney's Hyde Park.

On St Patrick's Day, 1825, the sport revived, with an officially recognized meeting somewhere between Bellevue Hill and Woollahra at what was known as Captain Piper's racecourse. This was right at the hub of one of the major centres of road match races. The five-race programme was so successful that Governor Brisbane next day agreed to become patron of the first Australian racing club, the Sydney Turf Club, which sometimes was also referred to as the Australian Turf Club. The new club's first meeting was held on 25 and 26 April 1825, when a bay called Junius won the major races on both days.

In September 1825, the club made the first attempt to produce a close finish by regulating the weights horses carried according to their merit. This first handicap race was won by Captain, which carried 7 st 12 lb in a field of twenty. But it was Junius, from a Hector mare by an Arab stallion, which established himself as the colony's outstanding racehorse by winning both the Town Purse and Town Plate. Junius confirmed his reputation by winning Governor Brisbane's Cup at the S.T.C. meetings in 1826 and 1827, after which his owner, Mr W. Nash, issued a

top: W.C. Wentworth, an ardent supporter of early race meetings, had a keen knowledge of good horses and an appreciation of good breeding. He became S.T.C. president in 1832.

above: Sir Thomas Brisbane who succeeded Macquarie as governor. At first he frowned upon racing, but eventually relented and in 1825 put the official stamp of approval on the sport by becoming patron of the Sydney Turf Club.

top right, right: A pair of old engravings—'Going to Botany' and 'Returning from Botany'—graphically illustrate the sad change in spirits often brought about by a day at the races. Botany was the starting point for the first Australian steeplechase event.

challenge to any horse in the colony for £1,000-a-side. There were no takers.

At a Sydney Turf Club dinner in 1827 Robert Waddell and W.C. Wentworth made speeches which the new governor, Darling, claimed insulted him. Darling withdrew his patronage from the S.T.C. and public servants in the club resigned, forming a new club, the Australian Racing and Jockey Club. The new club held successful meetings at Parramatta and this adversely affected the S.T.C., but despite an obituary notice in the *Sydney Gazette* the S.T.C. carried on for years. Wentworth was elected S.T.C. president in 1832.

Some historians believe that some of the privations which plagued early Australian explorers may have been prevented if they had had the same regard for good breeding in selecting their horses as had Lawson and Wentworth. They cite many examples of exploration mishaps caused by ill-bred horses and contrast these with the hardihood of mounts of proven colonial-bred stock. Exacting conditions culled the weak from the strong in the imported English stock, and a temperate climate and sunlit pastures gave this stock the great heart and constitution required to fully explore such a demanding country as Australia.

By then the first important studmasters had appeared, with Charles Smith at Doonside on the outskirts of Sydney, Dr D'Arcy Wentworth at Homebush, and John Macarthur at Camden among the leaders in establishing reputable breeding farms. From the early 1830s there was a sharp increase in the number of English-bred horses imported. Local owners were convinced of their superiority over Arabs but the Arab strains still survive today, and are accepted by the *Australian Stud Book*.

In 1832, the first Australian steeplechase event was staged over five miles between the Sydney suburbs of Botany and Coogee. In the same year the Hawkesbury Racing Club was founded and work began on Randwick racecourse. The first race on the course

right : Overlanders rounding up a straggler. Intelligent, nimble stockhorses were invaluable companions of the Australian pioneers, and many early racehorses, including the mighty Jorrocks, began their careers working in the bush.

was a private match between horses owned by Thomas Smithers and Edward Fagan. The first Randwick meeting was held in the spring of 1833, with Whisker winning the Governor's Cup. Whisker was a son of the Whisker which had won the English Derby in 1815 and whose ancestors included the great sire Eclipse.

Whisker had been mated in 1832 with Matilda, an outstanding race mare in the colony, and this mating in October of 1833 produced the great 'iron horse', Jorrocks. Matilda was a daughter of the English sire Steeltrap, which, like Whisker, traced back to Eclipse. Jorrocks was not broken until he was four years old, and was used at first as a stock horse in the Barwon River district. He had his first race as a five-year-old, but did not begin serious racing until he was rising eight years old. He changed hands so many times his precise record is obscure but he is known to have started at least eighty-eight times and won sixty races. He was placed twenty-four times. Most of these races were over two or three miles, he never carried less than 9 st, and he had to walk to race meetings from his training stable in Windsor. He was leading stake winner in New South Wales eight times, and lived until he was twenty-seven years old. Today there is a plinth marking his grave at Richmond airbase. Jorrocks was part Arab—on his mother's side. But with his retirement the influence of Arab horses on racing in the colony gradually waned. By the time the Australian Jockey Club was founded in January 1842, the Arabs had lost their dominance to English-bred horses.

One of the first acts of the A.J.C. was to make jockeys' costumes compulsory. The club held its first meetings at the Homebush course in September 1842 and raced there until 1859. Cossack, a chestnut by the locally-bred sire Sir Hercules, achieved wide popularity by winning the Queen's Plate at Homebush in both 1851 and 1852.

The A.J.C. moved to Randwick in 1860 and held its first meeting there in May. On the last day of the three-day meeting Mr G. T. Rowe's chestnut gelding Veno, which had won the A.J.C. Plate in 1857, distinguished himself by beating the New Zealand horse Strop for the Australian Plate. The A.J.C.

Death,

This morning, at Parramatta, after a lingering illness, **The Turf Club**, to the great grief of its few friends and supporters, and to the inexpressible regret of its creditors. The interment of **The Body** will take place in the afternoon, and move from Nash's Inn after the cloth is removed. The mourners, and only friends of the deceased, will wear a long sable train for the remainder of their lives, in commemoration of the death of their earliest prop and only friend.

BIRTH,

This morning, at Parramatta, to the gratification of the whole Colony, THE AUSTRALIAN RACING AND JOCKEY CLUB came into the world. The infant is as fine a looking an animal as could have been produced since January last. We have no doubt this hopeful scion will "ADVANCE AUSTRALIA."

top left : Parties of gentlemen leave for the Homebush races. From the beginning, racing was a popular sport in New South Wales, and important racing events became the highlights of the social year.

left : A sketch of the great 'iron horse' Jorrocks, an ex-stockhorse which was leading stake winner in New South Wales eight times. He was part Arab, and with his death in 1860 the Arab influence on Australian racing began to wane. A.J.C.

above : A column of the Sydney Gazette, showing the obituary notice inserted for the Sydney Turf Club as a practical joke in 1827. Despite the notice, the Turf Club carried on for many years, although the successful activities of its rival, the Australian Racing and Jockey Club, the birth of which was announced in conjunction with the obituary notice, did adversely affect it.

has remained the most powerful club in Australian racing, and from its Sydney headquarters has administered the *Australian Stud Book* since it first appeared in 1878. The club played a major role in establishing 1 August as the common birthday for Australian racehorses and in securing uniform rules on the registration of clubs, the licensing of trainers and jockeys, and the appointment of stewards. But the most important Australian horse race escaped its control.

HOMEBUSH RACES.

SEPTEMBER MEETING, 1842.

FIRST DAY, TUESDAY, 20TH.

THE CHAMPION CUP of One Hundred Sovereigns, with a Sweepstakes of Ten Sovereigns each, five forfeit if declared; Heats, Twice Round and a Distance; Weight for Age.

Mr. C. Smith's ch g Eclipse..............Black Jacket and White Cap
Mr. C. Roberts' b f Quail ....Scarlet Jacket and Black Cap
Sir J. Jamison's b c Sir Charles........Blue and Yellow Jacket and Black Cap
Mr. Rouse's b g Jorrocks ....Red Jacket and Black Cap

TWO YEAR OLD STAKES of Ten Sovereigns each, five forfeit if declared, with Thirty Sovereigns added from the Fund; Once Round; Colts, 8st.; Fillies, 7st. 11lbs.

Mr. C. Roberts' br c President ....Scarlet Jacket and Black Cap
Mr. Hunter's b f Marchioness ....Black Jacket and Crimson Cap
Mr. Abercrombie's b c Mozart ....Pink Jacket and Black Cap

AUSTRALIAN STAKES of Ten Sovereigns each, five forfeit if declared, with Fifty Sovereigns added from the Fund; Heats, Once Round; Weight for Age.

Mr. J. Pye's bk g Tommy Tickle ....Blue Jacket and Black Cap
Mr. C. Smith's ch h Tranby................Black Jacket and White Cap
Mr. C. Roberts' b h Eucalyptus ....Scarlet Jacket and Black Cap
Mr. Letsom's ch g Prince....................White Jacket and Black Cap

MAIDEN PLATE of Twenty-five Sovereigns, with a Sweepstakes of Five Sovereigns each added; One Mile and a Half; Weight for Age.

Mr. C. Smith's b h Chillington ....Black Jacket and White Cap
Mr. C. Roberts' b f Fancy ....Scarlet Jacket and Black Cap
Mr. W. Russell's b f Lady Jane..............Yellow Jacket and Black Cap
Mr. Oatley's b c Little Wonder ....Blue Jacket and Purple Cap

STEWARDS:
CAPTAIN BUSH; MR. LAWSON; MR. ICELY.

JUDGE—MAJOR HUNTER.

Clerk of the Course—MR. WAY.

W. HUNTER, Hon. Sec.

PRINTED AT THE "SYDNEY GAZETTE" OFFICE,
By Richard Sanderson, Proprietor.

far left: The A.J.C., founded in 1842, held its first meeting in the September of that year at the Homebush course. It continued to race there until 1859, and in 1860 moved to Randwick where its premises have been ever since.

centre left: Settlers who followed the explorers across the Blue Mountains found herds of brumbies, the progeny of strays from the colony. Brumby herds still roam the Australian countryside, often to be rounded up and used as stockhorses on large properties.

left: Charles Darling, the seventh governor of New South Wales. In 1827 Darling withdrew his patronage from the Sydney Turf Club because he claimed that he had been insulted by its members. This led to the formation of the Australian Racing and Jockey Club by public servants who resigned from the Turf Club in protest.

above: A view of Randwick racecourse in 1876. The first Randwick meeting was held in the spring of 1833, and the A.J.C. moved to the course in 1860.

HOMEBUSH RACES, 1851.

Stewards:

Captain Fitz Roy, R. A., Arthur T. Holroyd, Esq., Hon. E. Deas Thomson.

Judge:—Samuel Raymond, Esq.　　Clerk of the Course:—S. Samuel, Esq.

THIRD DAY, FRIDAY, MAY 30.

FIRST RACE.

THE GRAFTON STAKES of Three Sovereigns each, with Twenty-five Sovereigns added, for two-year-olds, T.Y.C., about half a mile. Colts, 8st. 7lbs. ; Fillies, 8st. 4lbs. The winner of the Trial Stakes to carry 7lbs. extra. Entrance, One Pound Five Shillings. *To start at half-past 12 o'clock.*

1. Mr. Outts ns. gr. c. **Vapour,** - - - - - - - - - tartan jacket and black cap.
2. Mr. De Clouet's br. c. **Surplice,** - - - - - - - - blue jacket and black cap.
3. Mr. Hall's ns. b. f. **Georgiana,** - - - - - - - - red jacket and black cap.
4. Mr. Holroyd's gr. c. **Vaccination,** - - - - - purple jacket and orange cap.
5. Mr. J. Robert's b. f. **Bessy Bedlam,** - - - - - - blue jacket and black cap.
6. Mr. T. Roberts' b. c. **Vanguard,** - - - - - - light blue jacket and red cap.

SECOND RACE.

THE QUEEN'S PLATE of One Hundred Sovereigns (without any deduction), for all horses. Two-year-olds to carry 5st. 12lbs ; three, 7st. 2lbs.; four, 9st. 2lbs.; five, 10st.; six and aged, 10st. 4lbs. Mares and Geldings allowed 3lbs. Three miles. Entrance, Two Sovereigns. *To start at 1 o'clock.*

1. Mr. Hillas' br. g. **Muleyson,** aged, - - - - - - green and white.
2. Mr. Arkin's ns. b. g. **Jorrocks,** aged, - - - - black jacket and red cap.
3. Mr. Ward's gr. f. **Sappho,** 3 yrs., - - - - green jacket and black cap.
4. Mr. Holcomb's ch. m. **Queen of Hearts,** 4 yrs., - - blue jacket and cap.
5. Mr. Minchan's b. g. **Bay Lottery,** 6 yrs., - - green jacket and blue cap.
6. Mr. De Clouet's ch. h. **Little John,** aged, - - - blue jacket and black cap.
7. Mr. Matthews' gr. g. **Almack,** aged, - - - - tartan jacket and black cap.
8. Mr. Reeve's ch. c. **Lieutenant,** 3 yrs. - - - green jacket and blue cap.
9. Mr. King's b. m. **Vanity,** 5 yrs., - - - - - red jacket and black cap.
10. Mr. Johnstone's br. c. **Rubens,** 3 yrs., - - plaid jacket and blue sleeves.
11. Mr. Gorrick's b. c. **Waxford** 3 yrs. - - - green jacket and blue cap.
12. Mr. Harris' b. h. **Plover,** aged, - - - - tartan jacket and white cap.
13. Mr. J. Roberts bl. g. **Jim-along-Josey,** 3 yrs., - - blue jacket and black cap.
14. Mr. J. Roberts' br. c. **Plover,** 3 yrs., - - - blue jacket and black cap.
15. Mr. Tait's ch. h. **Cossack,** 4 yrs., - - - black jacket and black cap.

THIRD RACE.

THE LADIES' PURSE of Forty Sovereigns, added to a sweepstakes of Five Sovereigns each, for all horses; weight for age. Maidens at the time of entrance allowed 5lbs. Once round the course. Entrance, Two Sovereigns. *To start at half-past 1 o'clock.*

1. Mr. Arkins' ns. c. g. **Volunteer,** 5 yrs., 9 st. - - - black jacket and red cap.
2. Mr. Lowe's ch. f. **Moss Rose,** 4 yrs., 8 st. 6 lbs. - - sky-blue jacket and purple cap.
3. Mr. Johnstone's b. h. **Euclid,** 4 yrs., 8 st. 9lbs. - - - plaid jacket and blue sleeves.
4. Mr. Ward's ns. b. c. **Bronze Wing,** 3 yrs., 7 st. 9lbs. - purple body, yellow sleeves and blue cap.
5. Mr. Hall's b. h. **Sir Charles,** 4 yrs., 9 st., - - - red jacket and black cap.
6. Mr. Bailey's b. g. **Young Jorrocks,** 4 yrs., 8 st. 11 lbs. - - scarlet jacket and cap.
7. Mr. C. Roberts' bl. g. **Sultan,** 6 yrs. 9 st. 9 lbs. - - scarlet jacket and black cap.

FOURTH RACE.

THE BURWOOD CUP AND SALVER, valued at Thirty-five Guineas, presented by Mosely M. Cohen, Esq., added to a Sweepstakes of Five Sovereigns each. The second horse to receive Twenty Sovereigns, and the third horse Five Sovereigns, from the Race Fund ; weight for age. St. Leger Course. Entrance, One Pound Five Shillings. *To start at half-past 2 o'clock.*

1. Mr. Arkins' ns. b. g. **Jorrocks,** aged, 9 st. 9 lbs. - - - black jacket and red cap.
2. Mr. Arkins ns. g. g. **Pasha,** 5 yrs., 9 st. 5 lbs. - - - black jacket and red cap.
3. Mr. Hillas' br. g. **Muleyson,** aged, 9 st. 9 lbs. - - - - green and white.
4. Mr. Holcomb's ch. m. **Queen of Hearts,** 4 yrs., 8 st. 11 lbs. - - blue jacket and cap.
5. Mr. Matthews' gr. g. **Almack,** aged, 9 st. 9 lbs. - - - tartan jacket and black cap.
6. Mr. Lowe's b. g. **Wentworth,** aged, 9 st. 9 lbs. - - - blue jacket and purple cap.
7. Mr. Gorrick's b. f. **Laura,** 4 yrs., 8 st. 11 lbs. - - - green jacket and blue cap.
8. Mr. Bailey's b. g. **Young Jorrocks,** 4 yrs., 8 st. 11 lbs. - - scarlet jacket and cap.
9. Mr. C. Roberts' bl. g. **Sultan,** (late Hercules) 6 yrs., 9 st. 9 lbs. scarlet jacket & black cap.
10. Mr. Rouse's br. h. **Dr. Syntax,** 4 yrs., 9 st. - - - - scarlet jacket and black cap.
11. Mr. Goodair's ch. h. **Paris,** 3 yrs., 8 st. - - green body, white sleeves, and scarlet cap.
12. Mr. J. Roberts bl. g. **Jim-along-Josey,** 3 yrs., 7 st. 11 lbs. blue jacket and black cap.
13. Mr. Tait's ch. h. **Cossack,** 4 yrs., 9 st. - - - black jacket and black cap.
14. Mr. Hurley's ch. f. **Mermaid,** 3 yrs., 7 st. 11 lbs. - - tartan jacket and black cap.

FIFTH RACE.

THE CORINTHIAN STAKES of Five Sovereigns each, for all maiden horses at the time of running. Four-year-olds and under, 11st. ; five ditto, 12st. ; six and aged, 12st. 5lbs. Twice round and a distance. Gentlemen riders. Ten subscribers. *To start at 3 o'clock.*

SIXTH RACE.

THE BEATEN STAKES of Three Sovereigns each, with Twenty Sovereigns added, for all beaten horses during the meeting ; to be handicapped by the Stewards, or whom they may appoint. One mile and a half ; post entrance, One Sovereign. *To start at half-past 3 o'clock.*

SEVENTH RACE.

A FORCED HANDICAP of Five Sovereigns each, with Twenty Sovereigns added, for all winners during the meeting (the winners of the Trial, Hurry Scurry, Hack, Grafton, and Beaten Stakes, to be entered at the option of their owners) ; to be handicapped by the Stewards, or whom they may appoint. Twice round—no entrance fee.

Horses to start by Flag precisely at the time named.

☞ The numbers of the winning and second horses will be telegraphed in front of the Stewards' Stand, immediately after each race.

[Published by Authority of the Australian Jockey Club by A. Mason, Printer.]

HOMEBUSH RACES,—1846.

STEWARDS:

MR. G. C. TURNER,
MR. R. FITZGERALD,
CAPTAIN APPERLEY.

JUDGE.

MR. NELSON LAWSON.

CLERK OF THE COURSE.

MR. A. WAY.

FIRST DAY, WEDNESDAY, MAY 27TH.

FIRST RACE.

THE METROPOLITAN MAIDEN PLATE of One Hundred Sovereigns, for all horses that have never won ; weight for age ; once round the course, to start at the three mile post. Entrance, five sovereigns.

SECOND RACE.

The ALL-AGED STAKES of five sovereigns each, with fifty sovereigns added, for all horses ; weight for age ; three miles. (Maidens allowed 5 lbs.) Entrance, three sovereigns.

THIRD RACE.

The TRIAL STAKES of ten sovereigns each, (five sovereigns forfeit if declared to the Honorary Secretary at the Royal Hotel, on the 1st of May, between the hours of one and two, P.M.), with forty sovereigns added, for two year olds ; once round the course. Colts 7 st. 7 lbs., fillies 7 st. 4 lbs. Entrance, three sovereigns.

FOURTH RACE.

The WELTER STAKES of three sovereigns each, with twenty sovereigns added, for all horses ; three year olds 10 st., four ditto 10 st. 12 lbs., five 11 st. 7 lbs., six and aged 12 st. Heats, twice round. Entrance, two sovereigns.

SECOND DAY, THURSDAY, MAY 28TH.

FIRST RACE.

The SQUATTERS' PURSE of Fifty Sovereigns, with a Sweepstakes of Three Sovereigns each, for all horses, carrying the same weights as in the Welter Stakes. Heats twice round. Gentlemen riders. Entrance, Two Sovereigns.

☞ The remainder of the day reserved for hack races and matches.

THIRD DAY, FRIDAY, MAY 29TH.

FIRST RACE.

The AUSTRALIAN PLATE of Seventy Sovereigns, for all horses ; weight for age ; twice round the course. (Maidens allowed 5 lbs.) Entrance, Four Sovereigns.

SECOND RACE.

The ST. LEGER STAKES of Ten Sovereigns each, (Five Sovereigns forfeit if declared to the Honorary Secretary at the Royal Hotel, on the 1st of May, between the hours one and two P.M.), with Fifty Sovereigns added ; for three year olds, one mile and a half. Colts 8st. 7lbs, fillies 8st. 4lbs. Entrance, Three Sovereigns.

THIRD RACE.

The LADIES' PURSE of Thirty Sovereigns, with a Sweepstakes of Five Sovereigns each, for all horses ; weight for age. (Maidens allowed 5 lbs.) Heats once round the course. Entrance, Two Sove-

far left: An A.J.C. race card of 1851, printed on silk with an embroidered border. Winner of the Queen's Plate on this day, Cossack, was to take the Plate again the following year, thus earning much popularity in the colony. A.J.C.

centre left: A column of The Sydney Morning Herald of 21 April 1846, announcing the programme for the A.J.C. three-day meeting to be held at Homebush in May.

left: John Macarthur, best-known for his activities in promoting the wool industry, was also one of the first studmasters in New South Wales.

above: Lassoing wild horses. Many bush horses achieved fame in the first days of racing in Australia, and stockhorses made a major contribution to the success of early meetings.

29

2. THE CLUBS

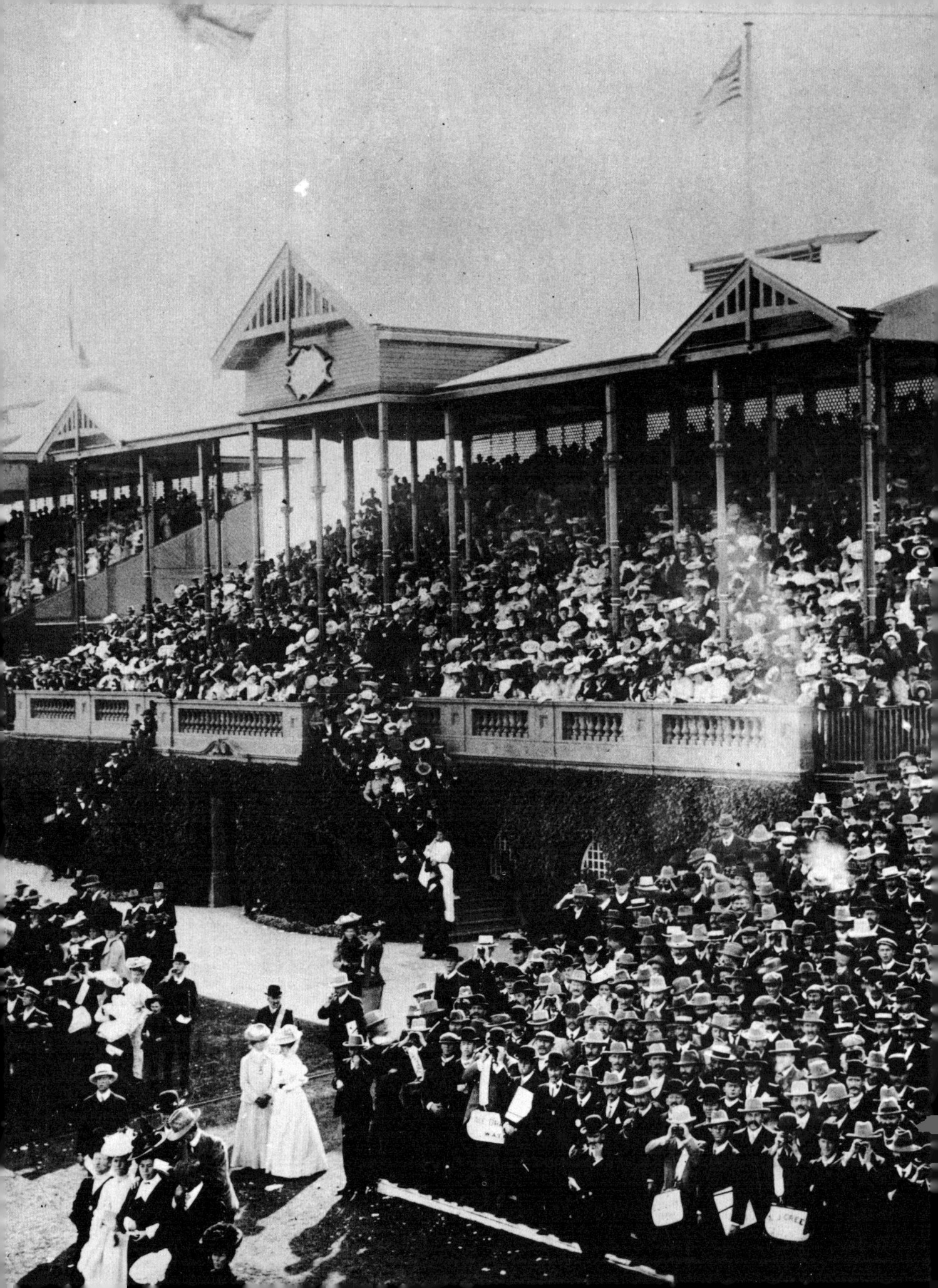

2. THE CLUBS

Settlement of other Australian cities followed a similar pattern to that of Sydney, and settlers took with them a deep pride in their horses and correspondingly keen desire to test them in races. Even in isolated areas horses of stamina and speed were essential. On the rough bush tracks some astonishing feats were achieved by both horses and riders. Races up to 100 miles were one of the main forms of entertainment. Indeed horses formed the only means of transport apart from walking, and stockhorses got used to covering 400 miles a week under heavy loads in tough conditions.

Bushrangers, whose operations had begun as early as 1796 among escaped convicts, had as a prime objective the theft of thoroughbred horses. To these outlaws who used the Australian bush as a base, good horses meant survival and improved their prospects of thwarting the hangman. Soon the horses the bushrangers rode became almost as famous as the bushrangers themselves. Troubadour, Mr C.M. Lloyd's well-performed racing stallion was reputed to have been stolen three times by Ben Hall the bush-ranger. Sapho, one of the most successful colonial-bred brood mares, was also 'lifted'. Some bush-rangers, like Jackey-Jackey (William Westwood), were so proud of their ability to ride vast distances in a few hours that they deliberately displayed themselves at the start and finish of these journeys so that the feats could be verified. Horse stealing was so prevalent that even respected property owners did not always acknowledge the pedigrees of their horses for fear of disclosing that they were the progeny of thoroughbreds that had been 'borrowed' by the breeders.

Many an early Australian racehorse first attracted attention by the speed it showed working in the bush. Petrel, the outstanding racehorse in the first decade of the turf in Melbourne, was an ex-stockhorse whose speed was first noted on an emu hunt. Petrel, sired by the English stallion Steeltrap, won big races in Melbourne, Geelong and Tasmania and was southern

pages 30-31 : An early race meeting in Hobart Town. Free settlers were few in Tasmania for years after its settlement in 1804, but such was their enthusiasm that meetings were held in that state as early as 1814. T.R.C.

left : Spectators pack the grandstand as they watch the Kalgoorlie Cup of 1906.

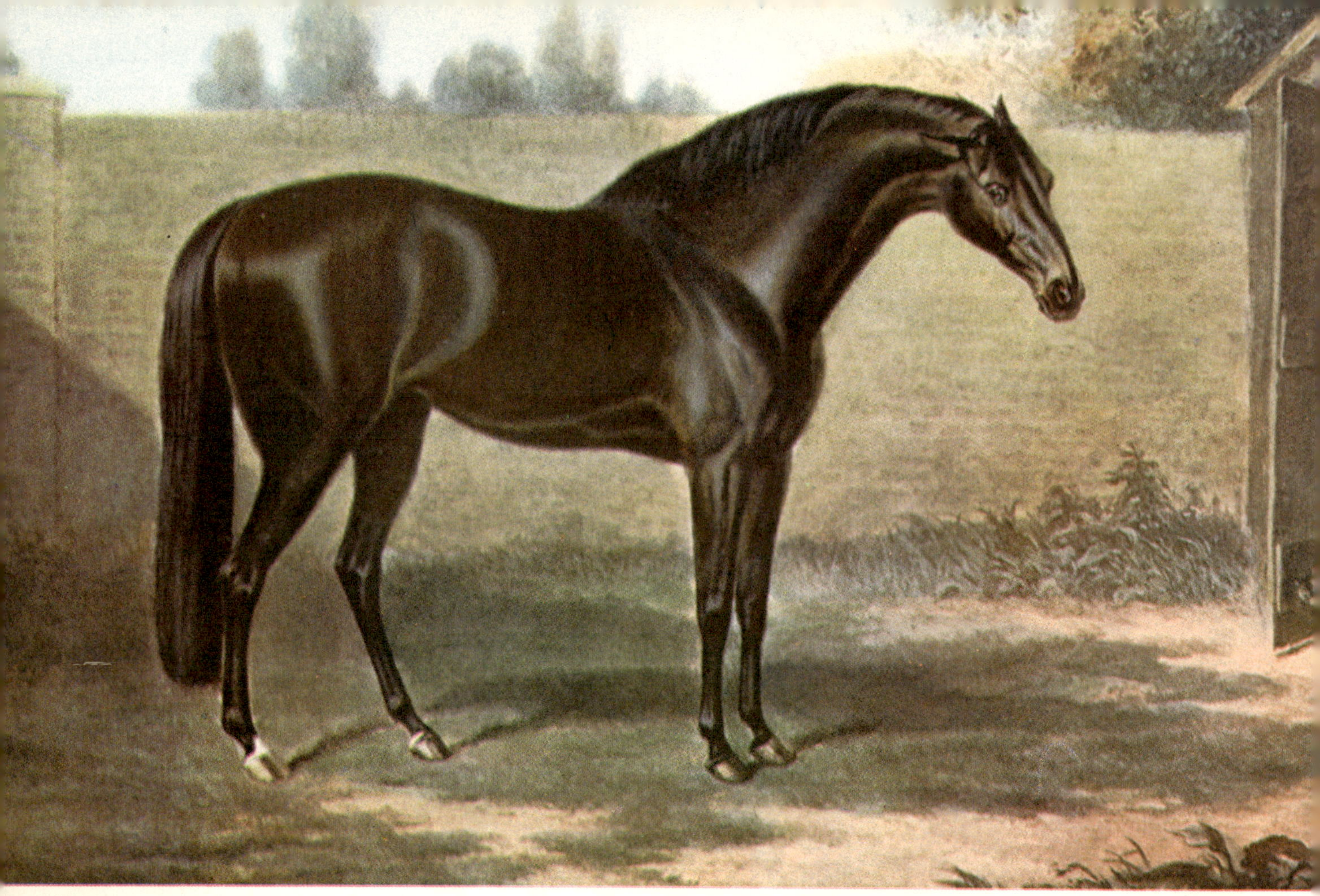

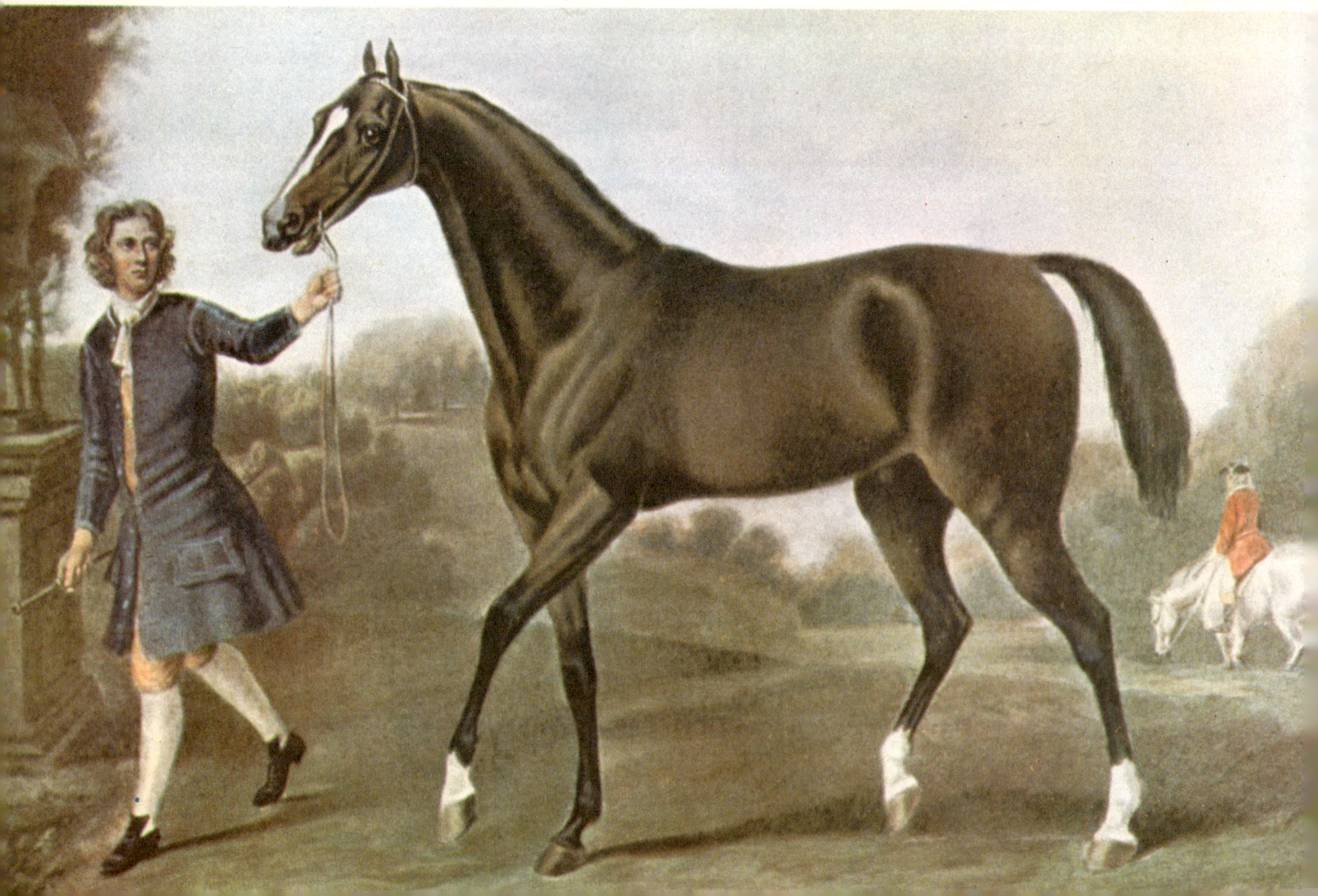

top left: The Godolphin Barb, a magnificent Arab and an ancestor of many great Australian horses. The description under this print, from the original by George Stubbs, claims that the Godolphin Barb 'contributed more than any other stallion to the improvement of the breed of horses.' *A.J.C.*

above: A horse hangs unhappily in his sling, waiting to be unloaded from the ship which has brought him to Australia. *Mitchell.*

left, right: The Darley Arabian (left) and the Byerly Turk (right), with the Godolphin Barb, were the foundation sires of the three great thoroughbred lines of the western world—the Eclipse, Matchem and Herod lines. All Australian thoroughbreds can be traced in their male lines back to these ancestors. *A.J.C.*

Australia's counterpart to Sydney's Jorrocks.

Racing officially began in Victoria in 1838 when a meeting in the inn owned by pioneer John Pascoe Fawkner, with Mr Henry Allen chairman, formed the Melbourne Race Club. Three years after Melbourne was founded this club conducted Victoria's first races on 6 and 7 March 1838, on a course marked out next to Batman's Hill. Spectators on the hill saw Postboy win the Town Plate worth twenty-five sovereigns. An added attraction was a grinning match, won by Mr Curwen, a carpenter so ugly that other ugly competitors shrank back abashed and promptly acknowledged defeat. On the second day almost the entire field for the Hunters' Stakes refused to start and there were no entries for the Beaten Stakes.

Carrying on the hard-drinking habits of their Sydney contemporaries, Melbourne racegoers celebrated this initial meeting with a dinner at Fawkner's inn and drank the place dry. One drunken woman guest wandered out of the inn, fell into the Yarra and was drowned.

Flemington racecourse opened on 3, 4 and 5 March 1840, the course taking its name from Fleming's butcher shop on a nearby road. The early grandstand was a makeshift affair but the first course administrators had their eye on progress and were sticklers for adherence to English Jockey Club procedures. Flemington, Caulfield and Randwick racecourses became the finest racetracks in the world at the time. They have been improved with new grandstands and other facilities but the conceptions on which they were based have been little altered, and they still compare favourably with courses anywhere in the world. Many English courses are primitive by comparison.

Australian race meetings were tough affairs in those days, not only for the horses, but for trainers, jockeys and spectators. At the 1845 meeting, in which Petrel beat the Tasmanian champion Paul Jones in the decisive third heat of the Melbourne Town Plate— they had previously won a heat each—a jockey named Dewing won a minor race on Wild Harry. As Dewing walked from the weighing stand after the race, a disgruntled punter rushed at him and knocked him down with a stick. Dewing almost died. On the

above: The Derby Day, in the early days of racing in New South Wales. A varied scene, full of excitement. The gentry prepare an elegant picnic while those not so fortunate look on. A.J.C.

right: Brumbies being roped in a station stockyard.

36

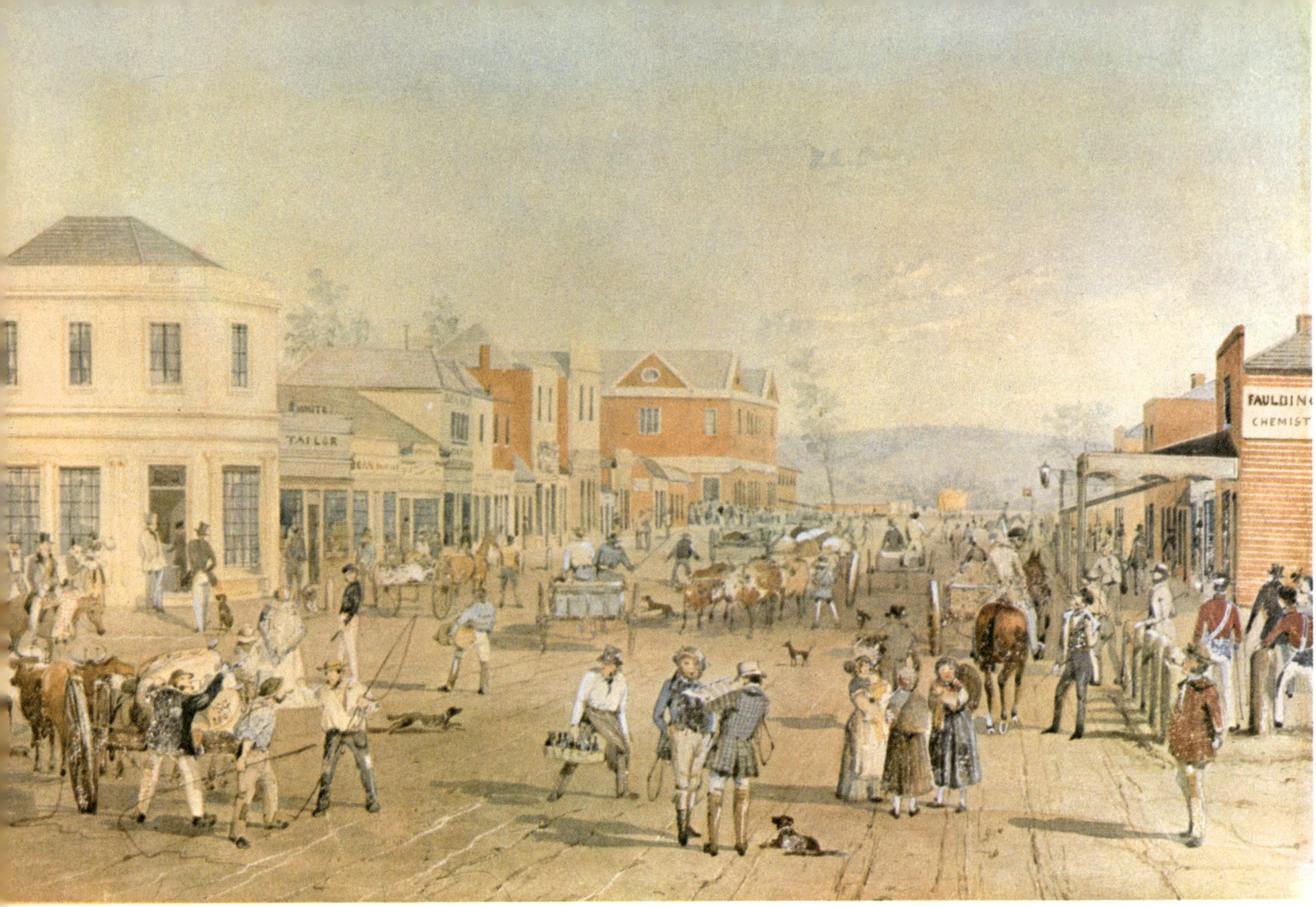
CHEMIST

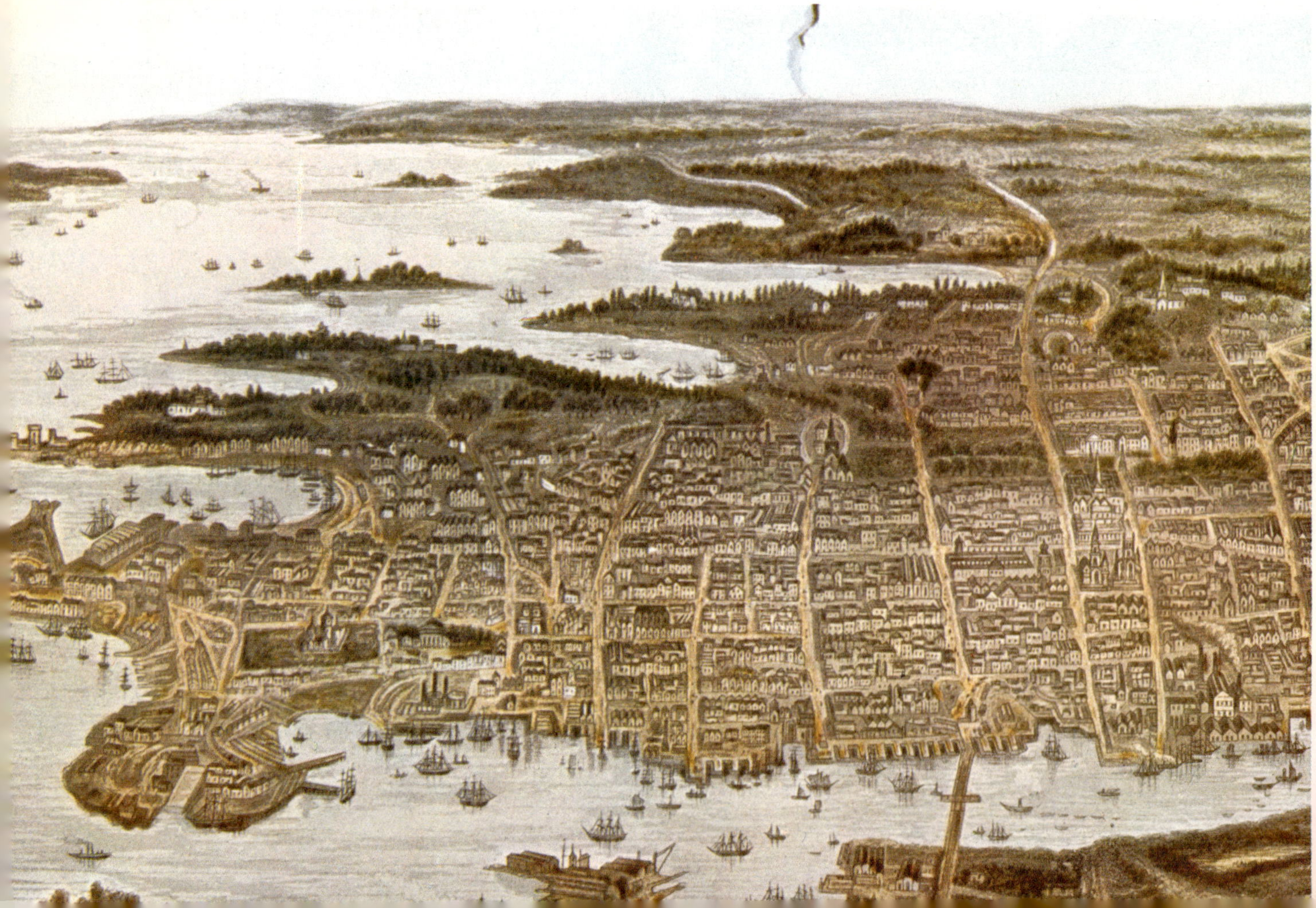

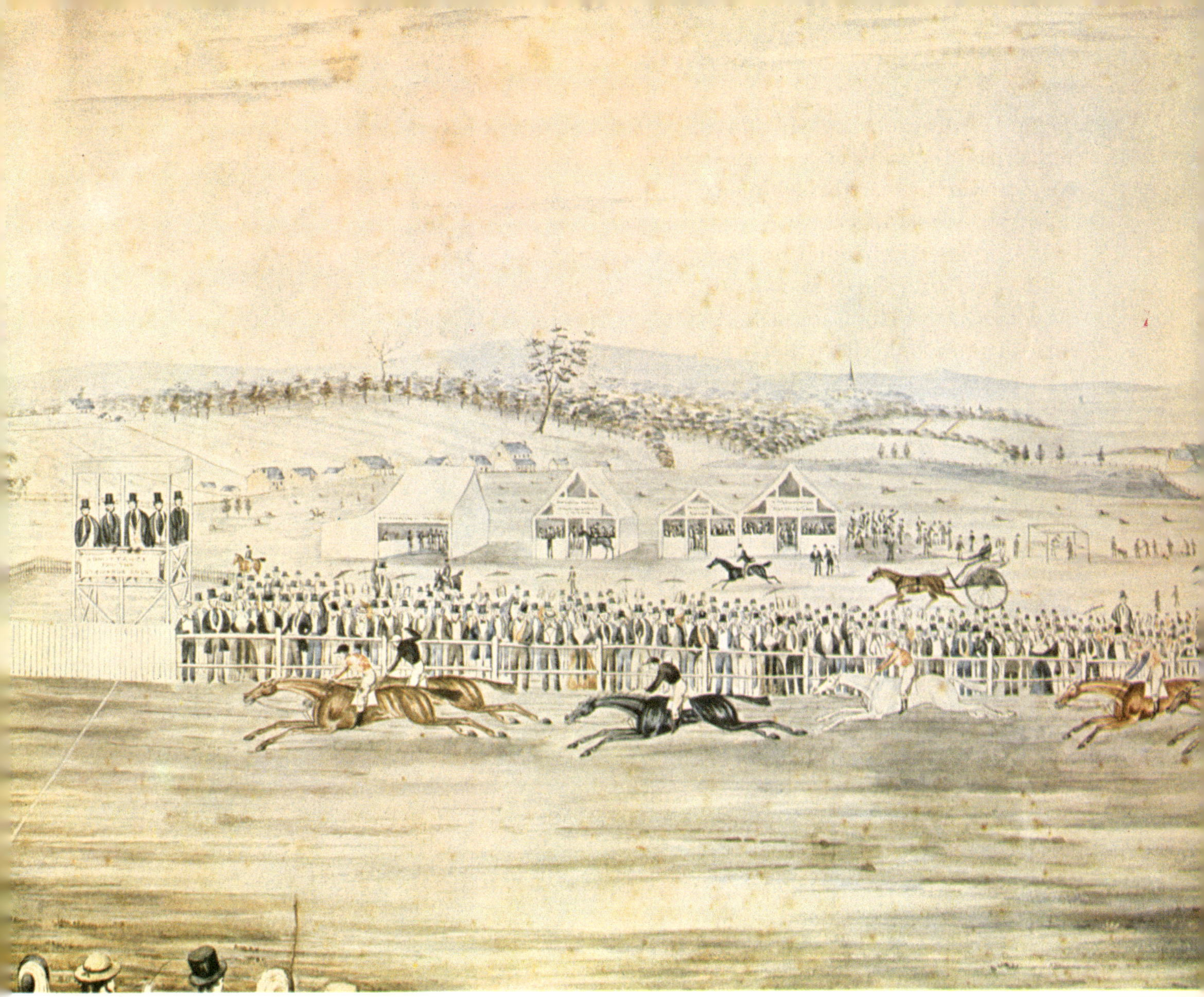

top left : This lively watercolour Rundle Street Adelaide 1845 by S.T. Gill, captures the spirit of the young South Australian colony. Collection, The Art Gallery of South Australia.

far left : Old Sydney town sprawling around the harbour. Australian racing began in Sydney, stimulated at first by the military, and later carried on by civilians with ever-increasing enthusiasm.

left : Lachlan Macquarie, the fifth governor of New South Wales, under whose watchful eye the 1819 Hyde Park race meeting was held. He later banned unauthorized race meetings, because they had become excuses for bad behaviour and low gambling. Photograph by courtesy of the Honourable J.C. Maddison, B.A., L.L.B., M.L.A., Minister for Justice for New South Wales.

above : A race meeting at Petersham in 1845. Mitchell.

evening of the same day Mr Edward Argyle was riding home from the races when three mounted ruffians pursued him to share his winnings. After a two mile chase Mr Argyle was knocked from the saddle by a blow from a whip handle and badly beaten up.

The year after Petrel had won the Melbourne Plate his owner, Mr Colin Campbell, decided to cash in on Petrel's glory and sell the horse in a sweepstake of forty tickets at £5 each. Mr Campbell's return of £200 was a big sum in those days. Lucky winner was a Mr Riddell who decided to celebrate his good fortune with a 'Grand Petrel Ball'. He decked the hall with Petrel's bridle, saddle and shoes and with the whip, bridle, saddle and spurs used by Petrel's jockey, 'Sandy the Butcher'. Immediately after the ball Mr Riddell, a socialite who had been more interested in the celebrity gained by his win than in the horse, sold Petrel at auction to a Mr Borradaile for 150 guineas.

By now racing had progressed enough for owners of successful horses to start looking for opposition outside their own cities. Petrel was taken to Sydney in 1849 to challenge the New South Wales champion, Jorrocks, but he was very sick on the sea journey to Sydney and was beaten by both Jorrocks and Blue Bonnet. In 1857 the owner of Alice Hawthorne, the best horse in Melbourne, challenged any horse bred in New South Wales to a match race over three miles for £1,000-a-side. Mr G.T. Rowe took up the challenge and his horse Veno easily defeated Alice Hawthorne. This inter-state rivalry persisted to such a degree that one of the conditions of early races at Flemington was that horses from Tasmania or New South Wales which had won races in their home states had to carry 7 lb extra weight.

The Port Phillip Turf Club, formed in 1840, and the Jockey Club, formed a few years later, both failed, and in 1864 the Victoria Racing Club was founded and took over the liabilities of both the defunct clubs. The V.R.C. has since become one of the world's outstanding racing clubs, second only in seniority

right : New Town racecourse in Tasmania as seen by Benjamin Duterrau in 1834. The Tasmanian Turf Club cleared the course in 1831. T.R.C.

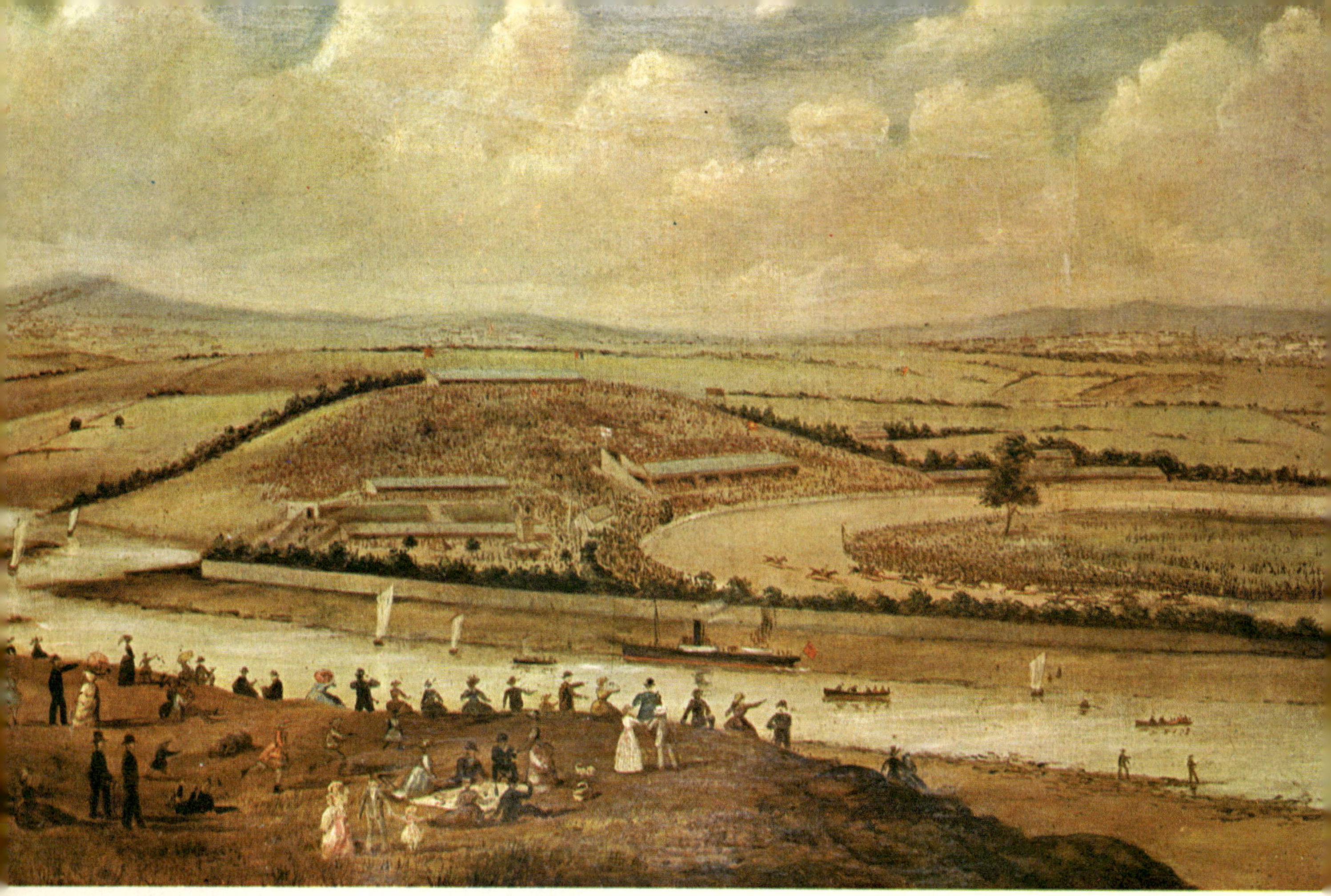

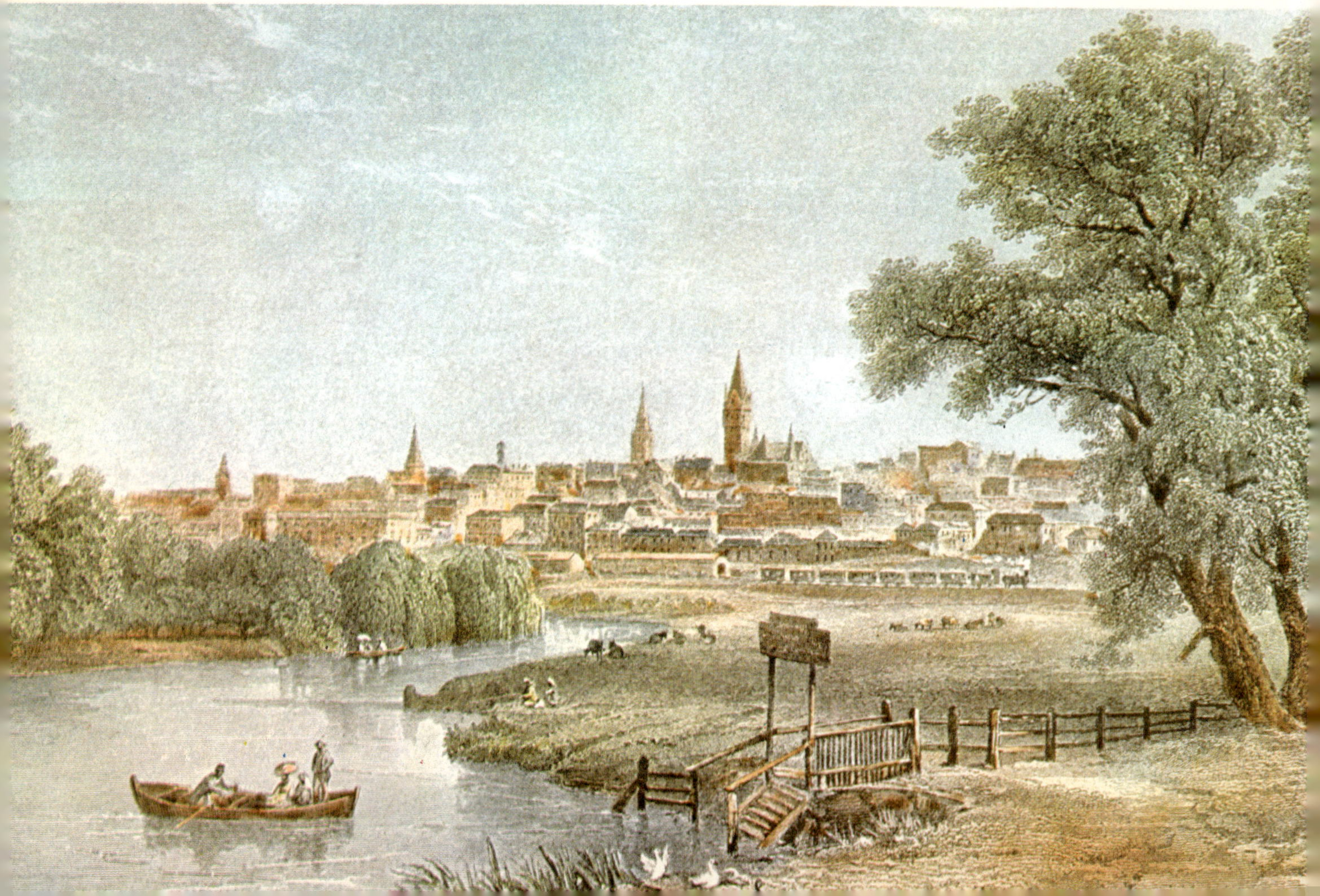

top left : Flemington Racecourse from the Footscray side of the Salt Water River, an oil painting by J. Ryan. Flemington opened with a three-day meeting on 3rd, 4th and 5th March, 1840. National Library.

left : A peaceful view of old Melbourne. Victoria had its first official race meeting in 1838, and in 1840 Flemington racecourse was opened. Almost from the beginning, inter-state rivalry was a feature of racing in Australia, with Melbourne and Sydney constantly trying to outdo each other.

above : The great English sire West Australian, the first horse ever to win the triple crown of Derby, St. Leger, and Two Thousand Guineas. Two of his sons were sent to Australia; Australian arrived in New South Wales in 1860, and Mazzini went to Victoria in 1864. An oil painting by Harry Hall. National Library

right : Aboriginal stockmen guide their mounts home. Horses were unknown in Australia until the arrival of the First Fleet, but the Aboriginal race has since become extremely skilled in horse handling.

in Australia to the A.J.C.. Victoria's other prominent racing body, the Victorian Amateur Turf Club began in Ballarat in 1875 and staged its first meeting at nearby Dowling Forest in March 1876. Later the same year the V.A.T.C. bought land for a new course at Caulfield, where it has run its major race, the Caulfield Cup, over one and a half miles annually since 1879.

The first racing club in Queensland was the Moreton Bay Racing Club formed soon after that state was opened up for general settlement in 1842. This club marked out a course at Cooper's Plains on the outskirts of Brisbane and held its first meeting there in July 1843, with total prize money of £147. A former stockhorse, Whig, won the main race, the Brisbane Town Plate. Other courses followed at Brisbane's New Farm and South Brisbane, both opened in 1852, and by the end of the 1805s Brisbane race meetings were attracting spectators from all the settled districts of Queensland and from northern New South Wales. The North Australian Jockey Club was formed at Ipswich in 1859. In 1861 at the town's course, The Grange, the club held a Champions' Stakes.

The Queensland Turf Club, now the leading Queensland club, began in 1863. Voluntary workers —jockeys, club members, and trainers—cleared land at Eagle Farm where the club had obtained a grant. There was all the fun of the fair for the Q.T.C.'s first meeting in 1865, with sideshows, three-card men, an Aunt Sally and a menagerie containing monkeys, a Tasmanian Devil and a lion. Nine publicans built booths on the course to slake punters' thirsts.

Country racing clubs were also springing up as white settlement spread. One of the oldest clubs in Australia, Wallabadah, ten miles east of Quirindi, New South Wales, was founded in 1852. Racing was then firmly established at country centres in other states such as Gayndah in Queensland, York in Western Australia, and Narracoorte in South Australia, where the poet Adam Lindsay Gordon rode in both hurdle and flat races.

Regular race meetings began in South Australia on 1 and 2 January 1838, less than a year after the city

top left : Sketches from The Queensland Figaro, 17 November 1888, depicting highlights of the Q.T.C. spring meeting.

left : The finish of the inter-colonial match race between Veno (New South Wales) and Alice Hawthorn (Victoria). This famous race, which was won by Veno, was run at Flemington on 3 October 1857.

above : A meeting of the Queensland Turf Club, now the leading Queensland racing club, in the late nineteenth century. Horses and jockeys enter the stewards enclosure.

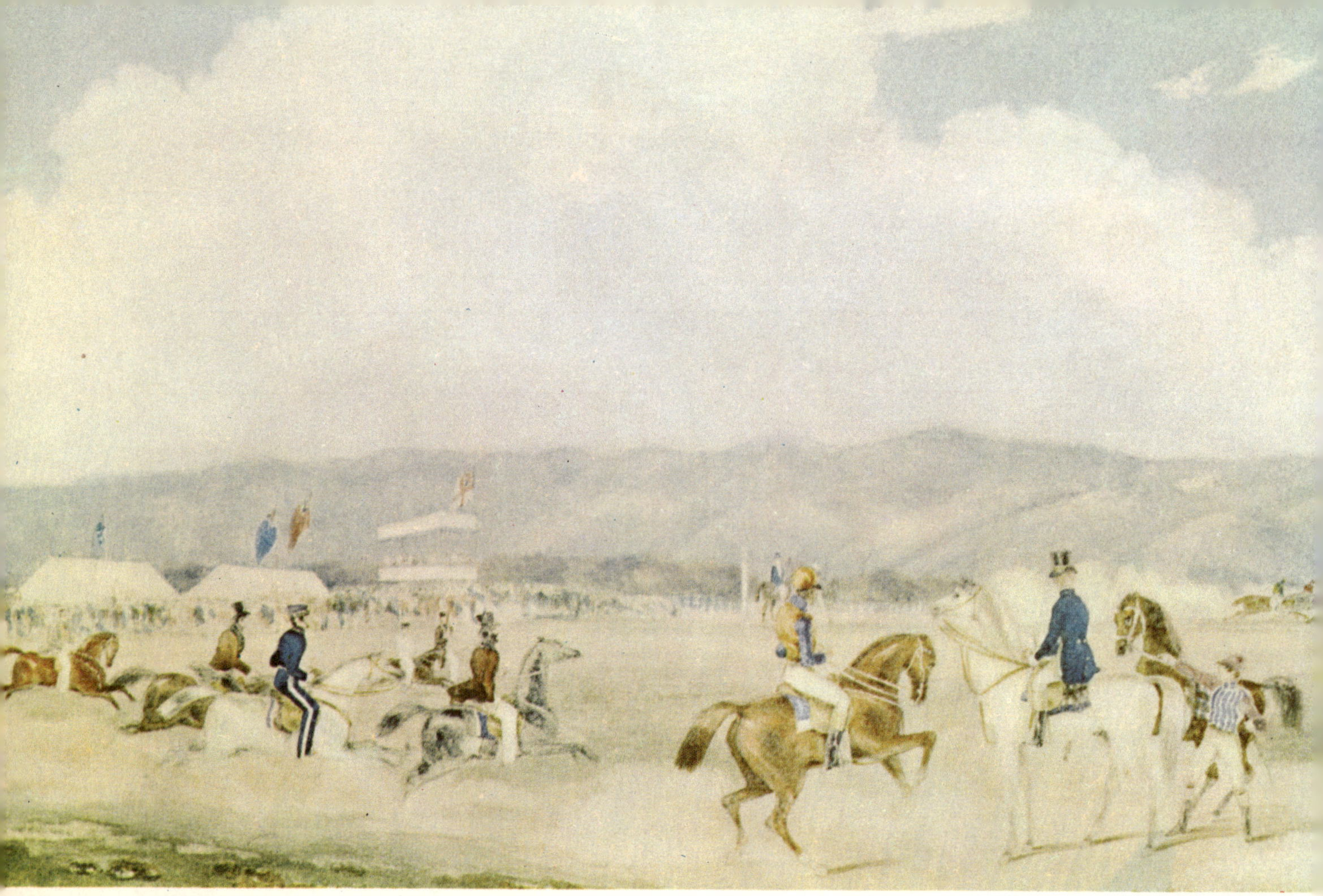

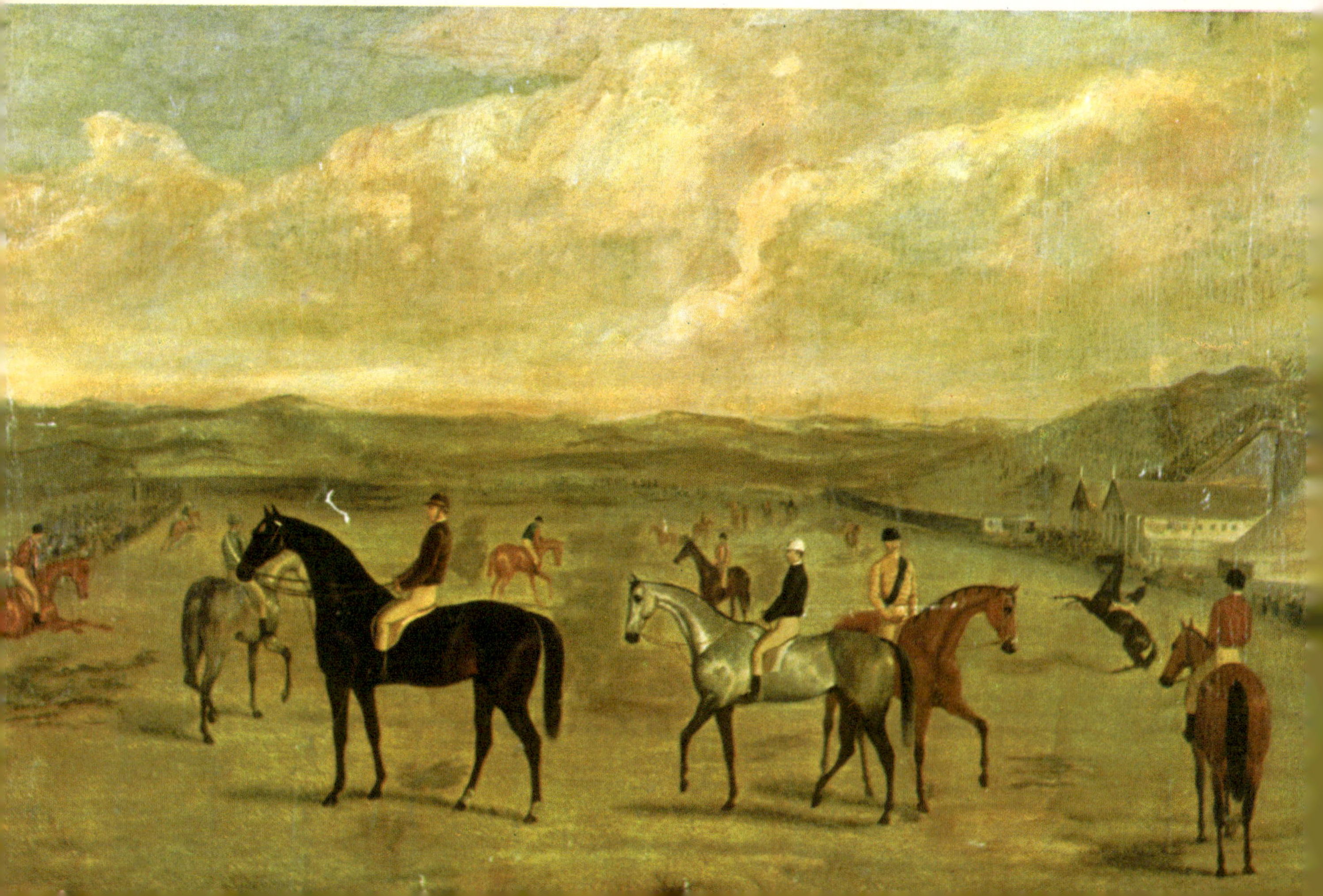

top left : The Adelaide Racecourse, painted in water-colours by J.M. Skipper on 1 January 1840, exactly two years after the first race meeting was held in South Australia. National Library

left : Before the 1865 Melbourne Cup—the nervous horses jump and prance. The small grey in the centre is the gelding Toryboy, which was to win the race. La Trobe

above : Veno, painted in 1857, the year of his tremendous win over Alice Hawthorne. His rider is J. Higgerson. A.J.C.

right : Brisbane town in its early days. The foundation of the first racing club in Queensland followed closely on the heels of general settlement. The first recorded race meeting was held in July 1843, on a course marked out at Cooper's Plains.

was first settled. Colonel Light, the city's founder, and James Hurtle Fisher acted as stewards at this meeting. The course was marked out in front of Fisher's house, and his horse Black Jack won the first official race run in the state. Horses were brought in by sea from Tasmania or across the rigorous land route from New South Wales and Victoria. But there were not enough horses of quality for officials of these first South Australian meetings to insist that each runner be of pure blood.

The South Australian Jockey Club, initiated in 1856, took over the staging of the Adelaide St Leger which had begun the previous year and is now the state's oldest classic. The S.A.J.C. disappeared for a time in 1861 but was later reorganized. It staged a notable meeting in 1869 on what was known as The Old Course in Adelaide when the Duke of Edinburgh was among the spectators. The club's problems persisted, however, and it lapsed in 1870 and 1871 when the Adelaide St Leger was not held.

For a time in the early 1880s, the Adelaide Racing Club challenged the leadership of the S.A.J.C. but in 1884 the A.R.C. conceded supremacy. Between them these two clubs have since dominated racing in the state. The S.A.J.C's main course is Morphetville, a few miles from Adelaide, where it conducts the South Australian Derby and the Adelaide St Leger as its major races. The A.R.C. conducts its meetings at Victoria Park. Steeplechasing, which began in Australia with the five-miler between Botany and Coogee in 1832, has always been very strong in South Australia, and is also maintained in Tasmania and Victoria. The annual Onkaparinga Great Eastern Steeplechase, held on Easter Monday at Oakbank, has frequently carried bigger prize money than any other Australian jumping event.

Tasmania started steeplechase and hurdle races in 1838, twenty-four years after the first flat races in the state were held at New Town, near Hobart. The first big race in Tasmania was a match between Cheviot and Diana, which won the 200 guineas side bet after a series of heats. Establishment of racing clubs there followed the pattern set by other states, with Lieutenant-Governor Arthur patron of the first Tas-

ADELAIDE RACES.

JANUARY 1st, 1838.

MATCH TWENTY GUINEAS—TWO-MILE HEAT.

1 Mr. Fisher's   bk. h. Black Jack   black body, white sleeves
2 Mr. S. Stephens's b. m. Polly   blue body, white sleeves

MATCH TEN GUINEAS—TWO-MILE HEAT.

1 Mr. Hill's   g. h.   Rainbow   white body, green sleeves
2 Mr. J. Fisher's b. g   Wilful   puce and white stripes

SWEEPSTAKES, FIVE POUNDS ENTRANCE, WITH TEN POUNDS ADDED FROM THE FUND—BEST OF HEATS—ONE MILE AND A QUARTER—ALL AGES.

Mr. Handcock's   bn. m. Taglioni   white body, green sleeves
Mr. Hill's   g. h.   Rainbow   white body, pink sleeves
Mr. Jones's   bn. g.   Bob   purple, black cap
Mr. J. Fisher's   b. g.   Wilful   puce and white stripes
1 Mr. Neale's   ch. m.   Nelly   plumb body, yellow sleeves
Mr. Sladden's   bk. m. Black Bess white body, green sleeves

MATCH TEN POUNDS—TWO-MILE HEAT.

2 Mr. Morphett's   b. m.   Fidget   mixed striped body, purple sleeves
1 Mr. S. Stephens's b. m.   Polly   blue body, white sleeves

TO COMMENCE AT TWELVE O'CLOCK PRECISELY.

(Signed)   F. HANDCOCK, c. c.

Stewards { COLONEL LIGHT.
{ JAMES HURTLE FISHER, Esq.

ROBERT THOMAS AND CO. PRINTERS.

top left : A view of the stand at Morphetville race-course, the main course of the South Australian Jockey Club, as it was in 1888. The South Australian Derby and the Adelaide St Leger are run at Morphetville, which is only a few miles from Adelaide. S.A.J.C.

left : A gas-filled balloon about to ascend—one of the extra attractions which added colour to early race meetings. The course pictured is Victoria Park, South Australia.

above : The race card of the first race meeting to be held in South Australia—less than a year after the city of Adelaide was founded. The course was marked out in front of the home of James Hurtle Fisher, who was one of the stewards at the meeting.

manian Turf Club and influential settlers such as
John Batman and William Field keen supporters.
The T.T.C. cleared the New Town course in 1831
and that same year saw the formation in Launceston
of the Cornwall Turf Club. These two clubs have
administered racing in the two main Tasmanian
centres ever since. The T.T.C. did have years when it
could not function but it has existed in its present
form since 1871.

The main problem facing those interested in racing
in Tasmania has always been to attract the best horses
from the larger Australian states and to retain outstanding horses which are developed at home. This
has been the Western Australian dilemma, too, with
horses which could pull in crowds heading for the
eastern states and a chance at richer prize money once
they had shown real speed or stamina. The first
Western Australian race meetings were, in fact, held in
1833 between ponies shipped in from the island of
Timor. Races between thoroughbreds did not begin
in the west until three years later.

Racing enjoyed one of its biggest booms in the west
when gold was discovered. Race meetings began to
proliferate almost overnight on makeshift courses in
Kalgoorlie and Coolgardie, where the 1896 meeting
had a race worth £1,000 in stakes. While the goldrush
lasted in the west, Western Australia had more racetracks than any area in the world in proportion to
population.

Keg-rolling races, camel races, wheelbarrow races,
shovelling contests and other novelty events were
usually staged in conjunction with race meetings on
the goldfields. The carnival atmosphere of the bush
picnic race meetings, and the madcap behaviour of
Territorians, who in Darwin rode horses into their
favourite bars, were joined in some of the most colourful race meetings held anywhere. In the 1890s Rufe
Naylor bobbed up on the goldfields to make a killing
between race meetings from professional footrunning.
Despite the heat Naylor acted as a bookmaker at one
meeting wearing his dinner suit and explained to
anybody curious that he had not had time to change
after gambling all night at two-up, cards and whatever
else was going.

above: A memorial commemorating the founding of
racing in Tasmania. Tasmania began racing only
four years after New South Wales and is, therefore,
the second oldest racing state in Australia.

top right: The card for the New Town races of 1840.
The clearing of the New Town course in 1831 was the
result of a campaign for better conditions conducted by
racing supporters in the south. T.R.C.

right: Elwick racecourse, Tasmania as it was in 1874.
The judge's box can be seen in the foreground and the
old Elwick Homestead in the distance. T.R.C.

NEW TOWN RACES, 1840.

STEWARDS:

Francis Bryant, Esq.—James Lord, Esq.,—T. Y. Lowes, Esq.

FIRST DAY, *Tuesday, the 17th March.*

THE TRIAL STAKES of 30 sovs., for two year old—Colts, 8st., Fillies 7st. 11lb. Entrance 3 sovs.—Heats, one mile.

W. Kearney's g.c. *Smolensko*, by Romeo.
R. Dry's, jun. b.f. *Creeping Jane*, by Little John.
Mr. Steele's b.c. *Alonzo*, by Hit or Miss.

THE TOWN PLATE of 100 sovs., for all ages, three-year old 7st. 8lbs.; four-year old, 8st. 6lbs; five year old, 9st,; six year old and aged, 9st. 5lbs.—Entrance 5 sovs.—Heats twice round.

E. Bryant's b.m. *Gulnare*, 5 yrs. old, by Buffalo.
W. Kearney's b.h. *Van Tromp*, 5 yrs. old, by Peter Finn.
Thos. Field's g.h. *Plenipo*, 5 yrs. old, by Wanderer.

THE MERCHANTS' PURSE of 40 sovs., the winner to be sold for 100 sovs., if demanded, in the usual way, within half an hour after the race, &c. Two-year old, 7st. 12lbs.; three-year old, 8st. 8lbs.; four-year old, 9st. 5lbs.; five-year old, 10st.; six-year old and aged, 10st. 8lbs.—Entrance 3 sovs.—Heats, once round and a distance.

W. Kearney's g.h. *Stranger*, 4 yrs. old, by Bolivar
S. Evans's b.h. *Waterloo*, aged, by Waterloo.
John Lord's ch. h. *Magic*, aged, by Buffalo.
J. Stephenson's r. g. *Randolph*, aged, by —————.

SECOND DAY.—*Wednesday, the 18th March.*

THE DERWENT ST. LEGER STAKES of 25 sovs. each, half forfeit for three-year old, with 30 sovs. added from the Race Fund. Colts, 8st. 6lbs.; Fillies, 8st. 3lbs.—Heats, once round.—Entrance, 3 sovs.

E. Bryant's b. c. —————, by Peter Finn.
Thos. Field's b.c. *Banker*, by Peter Finn.
R. Dry's, jun. g. f. *Zephyrine*, by Sepoy.
E. Abbott's b.c. *Don Giovanni*, by —————
E. Moore's b.c. *Counsellor*, by Bolivar.

A PURSE OF FIFTY SOVEREIGNS, given by Lieutenant-Colonel Elliott and Officers of the 51st K. O. L. I., added to a Sweepstakes of 3 sovs. each; three-year old, 8st. 2lbs.; four-year old, 9st. 6lbs.; five-year old, 10st.; six and aged, 10st. 5lbs.; the second horse to withdraw his stake—four to start or no race. No person to enter, either in his own name, or in the name of any other person, two horses of which he is wholly or in part the owner. The winner of any plate, or match, or Sweepstakes of 100 sovs. to carry 7lbs. extra ; if of 50 sovs. 5lbs. extra.—Mares and Geldings allowed 3lbs.—Two mile heats.

The Western Australian Turf Club was formed in Perth in 1852 with twenty leading citizens as members and, true to form, the state's governor, Charles Fitzgerald as the figurehead. The races the new club conducted were predictably given the same names as those in other states, with the Queen's Plate prevailing as the major race until 1879 when the Metropolitan Handicap for some reason pinched its status. Although other well-supported race clubs appeared in Bunbury, Busseltown, Champion Bay and Geraldton (the latter bearing the incongruous name of Victoria Racing Club), it was obvious that control of racing in the state should remain in Perth. This control was passed to the W.A.T.C. in 1917.

Australia's major race meetings have always remained vulnerable to the hot-shot country horse whose true abilities are known only to the people who have helped to prepare him out in the bush. When one studies the histories of our race clubs and examines the major contribution which stockhorses have made to early meetings, it is hard to deny country horses and owners these killings. But as the conditions of Australian classics have been refined and revised Australians have come to believe completely in the mastery of the thoroughbred and deny the brumby from the bush his opportunity for the big prizes.

The Australian racehorse's birthright is that he came from tough, incredibly durable stock, with a lot of his staying power stemming from Arabs. But in a sport in which Derby-winning stallions mated with Oaks-winning mares repeatedly fail to produce winning horses, the Australian mug punter can only remain bemused at his country's allegiance to English blood for the past century and a half. Out in the bush, horses whose lack of pedigree, or their owners' inability to disclose it denied them a chance to run for some big race club prize money, helped build the nation through their toughness. Purity of blood is commendable, but according to our romantic fiction the earthy Australian racegoer has always responded most to the idea of a wild bush horse bobbing up and winning even the biggest of our races...even the Melbourne Cup.

top left : A sketch of the grandstand at Elwick race-course, Tasmania. T.R.C.

left : The grandstand as it was in later years—crowded with racegoers, the ladies shielding their complexions from the summer sun with a multitude of parasols. T.R.C.

above : After the cup race at the Kalgoorlie Racing Club's meeting of 1903. Racing in the west boomed after the discovery of gold, and during the goldrush Western Australia had more racetracks in proportion to its population than anywhere else in the world.

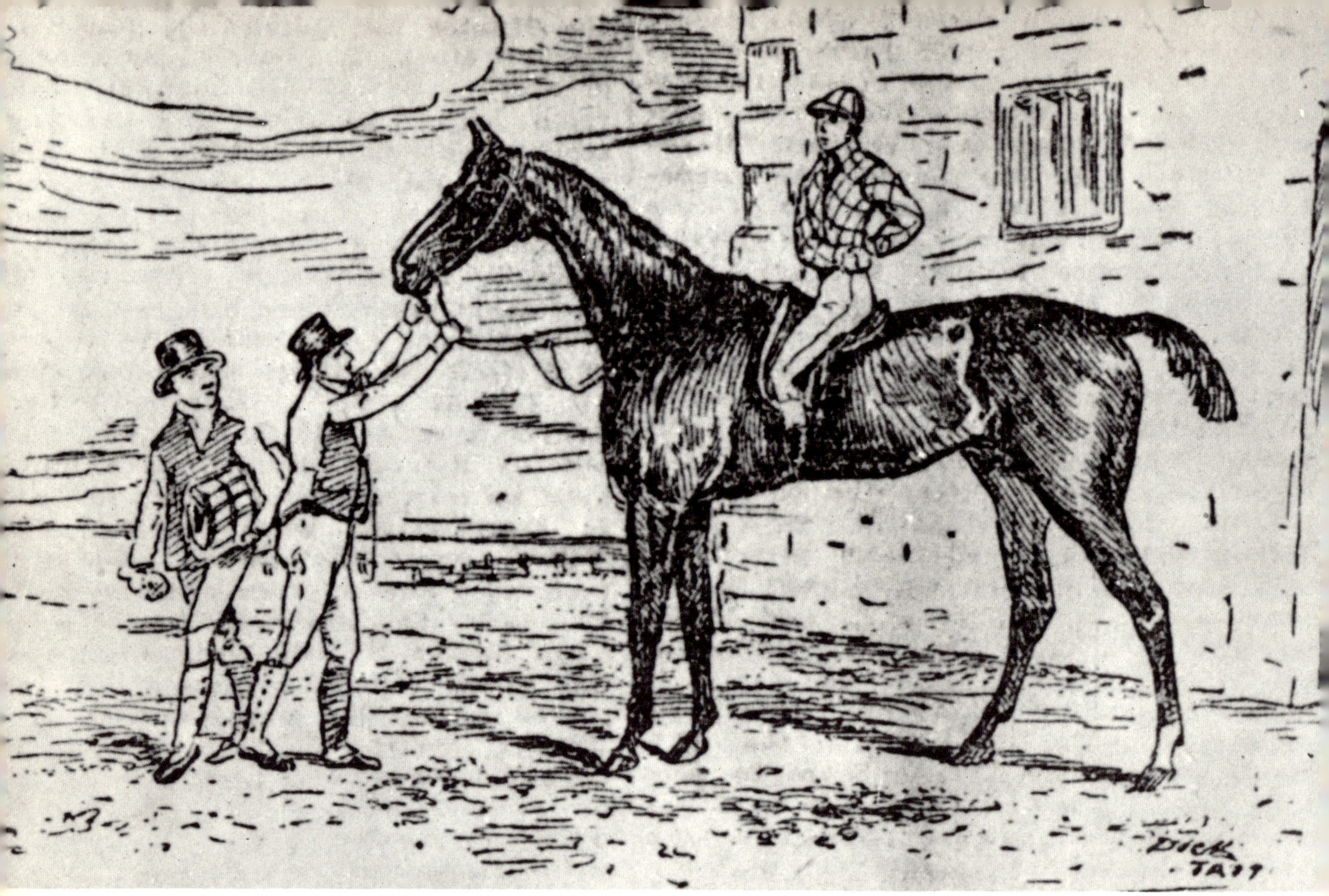
Dick
Tait

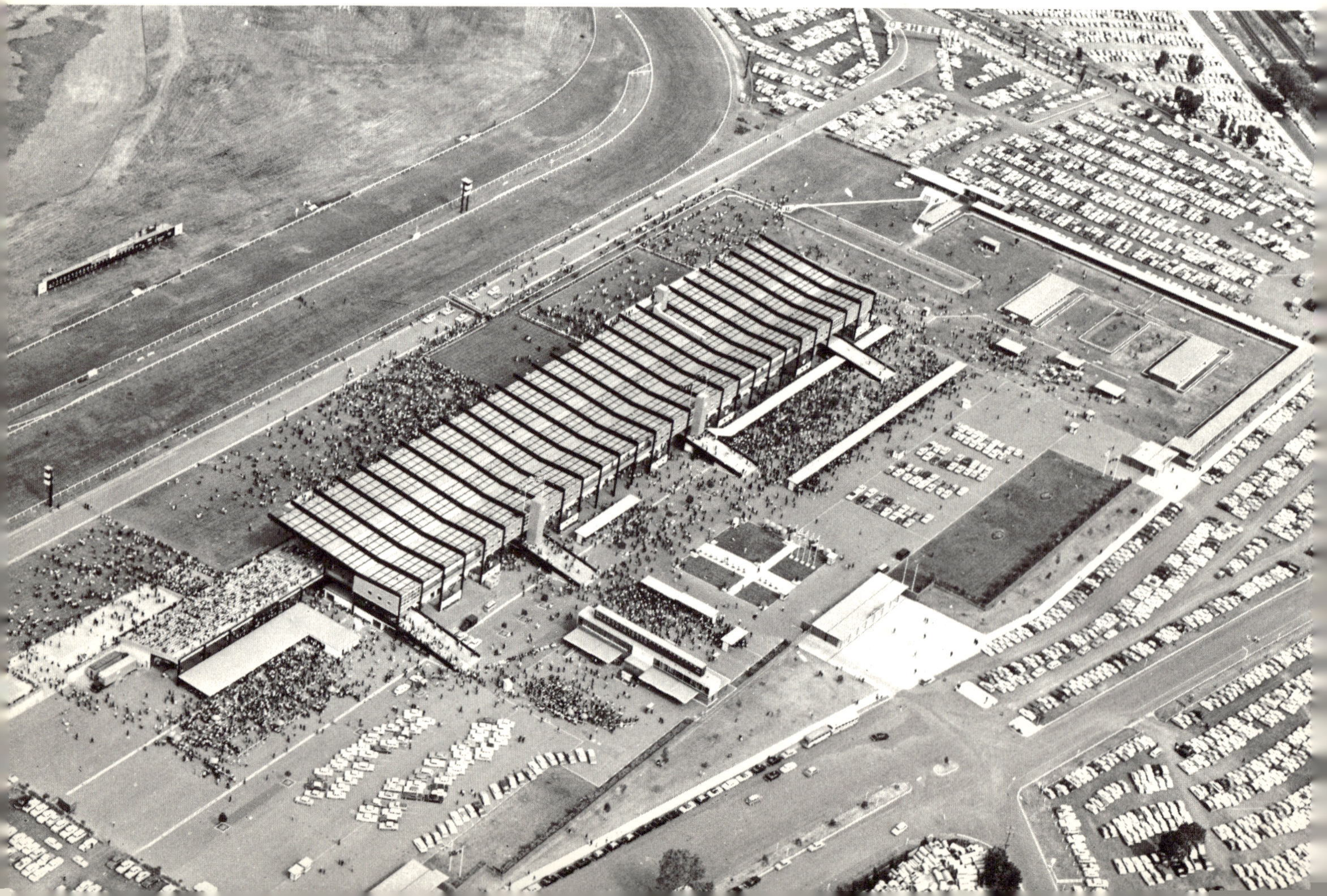

top left : Blacklock : 'A Pillar of the Stud Book'.
The English horse Blacklock was an ancestor of the
great sire St Simon, and himself sired many winners
including Bolivar, bred in 1826 and exported to
Tasmania two years later.

left : Cup Day at Sandown racecourse, which, like
Caulfield, is controlled by the V.A.T.C.. Sandown
Course is about fifteen miles south-east of Melbourne.
V.A.T.C.

above : In 1869 the South Australian Jockey Club
organized a notable meeting at 'The Old Course' in
Adelaide. To the club's delight, the visiting Duke of
Edinburgh decided to attend the meeting. Since that
time, it has become almost standard practice for
members of the Royal family to attend important race
meetings during visits to Australia.

right : The Wagga Wagga Gold Cup as pictured in an
Australasian Sketcher of 1876.

KILPATRICK & C°.

far left: Mr E.M. Bagot, secretary of the South Australian Jockey Club from 1861 till 1869 when the club, after years of financial difficulty, was dissolved. S.A.J.C.

left: The saddling enclosure of the Rockhampton racecourse, Queensland, during a meeting organized by the Rockhampton Jockey Club.

above: A group of settlers returning from a Kangaroo hunt. Hunting was both a sport and a necessity in the early days of the colony, and a hunt was always a good opportunity for a horse to show his stamina. The famous racehorse Petrel was a stockhorse whose speed was first noticed on an emu hunt.

3. THE CUP

3. THE CUP

Six days before the running of the first Melbourne Cup, news reached Melbourne that the explorers Burke and Wills had perished on their expedition into Australia's north. Melbourne was a buoyant city. It had grown from a population of 20,000 in 1850 to 140,000 by 1860, a bustling exciting major staging post for the migrants who landed by the thousands and headed for the goldfields at Ballarat and Bendigo. Now the death of the explorers cast it into gloom and when the first Cup was run neither newspapers nor a mourning population felt like going to the races. Just 4,000 saw the race.

The Cup had sprung from the rivalry which existed between the Victoria Turf Club and the Victoria Jockey Club. The Jockey Club had responded to a suggestion in *Bell's Life* that there should be a race for the championship of the Australian colonies by staging such a race in October 1859. This race went off successfully despite the loss of several horses on their way from Adelaide to run when the ship *Admella* was wrecked. Another Victoria Jockey Club venture, the Corporation Cup, run on 3 November 1860, caused Melbourne publicans to put up gaudy flags and sent showmen out to Flemington to stage a gay carnival which thousands enjoyed in a picnic atmosphere. Clearly, the Victoria Turf Club had to match these promotions, and they did so by announcing the Melbourne Cup.

According to the latest researches, the Melbourne Cup was the brainchild of the chairman of the V.T.C. at the time, Captain F.C. Standish, Chief Commissioner of Police in Melbourne, whose striking presence had enabled him to overcome criticism of his abysmal failure to catch the bushranger Ned Kelly. Standish, it was said, had come to Australia following a disastrous betting plunge on the English Derby. He was widely known as a prodigious and brave gambler. He was well-connected. Admiral Rous, who masterminded the weight-for-age system, still in use all over the world, was a personal friend.

pages 58-59: The nineteenth century Flemington crowd watches as a winning horse is decorated with a sash. This is one of the several Flemington scenes painted by Carl Kahler. La Trobe

left: The battered cover of A Record of the Melbourne Cup. Published in 1888 this book covers every Cup run till that time, and contains pictures of all the winners, including a sketch of Archer reproduced in this chapter. The very existence of such a publication shows the interest generated by the famous race. A.J.C.

There were seventeen starters for the first Melbourne Cup, which was the third race in a four-race programme —it was followed by a hurdle race—and the second leg of a betting double. The winner gained £710 in prize money. There was no trophy but the winning owner got a hand-beaten gold watch. Badly affected by the news of Burke and Wills' deaths, the race did, however, have one big advantage—for the first time racing devotees could go out to Flemington in a train from Spencer Street Station. This train, return fare 1s 6d, was crowded, but many preferred the river— some rowed out—or the road.

Among the women in bonnets and flounced skirts hanging on the arms of well-washed men in beaver hats and frock coats, the word was that the smart betting fraternity had picked out a horse called Archer as their big betting medium in the Cup. As they tried to sustain their good manners walking in high grass —the course for the race was roughly scythed, else-where it was up to two feet high—the sideshows offering everything from thimble-and-pea to fortune-telling, performing monkeys and astrologists diverted them. It was fun, there was a buccaneering spirit in the air and everyone wanted to see Archer.

They may not have been so curious about Archer had they known that he had walked 550 miles just to race. Archer came from Braidwood, about fifty miles from Canberra, and was trained by Eteinne Living-stone de Mestre at his 1,300-acre Shoalhaven farm. Although he was still in his twenties, de Mestre had a reputation as one of the best trainers in New South Wales and in 1857 had trained Veno to beat the Mel-bourne champion Alice Hawthorne. The ownership of Archer is clouded, but he raced in de Mestre's colours, all black.

Archer was taken to Melbourne from Nowra, New South Wales, a month before the Cup. His strapper Dave Power walked or rode him in twenty-five-mile daily stages over rough tracks from one town to the next. Just before dusk each night Power found a paddock and took Archer into it and worked him. Then he gave him a brisk rub down before they went into the next town for the night. In Melbourne de Mestre trained Archer away from the eyes of racing

above : Etienne de Mestre, the trainer of four Cup winners including Archer and Tim Whiffler. Because Archer took the Cup twice, de Mestre is credited with five Melbourne Cup wins in eighteen years, a record which has remained unbroken.

top right : Archer, the winner of the first and second Melbourne Cups, with his jockey J. Cutts who rode him for both wins. A horse of exceptional stamina, Archer won the first cup after a walk of 550 miles from his stable to the course. The second time he won by 8 lengths with a weight of 10 st 2 lb.

right : A scene at the first Melbourne Cup meeting, before the big race. Horses and jockeys move around nervously, as owners and trainers look on. La Trobe

63

writers at St Kilda Park, South Yarra.

Archer kept winning races despite tremendous weights, but he was spared a start in the third Melbourne Cup in 1863 with 11st 4lb because of a peculiar flare-up of inter-state jealousy. His entry was lodged in Sydney late on the last day for nominations and was wired to Melbourne well before the Victoria Turf Club's normal closing time. But officials in Sydney had been unaware that it was a public holiday in Melbourne to celebrate 'Separation Day', the day Victoria had parted from New South Wales in 1851. When the telegram boy arrived at the V.T.C. rooms the doors were shut. He delivered the telegram containing Archer's entry the next day, but the V.T.C. refused it on the grounds that it was a day late. This caused a quite justified outcry in Sydney among Archer's supporters, but the V.T.C. remained unmoved.

Despite the handicappers Archer continued racing until 1866, sometimes starting two or three times in one day. He retired at the age of ten. Until 1969, when Rain Lover won a second successive Melbourne Cup, Archer was the only horse to have won it two years in a row. Had he run a third time in the Cup it is likely that Archer would have won three straight— a feat probably beyond modern racehorses—but his absence did not spoil the great run of trainer de Mestre who won later Cups with Tim Whiffler (1867), Chester (1877) and Calamia (1878) for a total of five Cup winners in the race's first eighteen years. No other trainer has approached that feat.

Etienne de Mestre was the son of Prosper de Mestre, the first American merchant to settle in Australia. Prosper was given his 1,300 acres at Shoalhaven in a government grant 'for each of the children born in the colony'. Etienne trained his first winner at Bathurst when he was fifteen and subsequently converted his father's property into the best private training ground in the colony, complete with a racetrack, stables, and brood mares. He grew into a commanding figure,

The starter orders horses and riders into line before the running of the 1869 Melbourne Cup. Victorian Tourist Development Authority

with a handsome white beard. But droughts devastated properties in which he invested and a benefit was held at Randwick races to help him retire to Sutton Forest, where he died in 1916, aged eighty-four.

The start of the first Melbourne Cup was delayed when Twilight bolted at the start and galloped a full circuit of the course before he could be returned to the starter, George Watson. Flatcatch led at the start from Archer, with the other fifteen starters well back. Turning into the straight for the first time Medora fell and brought down Despatch and Twilight. Archer sprinted right away from the field in the finishing straight to win by six lengths from Morman, with Prince two lengths further back third. Medora and Despatch had to be destroyed as a result of the fall.

Archer's win was a tremendous blow to bookmakers. Despite de Mestre's efforts to conceal Archer's true ability the public had heavily backed the horse, and he started second favourite at 6 to 1. The second horse, Morman, was favourite at 3 to 1. 'Without exception, the settling on the Turf Club races just concluded was the worst we ever remember, and it will be a long time before the ring recovers itself from the severe blow which Archer's victory in the Cup administered,' read the report on the meeting to the Victoria Turf Club. 'Altogether the betting world just now is in a fog. The solvent members of the room will meet on Monday next to decide what can be done.'

Strangely enough, de Mestre did not have a high regard for Archer, which was bred at Exeter Farm, Braidwood, the home of de Mestre's schoolfriend, T.J. Roberts. When Roberts asked de Mestre to decide whether Archer or a horse called Exeter should be sent to China, de Mestre picked Exeter to go. Although Roberts said he was wrong de Mestre always said he had chosen the better horse and stressed that Exeter had done exceptionally well in China. When he first learned of the staging of the first Melbourne Cup de Mestre nominated Inheritor as well as Archer and told his friends Inheritor was the best of the pair.

In 1862, de Mestre again sent Archer to Melbourne with Dave Power to run in the Cup. Prize money had risen to £810, and this time Melbourne racegoers

above: The starter moves away as the field for the first Melbourne Cup leaps ahead. This picture is somewhat inaccurate, as it shows twenty horses and riders competing when in fact only seventeen started in the historic race.

right: The running of the first Melbourne Cup, which was won by Archer from Mormon. There was a bad fall during the race, and two horses had to be destroyed. Herald and Weekly Times

made Archer firm favourite at 2 to 1 despite the fact
that he had to carry 10st 2lb. Archer's jockey was
again J. Cutts, who had ridden him the previous year.
Archer won by eight lengths this time, and cut his
time by five seconds to 3 min 47 sec despite his big
weight. Mormon was again second, the only time in
Cup history that the same horses have run first and
second in successive years. The crowd was 7,000.
To prevent a repetition of the smash which had marred
the first Cup the organizers moved the starting post
so that the horses had a straight run for four furlongs
before they had to make a turn.

The first three Melbourne Cups were conducted by
the Victoria Turf Club, which also conducted incessant
guerilla warfare against the rival Victoria Jockey
Club. In 1864, members of both clubs decided they
had had enough of this folly and held a conference
which agreed to sink both clubs without trace and
form the Victoria Racing Club. This club took over
control of the Melbourne Cup in 1864 and has run
the race with unqualified distinction ever since,
building it to a superb test of horses and a beguiling
social occasion. The V.R.C. was lucky in its choice
of its first secretary, R.C. Bagot, an Irish-bred son of
Canon Bagot, who had done distinguished work in
relieving distress in the Irish famine back in 1849.

Bagot first became interested in Flemington as the
engineer hired to survey the course and recommend
improvements. Bagot was not a racing fan when he
began but his education in architecture and engineering
gave him invaluable experience when improvements to
the Flemington crowd facilities were discussed. His
first stand was labelled 'Bagot's cowshed', for it lacked
beauty, but it was cheap, ideally positioned, and it
helped bring thousands of people to Flemington. In
the early days of the V.R.C. Bagot acted as unpaid
secretary. As the club prospered he gave up his
profession to become full-time paid secretary. It was
Bagot who persuaded the V.R.C. committee to give
each member of the club two ladies' tickets. 'Where
the women go, the men will follow', Bagot said, and
long before he died in 1881 he had made the Melbourne
Cup meeting a highly popular event for women from
all states. Bagot died of pneumonia following a flood

No. 9.—VOL. I. MELBOURNE, SATURDAY, NOVEMBER 29, 1873. PRICE 6

top left : A bird's eye view of Flemington racecourse on Cup Day, 1877. Excited spectators barrack from the hill in the foreground, while others observe the race from boats on the river.

left : Rounding the turn by the river in the Melbourne Cup of 1883. In the background stands 'Bagot's Cowshed', the functional, inexpensive grandstand erected by the first secretary of the V.R.C., R.C. Bagot.

above : Fashion plates on the lawn on Cup day 1873. Enormous bustles, bows and flounces, small plumed hats and tiny parasols were in vogue for the well-to-do in this period, and newspapers seemed to devote as much space to the fashions as they did to the races.

at Flemington and was succeeded by his friend Henry Byron Moore who applied for the job at the insistence of the widowed Mrs Bagot.

'I am an applicant for the appointment of secretary of the Victoria Racing Club,' Moore said in his letter of application—and left it at that. He didn't have to say any more because his merit in highly diversified fields was known to all. He was not a racing man in the sense that he doted on betting and making a killing, but he loved the spectacle of a well-bred, carefully-trained thoroughbred at full flight. He played violin and piano splendidly, confessed he knew more about roses than horses, was an outstanding amateur engraver, at one time had been Victoria's assistant Surveyor-General, had run his own telephone exchange before these were organized officially, wrote and published fairytales for children's hospitals, and had a reputation for honesty that meant trouble for all race-track crooks.

One of Moore's first actions as V.R.C. secretary was to arrange for a large group of Melbourne detectives and constables, accompanied by a plain clothes man from each of the other colonies, to go to the races and swoop on all known criminals. Most of the inter-state crooks were stopped at the gate and prevented from entering. Nineteen were arrested and gaoled for a week—the duration of the meeting. Thereafter criminals from other colonies were loath to visit Melbourne. This prompt work helped foster the feeling that people of quality could attend the races with their children without worry from hoodlums.

Moore also put his knowledge of roses to good use. On Cup days Flemington was always resplendent with roses. There were fountains and comfortable benches on the lawns, needles and cotton in the ladies' rooms for those unlucky enough to tear a prized dress, a Temperance Pagoda for those who did not drink hard liquor—it later became a wine bar—and huts which offered hot water for tea-making and supplies of fresh cream and milk. Moore's musical background enabled him to bring in the best brass bands to play between races. He was always improving facilities, adding an oyster pavilion here, a fruit kiosk there, or altering traffic arrangements to prevent crushes. Even the

above, top right : Contemporary caricatures of Flemington racecourse personalities.

top far right : Henry Byron Moore, the second secretary of the V.R.C., photographed at Flemington racecourse. During his years as secretary, Moore constantly improved facilities at the course, attracting large numbers of people to the races, particularly the Melbourne Cup.

right : Despite official surveillance, the excitement of the races provided an ideal cover for petty thieving. Here a pickpocket (circled) is photographed in the act of lifting an unsuspecting gentleman's wallet. The photographer, intent on recording the finish of this exciting Cup race in the 1890s, was unaware that he was also recording a crime in the making. Racecourse Hotel, Flemington

MR. LLOYD (Committeeman).

smallest details did not escape him—he arranged with a Melbourne store for it to accept hampers on race days, take them to the course for lunch and deliver them later to the owners' homes. By 1890 he had 500 stalls for carriage horses.

Perhaps the most successful owner of this period was 'Honest John' Tait, who between 1865 and 1874 won 139 races, four of them Melbourne Cups. Tait had trained as a journalist and then become a jeweller, migrating from Scotland to Tasmania when he was in his mid-twenties. He next turned to the hotel trade, seeking out the toughest districts because he said that was where his best customers would reside. He could fight like a thrashing machine when he had to, and the *Melbourne Herald* once commented that he served excellent rum with beer chasers and even better left hooks.

When he moved to the mainland, Tait made his pubs the meeting places of sportsmen. The first horses he bought won races and about 1860 he moved them into Byron Lodge at Randwick, which had been built by the musician Isaac Nathan. Tait had two horses in the 1866 Melbourne Cup, the winner, The Barb, and Falcon which gained third place. The field of twenty-eight was the biggest that had ever contested a race in Australia. The Barb raced to the post level with Exile but found just enough extra to win by a head. The judge Mr J. Dougharty, caused a furore by naming the first and second horses but refusing to name a third because Falcon had run in colours that had not been officially notified. The stewards held a hurried meeting and placed Falcon third, but some bookmakers on the course refused to pay place bets on Falcon, claiming his placing was not official under the rules of racing.

The Barb had won the A.J.C. Derby in brilliant style a few weeks earlier, defeating Fishhook, then the highest-priced two-year-old in Australian history. Fishhook had been taken to Sydney by Mr C.B. Fisher, who had paid 3,600 guineas for the colt at the sale of the Maribyrnong Stud stock, owned by his brother Hurtle. The sale had realized 26,000 guineas, an unheard-of sum in Australian bloodstock sales, and Fishhook had been the prize buy of the forty-five

above: The lawn at Flemington on Cup Day, 1867. A lithograph of a painting by Carl Kahler. The gracious and attractive surroundings created by the first two secretaries of the V.R.C. attracted whole families to the races. Fountains, flowers, grass, comfortable lawn benches and a pleasantly social atmosphere prevailed. La Trobe

left: The Australian band adds to the Flemington festivity in 1880.

lots offered.   Fortunes were lost when The Barb beat Fishhook in the A.J.C. Derby and Melbourne Cup.

The Barb's great success in the Melbourne Cup did a lot for Australian racing.   He was clearly the best horse foaled to that time in Australia, which boosted our breeding reputation, but he was also what racing always needs—a brave and fast horse that thrills the public and attracts them in large numbers to the race-tracks.   The Barb, nicknamed 'The Black Demon', was almost unbeatable in weight-for-age races, and ignored the attentions of handicappers in winning the 1868 Metropolitan Handicap and the Sydney Cup in 1868 and 1869, carrying the impressive weight of 10 st 8 lb.   He remains the only horse to win the Sydney Cup with more than 10 st.

The Barb was a small, but splendidly framed jet-black horse by Sir Hercules, whose renown as a sire was of great value to Australian racing.   The Barb won fifteen times in twenty-three starts.   His emergence as a champion made 1866 a year to remember in Australian horse racing.   In addition to Hurtle Fisher's shock decision to retire from racing by selling his Maribyrnong Stud, the record prices obtained, and a controversial Melbourne Cup incident involving Falcon, this was the year that big races, the Sydney Cup and the Metropolitan Handicap, were started in Sydney.   It was in this year that New South Wales made a belated effort to emulate the success of the Melbourne Cup.   These efforts have never succeeded, largely, one suspects, because the shrewdness of Robert Cooper Bagot and Henry Byron Moore, backed by wise committees, gave the Melbourne Cup too big a start.

top: A panoramic view of Flemington racecourse and the finish of a Melbourne Cup in the last half of the nineteenth century.

right: Cup Day: a sketch on the road. From an Australian Sketcher of 1876.

far right: John Tait's Fireworks, winner of two Victoria Derbies, in 1867 and 1868, the Victorian Champion Stakes and St Leger and the Derby Stakes and Spring Metropolitan Maiden Plate at Randwick in 1867.

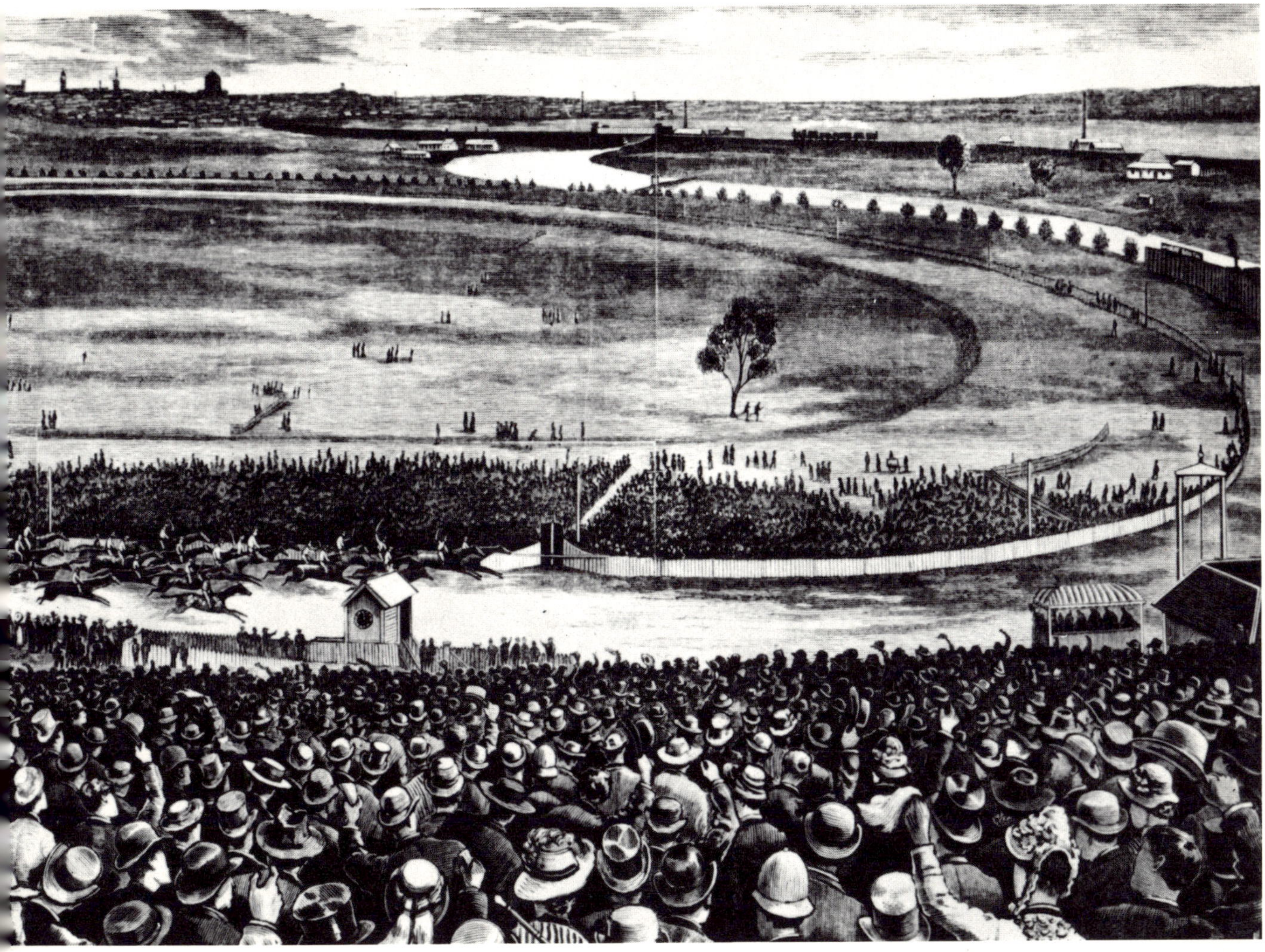

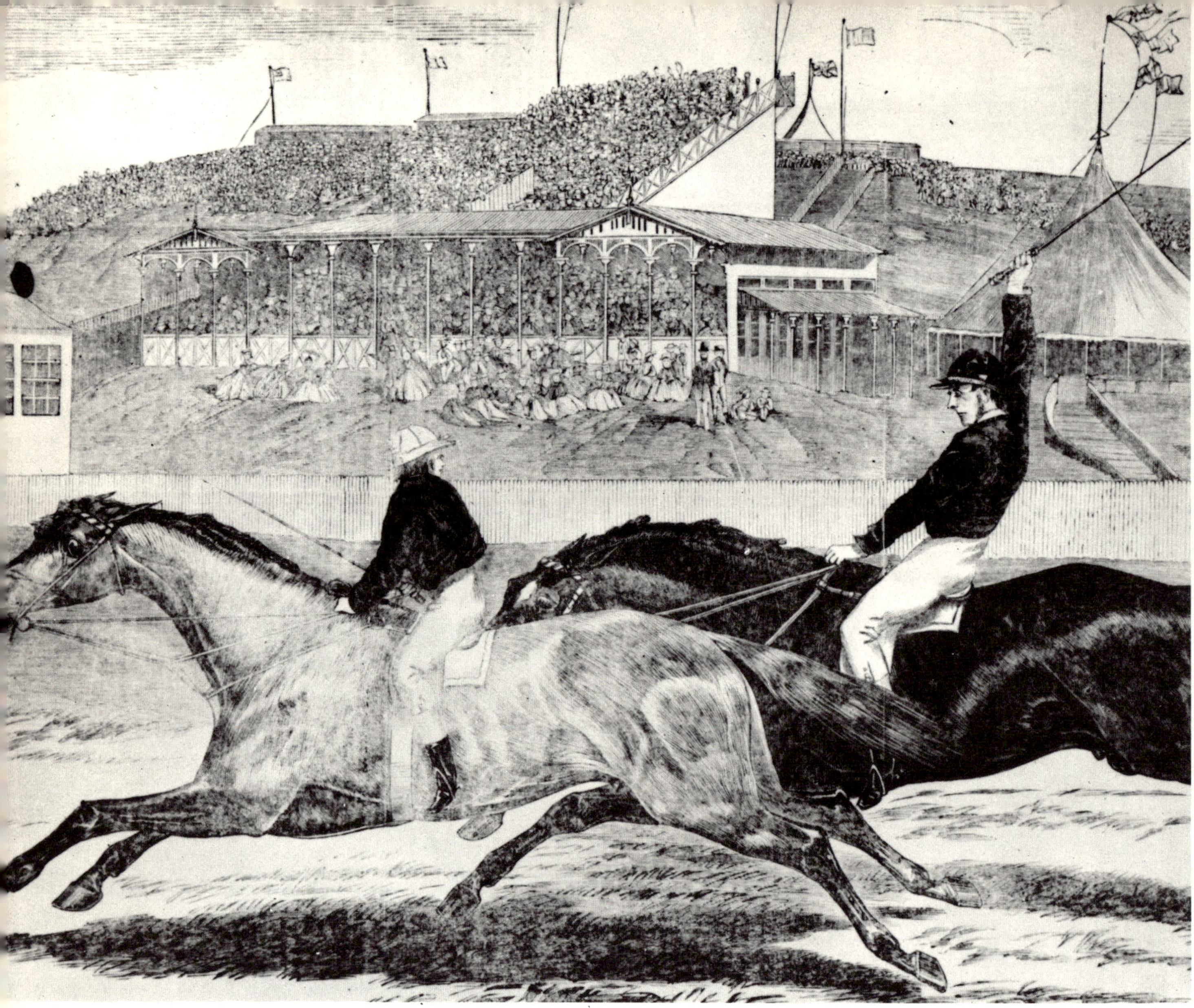

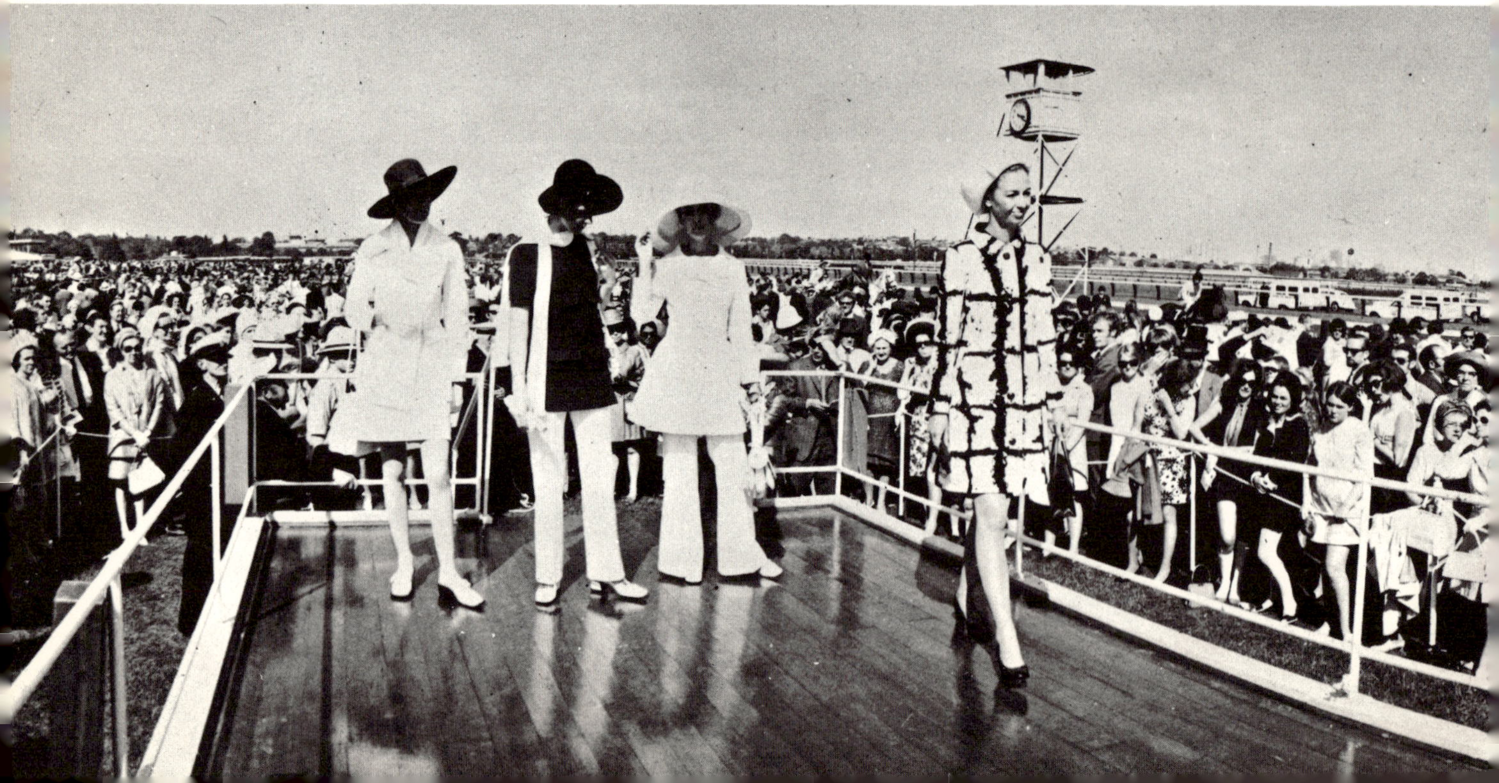

*top far left : The grey gelding Toryboy winning from
Panic in the Cup of 1865.*

top left : The elaborate Melbourne Cup of 1876.

*left : The fashion scene is still important at the Cup.
Here ladies parade in their carefully chosen outfits,
competing for fashion prizes. V.R.C.*

*above : On the lawn at Flemington in 1884, these
rather stiff ladies and gentlemen seem to be eyeing one
another's outfits rather critically. The Melbourne
Cup and other big racing events have always been
excuses for excursions into high fashion, and at this
time in Australia fashion meant English fashion,
with very few concessions to boiling summer heat.*

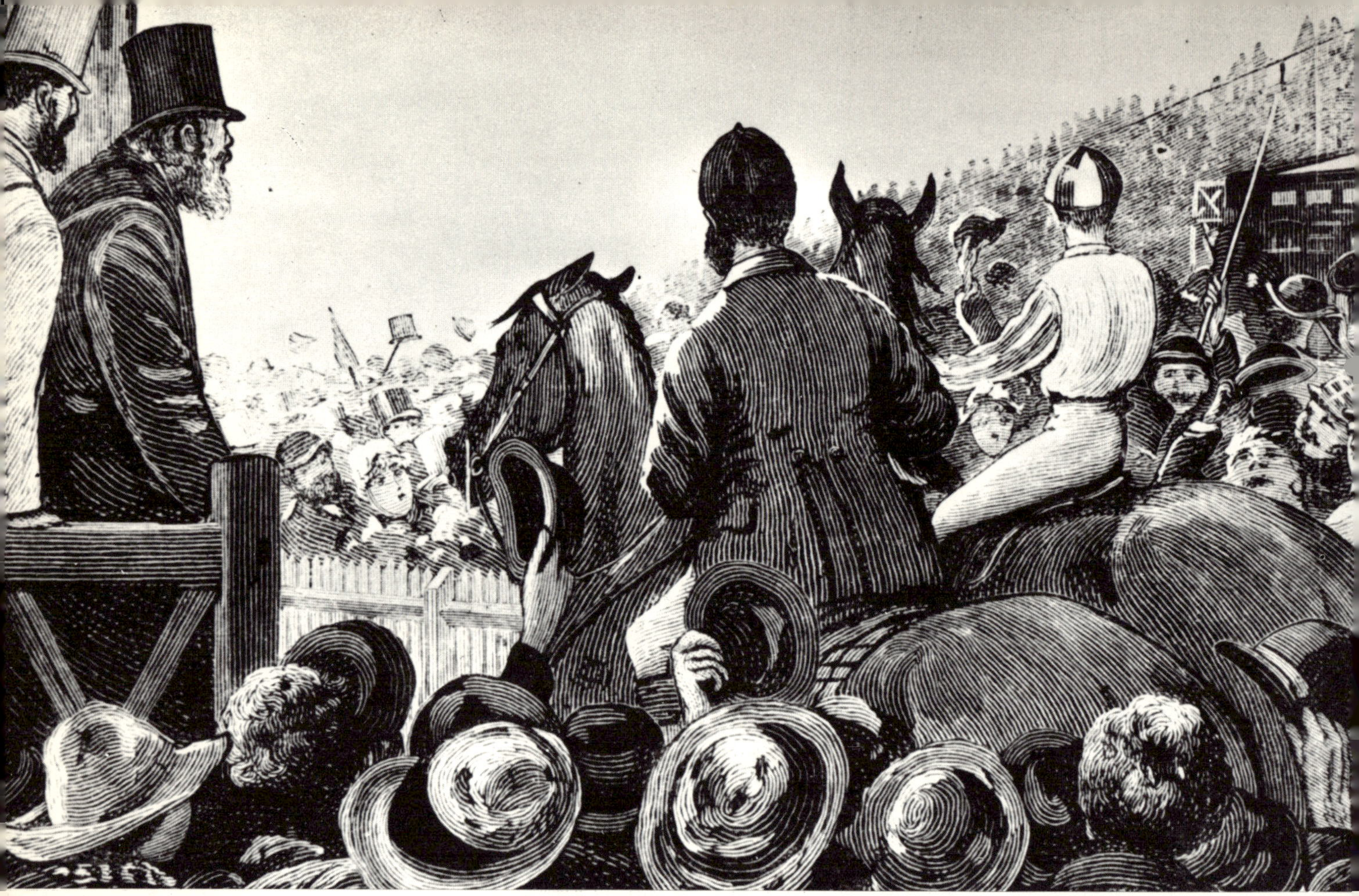

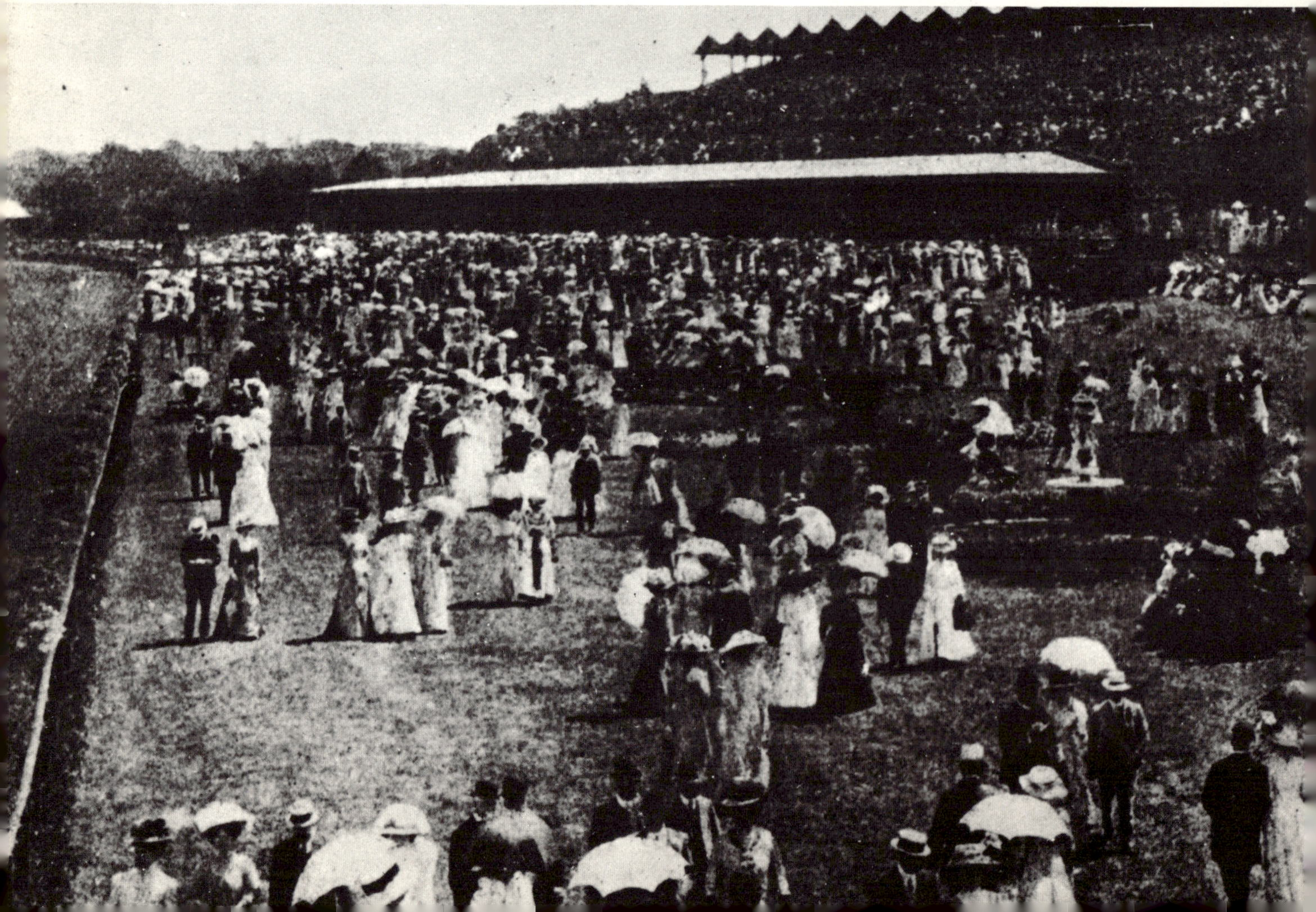

top left: *Bringing in the winner, Zulu, after the running of the Melbourne Cup of 1881.*

left: *Flemington on Cup Day: the lawn, the grandstand and the hill. This old photograph, when first published by the Sydney Mail, was regarded as the most successful photographic view ever obtained of the course on Cup Day.*

above: *Jottings about the Cup from an Australian Sketcher 1876. Horses, touts, bets, and sweeps are caught by the artist's pen.*

BELL'S LIFE
AND SPORTING

VOL. 4, No. 107.   MELBOURNE, SATURDAY

BELL'S LIFE IN VICTORIA,
AND SPORTING CHRONICLE.

SATURDAY, 22ND JANUARY, 1859.

Now that the Inter-Colonial Cricket Match is exciting the greatest interest in Sydney and Melbourne, it appears to be a favourable moment to make a proposition for a grand Australian Turf Tournament. The former Champion race having resulted in favour of New South Wales, the sportsmen of Victoria may be (but we believe they will not be, when brought to the scratch) afraid to venture upon a new trial of strength. At all events, it must be ultimately beneficial to the turf of all the Australian colonies, if some great annual race could be established, where, in friendly rivalry, the leading sportsmen of each country could meet and test the merits of their respective stock. Apart from any selfish home considerations, it appears to us that the central position of Victoria, and the very fine course which Melbourne has, point out our city as the best locality for the rendezvous of all the parties interested.

We therefore propose (and we are authorised to state that the affair shall not fall through on the part of Victoria) that an annual race shall be established, with a good bonus added to a sweepstakes of a sufficient amount to test the confidence of owners of horses, but not so high as to bar out some whose pockets are not thoroughly well lined; a stake which will realise about a thousand pounds, and perhaps more, to the winner, in addition to "the honour and glory of the thing."

In suggesting the terms of the race, we have endeavoured to guard against the possibility of a fluke and a sham being substituted for what we desire—a sterling, honest and honourable race. We have offered what appear to us to be liberal terms to competitors from the other colonies, having secured to them the whole stake, if any one of them can win it, and expenses if only able to secure second place. This advantage to our visitors will probably recompense them for the additional charges and risks consequent upon a sea voyage. At the same time, we have plenty of other money which awaits their winning, if our guests from abroad will condescend to attend the regular meetings now appointed and advertised.

Perhaps some day, other than that we have named, would better suit the convenience of our outside neighbours. In which case, upon their suggestion, we will alter the date. It may be advisable to collect opinions upon this subject, and we hope to receive communications thereanent, especially from gentlemen likely to take part in the affair, if it assumes an aspect satisfactory to them.

There can be little doubt that the public money would be readily obtained by subscriptions, by assistance from the Racing Clubs, by the revenues of the Course upon the great day of trial; more especially if the affair were left to the management of the gentlemen whose names have occurred to us as the most appropriate Stewards of this very important occasion. They would probably assist with themselves some of our visitors who

ourably, and whom we shall be happy to see
mongst us again and again.

Our proposal for the contests would run as
llows :—

SATURDAY, 28TH MAY.

THE AUSTRALIAN CHAMPION SWEEPSTAKES of
0 sovs each, half forfeit, with 500 sovs added by the
ewards, if two horses start for the race, and 100 sovs
dditional for every horse up to the number of seven
arting. Distance, three miles. Weight for age :
yrs, 5st ; 3 yrs, 7st 8lb ; 4 yrs, 9st ; 5 yrs, 9st 7lb ;
yrs and aged, 9st 10lb : 3lb allowed to mares and
eldings.

Any horse who shall run second, if he be the property
a non-resident in Victoria, and shall have been bred
another colony, and imported here by sea within
ree months of the 1st of May, shall receive back 200
vs out of the stakes if two only start ; and 100 sovs
dditional if more than two start.

The public money will not be given, unless at least
vo horses enter ; one of which must be a non-Victorian
orse, as expressed in the foregoing condition ; nor to any
orse walking over for the stake, unless a non-Victorian
orse as previously expressed.

Nominations to be made between the hours of nine
nd ten o'clock on Monday evening, February 21st, at
e Union hotel, Melbourne. sealed and addressed to
e stewards of the appointed race-day (Dal. Campbell,
sq., R. Goldsbrough, Esq., and three others to be
lected by them).

As the object of founding this race is to give the
olonies of Australia an opportunity of testing the rival
erits of their best horses, the stewards will reserve to
emselves the power to reject any nomination, which
ay appear to them to be made not in good faith, but
r the purpose of securing the added money without a
ntest.

One hundred sovs. to be paid with each nomination
the night of entry (February 21st), and the remain-
r of the stake to be paid by nine o'clock on the Mon-
y evening, before the race, at the Union hotel.

We have proposed the scale of weights to suit
e custom of New South Wales, and have taken
e measure of the allowances to young horses
om the rules of the Victoria Jockey Club. Upon
is point we should like to gather opinions, but
om what we can learn, we are not likely to see
ny but aged horses in the field on the day named.

It is highly probable that a good handicap
veepstakes for two-milers, of 50 sovs. each, half
rfeit, might arise out of the enthusiasm of the
me, so that a great turf tournament might be got
p at the intercolonial *concours.*

Champion two-year-olds might also meet with
liberal bonus to recompense them for the late-
ss of the season at which they must be kept up.
great day's sport might in fact be realised ;
ch as has never before been seen south of the
ne.

Such a turf gathering would do good to the
eeders of all Australia ; would improve the stock
every competing locality ; and would improve
d extend friendship between people who now
ow little or nothing of each other. It is diffi-
lt to see the limit of advantage which these
ercolonial visits bring about ; and why should
t our noble sport of the turf contribute its
are of good to the people and the land of our
oice ?

Since the above was in type, we have received
e sanction of the two gentlemen named, to an-
unce that they are willing to act and to carry
t the above proposal. The management can-
t be in better hands, and it would be very
ficult to imagine that under their direction

*far left : Admiral Rous and Mr Payne. Admiral Rous
was responsible for the weight-for-age system still in
use all over the world. He was a good friend of Captain
F.C. Standish, the Melbourne police commissioner,
who, it is claimed, conceived the idea of the Melbourne
Cup. A.J.C.*

*left : The newspaper Bell's Life suggested that a race
for the championship of the Australian colonies should
be organized. This led to the Victoria Jockey Club's
staging such a race in October 1859, stimulating the
rival Victoria Turf Club to cap this effort by announcing the Melbourne Cup.*

*above : The Governor's Box at the V.R.C. meeting of
29 November 1870. From left to right; Sir George
Bowen, Sir Hercules Robinson, Sir Anthony Musgrave.*

4. CONSOLIDATION

THE WEIGH
TO OWNER

AUSTRALIAN

NEWS

377.   MELBOURNE. SATURDAY, NOVEMBER 13, 1886.   PRICE { WITH TWO SUPPLEMENTS } 1s.

4. CONSOLIDATION

Away from the racetracks, starting to spring up in the big cities, picnic race meetings were flourishing. This was a tribute to the hardihood and flair for improvization of the early bush settlers. From hazardous beginnings the picnics became an integral part of the Australian racing scene. They developed from the desire of country people, many of them isolated, to briefly fraternize with people facing similar problems. The common talking point was the horses in which they all had so much pride. In time they became an attraction for city folk eager to get out into the country and enjoy a good social booze-up with sophistication and manners intact.

Some of the most unusual horse races in Australian history began, naturally enough, over arguments in bush pubs. There was, for example, tremendous interest in how far a horse could race. The Melbourne Cup had been set at two miles and it was well known that the English Derby was over what was regarded as a classic test of stamina and speed, a mile and a half. But with bushrangers covering vast distances in short times, troopers' horses not far behind, and the speed and strength of stockhorses well proven, there seemed a strong case for Australian horses being able to race over longer distances than those set by the city race clubs.

On 20 November 1868, a race over ten miles was held on the third day of the annual Wagga races. Twelve horses were entered and they had to run seven and a half times around Wagga racetrack. The race was won by a horse called Australia, who averaged more than twenty-five miles an hour for the ten miles. Many of the starters were distressed at the finish and most showed no further fondness for racing, but the race aroused such interest that ninety-six mile match race was organized between Dubbo and Orange on 15 July 1870.

The starters, a mare called The Barmaid and a gelding called The Colonel, stayed together for almost six hours before The Colonel surged ahead. About thirty miles from home The Barmaid was pulled up exhausted, leaving The Colonel to complete the ninety-six miles unchallenged in 10 hrs 29 min, an average speed of nine miles an hour. Both horses carried 9st and the losing owner parted with £1,000. The horses were frequently rested on the way. They raced over tough terrain, crossing streams, climbing hills, galloping down muddy roads.

One outcome of this and other displays of stamina away from the racetracks—in 1853, a man named Mossman raced his horse the 140 miles from Sydney to Maitland in twenty hours—was the acceptance of the humanity of the race clubs in sticking to shorter distances. Barmaid was very much the worse for wear after her defeat by The Colonel and Mr Mossman's horse died soon after reaching Maitland. But in 1966 Tom Quilty, a Queensland station owner, revived 100-mile horse races and these have been held each year since despite protests from the R.S.P.C.A. The winners have usually covered the distance in under twelve hours.

A major problem of the early race clubs, as they gained strength and started to stage regular meetings, was that of sorting out the names of horses. There were often several well-performed horses around at the same time carrying the same name. One fashion was for owners to call their horses after champion English or colonial horses. When Hector was winning races early in the early nineteenth century there were Hectors all over New South Wales. In 1867, there were two Tim Whifflers entered in the Melbourne Cup. One, owned by Ballarat publican Walter Craig, had won the 1867 Australian Cup. The other was the Sydney-bred Tim Whiffler which had won the Metropolitan Handicap at Randwick in record time. To avoid confusion, bookmakers dubbed them Sydney Tim and Melbourne Tim. Sydney Tim won the Melbourne Cup easily and then had a son which was also named Tim Whiffler. In Perth in the 1870s another Tim Whiffler won several races. Yet another Tim Whiffler was imported from England in 1871 and sired Briseis, who won the 1876 Melbourne Cup and Darriwell, winner of the 1879 Melbourne Cup. Surprisingly, this problem of identification was not

left : A series of three cartoons depicting the misfortunes of a pompous city slicker, Mr Blowhard as he tries to deal with bush horses. Property owners were very proud of their tough, fast stockhorses and picnic races were, and still are in some areas, the highlight of the country social year.

above : The Melbourne Cup of 1867, won by de Mestre's Tim Whiffler, and now in the possession of Mr J.M. Royds of Sydney whose great-grandfather, T.M. Royds, bred the horse. The silver cup, imported from England, is richly ornamented and extremely elaborate in design.

solved until 1911 when uniform name registration came into force in all states.

From the start of racing in Australia, there was far more hero-worship lavished on jockeys than there had ever been in England. The first Australian professional jockey, John Fisher, was reported to have ridden at eighty years of age and lived to ninety-nine. The men who rode the early champions such as Hector, Junius, Jorrocks and Archer were far from under-privileged lackeys. John Cutts, who won the first two Melbourne Cups on Archer was well set up. Owners consulted their jockeys freely and good horsemanship was well rewarded. This tendancy to lionize jockeys was reflected in the space journals gave to successful race riders. Race descriptions invariably included lines about the 'leathering' of the horses involved. Garryowen, in reporting the first Flemington meeting, noted that the jockeys were quite proud of their colours and rode with an utter recklessness to themselves and their mounts.

In 1828, after Junius had won another Brisbane Cup in Sydney, his owner, Mr Murray, offered 500 guineas to any horse that could beat Junius in a race 'three times around the Sydney course'. Junius's regular jockey, James Spinks, hearing of this challenge, publicly increased the offer to £1,000. Spinks had won on Young Junius at Campbelltown and again at the Bellevue Hill track despite a broken stirrup-iron. A fine horseman, he was the predecessor of the colony's most notable rider, John Higgerson, who rode Jorrocks and many other star performers to victory. Higgerson was the rider Etienne de Mestre chose to take with him to Melbourne to ride Veno in the famous 1857 match race against Alice Hawthorne. Higgerson died in 1905, aged ninety-five at Heathcote on the outskirts of Sydney, where there is still a Veno Street.

In the years when most of our major races and clubs were consolidating, the great virtuoso of the saddle was Tommy Corrigan, who rode his first winner in the Victorian town of Woodford in 1865, his last at

top. Dust Cloud, owned by Mr Ben Osborne Junior, winning the Mulwaree Stakes by three lengths at the Tirranna picnic races of 1912.

centre: Interested spectators watch a race at the Tirrana picnic meeting, January 1912.

bottom: Hake, also owned by Mr Ben Osborne Junior, wins the Tirranna Cup by four lengths.

Caulfield in 1894. Corrigan was born in County Meath in 1854 and migrated to Victoria with his parents who took up farming at Woodside. Tommy wagged school to ride his first winner and over the next twenty-eight years became a public idol by winning almost every major race in both Victoria and New South Wales and showing equal skill across country, on the flat or over jumps.

Corrigan's great popularity stemmed from his fearlessness and his honesty. Warned of a horse's reputation for throwing his jockeys, he would insist that only badly-handled animals remained bad-tempered. He was a devout churchman and a devoted father and husband. When he walked the streets of Melbourne people stopped to pay their respects to the 'merry-hearted little Irishman'. The poet Banjo Paterson wrote of him in hurdle races:

When any slip means sudden death—with wife and
    child to keep—
It needs some nerve to draw the whip and flog him
    at the leap—
But Corrigan would ride them out, by danger
    undismayed,
He never flinched at fence or wall, he never was
    afraid;
With easy seat and nerve of steel, light hand and
    smiling face,
He held the rushing horses back, and made the
    sluggards race.

Corrigan had his first ride at Flemington on Melbourne Cup day, 1867, when he was thirteen. He grew a seven-inch moustache, of which he was inordinately proud, that became known to racegoers throughout Australia, as did his flair for a quip. On an August day in 1894 before the start of an important steeplechase at Caulfield, the Governor, the Earl of Hopetoun, wished him luck and Corrigan said, 'Wouldn't you like to be coming with us, sir'? Corrigan's mount Waiter, which he owned, fell at the fourth hurdle, throwing Corrigan on to his head. His brain was damaged and he died next day, aged forty.

Corrigan's funeral was a remarkable event which stirred all Melbourne. But the V.A.T.C. had to pay

top left: Racing over the jumps—a thrilling spectacle, and a dangerous sport. This Daryl Lindsay drawing shows the possibly fatal consequences of a fall. The great jockey Tommy Corrigan was killed in this way during a steeplechase in 1894. Sir Daryl Lindsay

left: Tim Whiffler, Sydney-bred winner of the Melbourne Cup of 1867 in which there was another Tim Whiffler running. The successful horse, nicknamed 'Sydney Tim' was trained by Etienne de Mestre, the trainer of Archer.

above: Tom Corrigan.

for it because Corrigan had died penniless after a
lifetime of giving his money away to touts and racecourse urgers. Thousands lined the streets to the
cemetry and 150 jockeys and trainers marched ahead
of the hearse. All Melbourne shops closed, flags were
at half mast, and the city mourned. From a career
total of 788 mounts Corrigan had ridden 239 winners,
135 seconds and 95 thirds. His wins included seven
Grand Nationals.

Gambling, which began with private wagers between
officers of the 73rd Regiment and among settlers who
started their horses in our first meetings, spread
rapidly with the establishment of race clubs. 'Many
pairs of gloves changed hands; a mode of gambling to
which the ladies were by no means averse', wrote
Garryowen of the first Flemington meeting. Betting
was confined initially to the clubs and to establishments such as Kirk's Bazaar, the Melbourne horse
market which became a great meeting place for horse
fanciers. Welching was not uncommon.

Betting for cash at the course was practised from
the 1860s, but meetings were so infrequent that
bookmaking could not provide a livelihood. Newspapers published lists of odds from the time fields for
races were known. The four or five bookmakers at
the course offered very tight prices and co-operated
closely to ensure their odds were uniform. Outsiders
were not admitted to their ranks. They moved about
entering wagers in pocketbooks and only occasionally
did a bookie hand out a ticket to a client with his name
on it.

The modern conception of bookmaking began with
the arrival of the Englishman Robert Standish Sievier
in 1882. Siever was the first to wear a big black bag
in which to hold money, the first to issue numbered
tickets bearing the initials of horses backed to punters,
and the first to stand at a regular pitch with a clerk.
He began with little cash but he had sensed an opportunity to get rich. When winning punters presented
their tickets after the first race on which he fielded at
Flemington, he told them to come back for their money
after the second race. He handed out money to
winning bettors in flamboyant style and word of this
dashing and honest bookmaker swept the course.

*top: The Grand National Steeplechase, one of the
most important Victorian races, first run in 1866.*

*above: A prodigal husband returns, somewhat the
worse for wear, from a day at the races. His wife
doesn't look very sympathetic! This Punch sketch
appeared in 1891.*

*right: Bookies on the flat, resplendent in striped coats,
call their odds at the V.R.C. spring meeting of 1891.
By this time the practice of standing on a little platform
to do business had been adopted by most bookmakers,
and their activities added colour and flamboyance to
the racing scene.*

93

Just before the 1886 Melbourne Cup, the Sydney colt Arsenal arrived for the race in bad shape. The horse had very tender feet and the journey had upset him so much that when he was stalled he refused to touch his oats. Sievier advised Arsenal's owner, W. Gannon, to put a pony in Arsenal's stall with him, reasoning that if the pony ate hungrily the colt would copy him. Arsenal had been prepared for seven months for the Cup, working out daily on the tan to protect his feet without once risking them on the hard surface of a racetrack. Following the pony's lead he ate well in the few days preceding the Cup, building enough strength to win the big race by a neck from the celebrated New Zealand stayer Trenton. Gannon sent Arsenal back to Sydney for the Australian Cup the following autumn but he broke down during the race.

In the process of introducing new bookmaking techniques, Sievier prospered. He returned home to England where he became a sensation as a punter and buyer of racehorses. In one purchase, he paid out £21,000 for three untried yearlings, an astonishing sum at that time. At the yearling sales in 1901 he paid the unheard-of price of 10,000 guineas for the filly Sceptre, which vindicated his judgment by becoming one of the greatest race and brood mares in the Stud Book. Eventually Sievier was warned off by the English Jockey Club, but his influence on Australian racing has persisted through a long succession of bookmakers, colourful personalities whose behaviour has enriched the lexicon of the Australian turf. To many, dealing with them remains more appealing than poking money through a grill to be fed into a machine.

One of the men whose betting sprees brought rich colour to the betting ring was former cabin boy Joe Thompson, who deserted when the sailing boat that brought him from England reached Hobson's Bay. Thompson headed for the goldfields at Ballarat where he spent six years and made enough to enable him to

right : 'The Ring' at Randwick in the 1890s, the grass littered with discarded tickets. A.J.C.

94

return to Melbourne in 1860 and take out a bookmaker's license. He was widely known for the great power of his voice in shouting the odds and for the enormous bets he laid. He won a bet of £20,000 to £1,000 against Whakawai winning the 1887 Melbourne Cup.

Horses owned by Thompson, who openly referred to himself as King of The Betting Ring, won many races. They were usually trained by James Wilson at the St Alban's stables. Thompson and Wilson prospered in joint racing ventures for more than twenty years but sustained an intense dislike for each other. This simmered until they brawled in the paddock at Flemington and were charged with disturbing the peace. They were fined £50 each. Once when it was rumoured that he was in financial difficulties, Thompson laid a winning double of £10,000 and, following a burst of publicity, paid the winner in gold sovereigns on the steps of his Collins Street office.

The greatest Australian bookmaker of this time, however, was Sol Green, a Cockney who migrated to Australia in 1880 when he was sixteen. Green worked hard as a general trader to get enough money to start as a bookmaker at the age of twenty. He had a remarkable memory and could assess almost instantly his prospects in a bet. He was also an intense student of racehorse form, prepared to back his judgment when the odds were favourable. Often he took bets with such speed even skilled punters watching him could not follow the dealings. From bookmaking he branched out into buying and breeding horses, then to property dealing. He died a millionaire.

Sievier, Thompson, Green and other prominent bookmakers like E.N. Thompson ('The Count'), Maurice Quinlan and Tot Murray helped build Australians' reputation as the world's greatest gamblers. They were ready to accommodate the biggest bettors. Many historians believe the gambling instinct sprang from the goldfields, where men who had been broke suddenly found themselves wealthy. Whatever the taproots of the habit, there is no doubt that horse racing provided a most attractive gambling medium, more appealing to the punter than dice, roulette or the other illegal game which became an Australian tradition, two-up.

top left : A caricature of Flemington bookmaker, M.J. Healey, his big black money bag prominently displayed.

far left : A caricature of Sol Green, well-known colourful racecourse personality and skilful bookmaker. A remarkable memory and careful study of racehorse form helped him to build a fortune.

left : Trenton, the best son of Musket next to Carbine. Bred in New Zealand, he started thirteen times in four seasons for eight wins, three seconds and a third. He sired many great winners, including the gallant mare Wakeful. A.J.C.

above : The horses move off to line up for the 1887 Melbourne Cup. Joe Thompson, 'King of the Betting Ring' had bet £20,000 to £1,000 against Whakawai winning the race. His must have been the loudest cheers of all when Dunlop came in at 20 to 1 in record time, beating the next horse, Silvermine, by a length.

97

Nothing quite stimulates a punter's willingness to bet, however, like the chance to back a really good horse. Picking good horses out in advance had always been a problem, but even after a fine horse's ability was known Australians have always backed their respect for a class thoroughbred in hard cash, prohibitive odds notwithstanding. Such a horse was Carbine, who probably did more to boost the prestige of Australian horse racing internationally than any other horse.

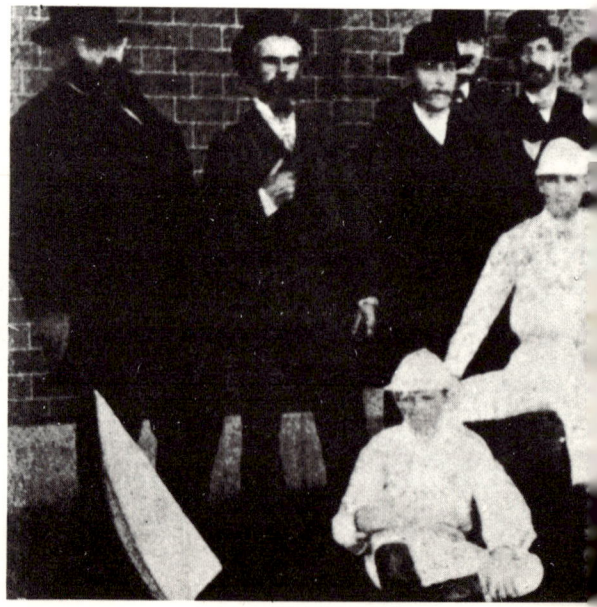

far left : A milling crowd at Elwick Racecourse, Tasmania, jostles to place bets at the ticket windows. T.R.C.

left : An old, faded photograph of a group of racecourse personalities taken in the late nineteenth century. Standing at back : Arthur Devlin (starter), T. Lamond, J. Allsop, M. Fennelly, T.S. Clibborn (A.J.C. secretary), M. O'Brien, J. Monaghan, M. Gallagher, T. Payton, I. Earnshaw (in window), T. Nieriker, W. Kelso, H. Rayner. Seated : D. Bowes, E. McGrade, 'Brickey' Volley, Tom Hales, A. Robertson, R. Ellis. On ground : R. and J. Gough.

above : A crowd watches intently as jockeys dismount after a race at the Elwick course, Tasmania. In Tasmania, as in the other Australian states, successful jockeys often became public heroes. T.R.C.

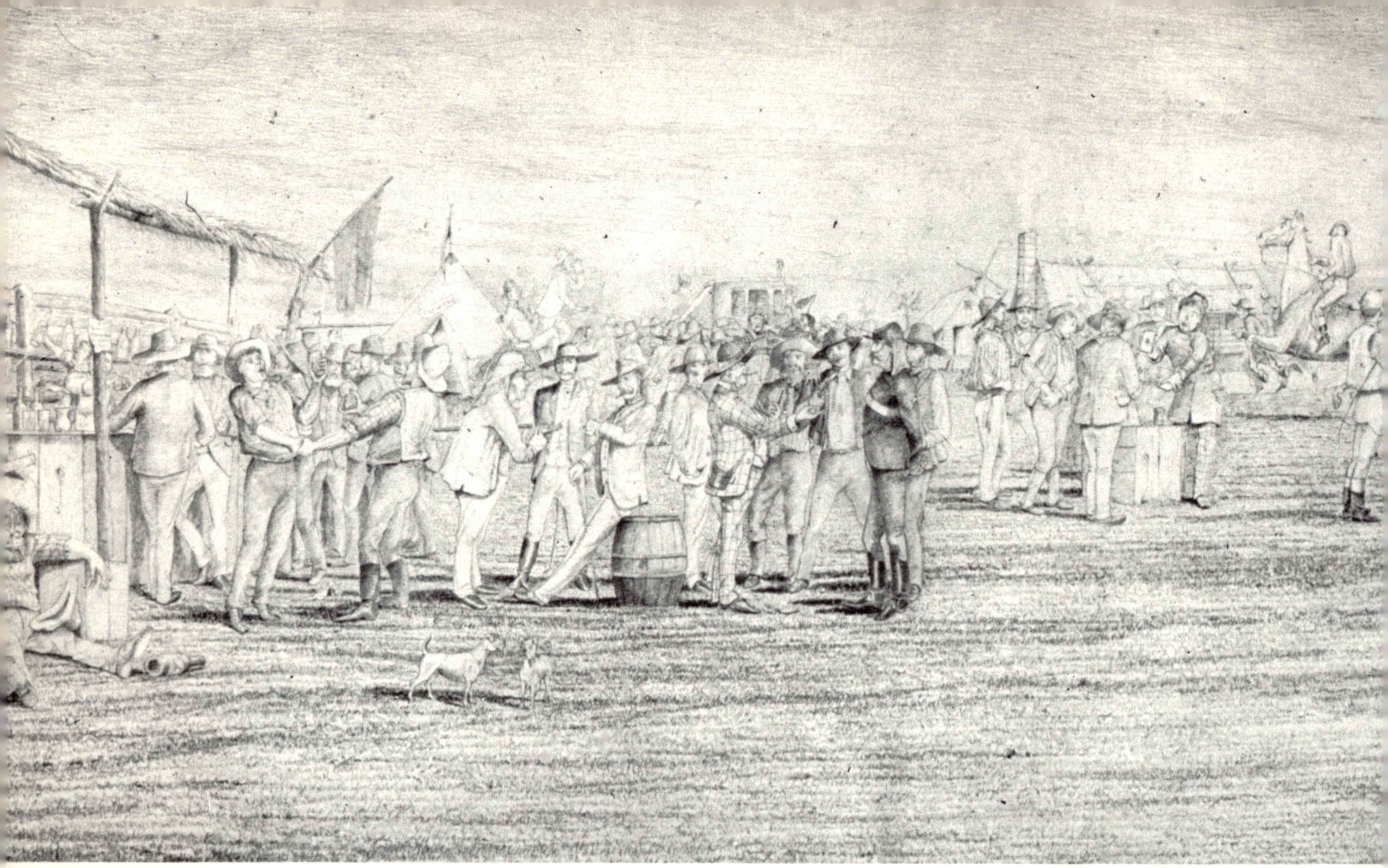

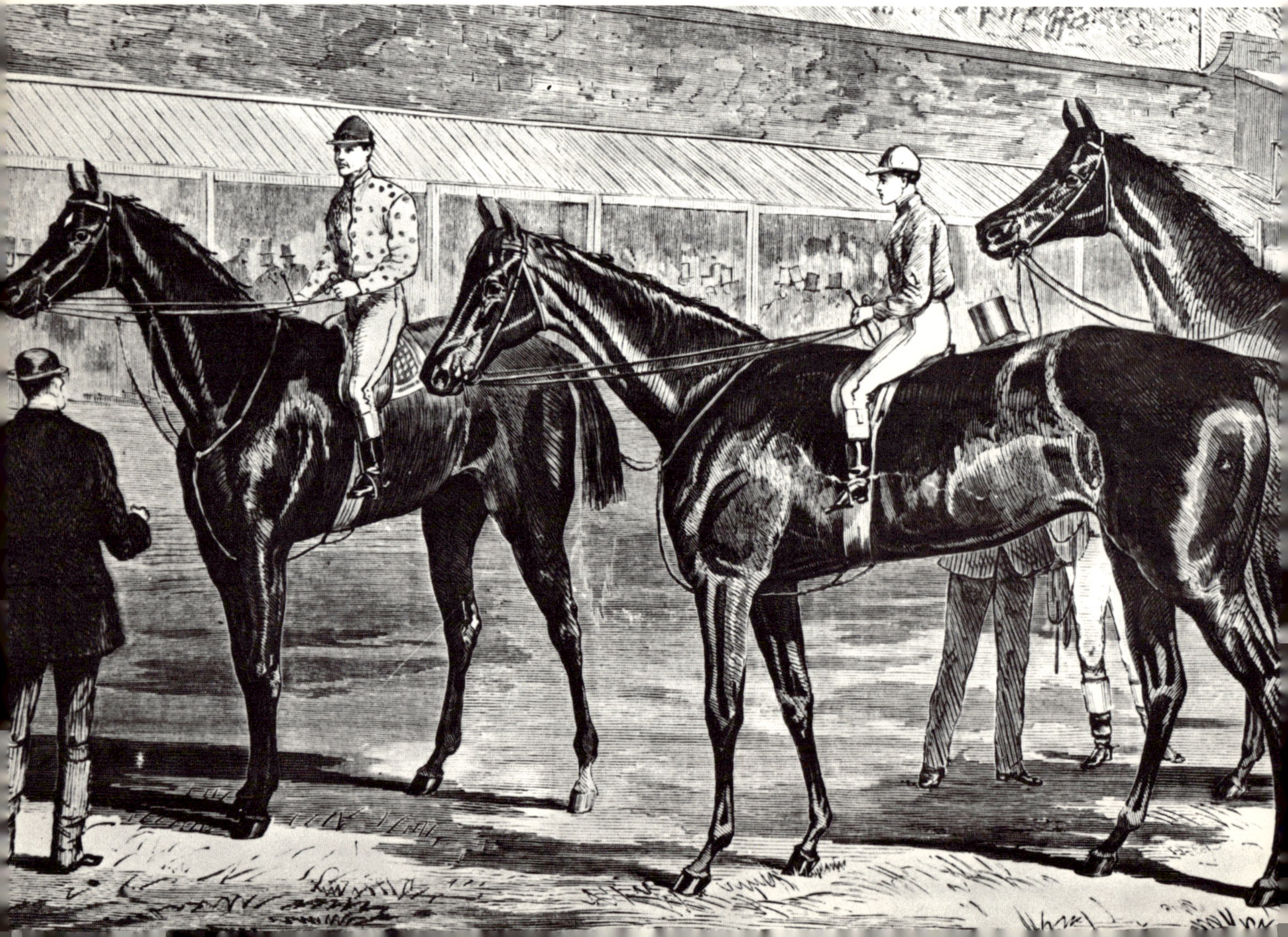

top left : A lively pen drawing of a country race meeting. La Trobe

left : The winners at the V.R.C. spring meeting of 1876. From left to right : Habena, winner of the Maribyrnong Plate, Briseis, winner of the Derby, the Cup and the Oaks and Lansdown, winner of the Steeplechase. Briseis set a record at this meeting by becoming the first filly to win the three races, after having won the A.J.C. Doncaster at the end of her two-year-old career.

above : The betting rooms at night in 1873. Betting for cash on the course was practised from the 1860s, although bookmaking was not big business until the 1880s.

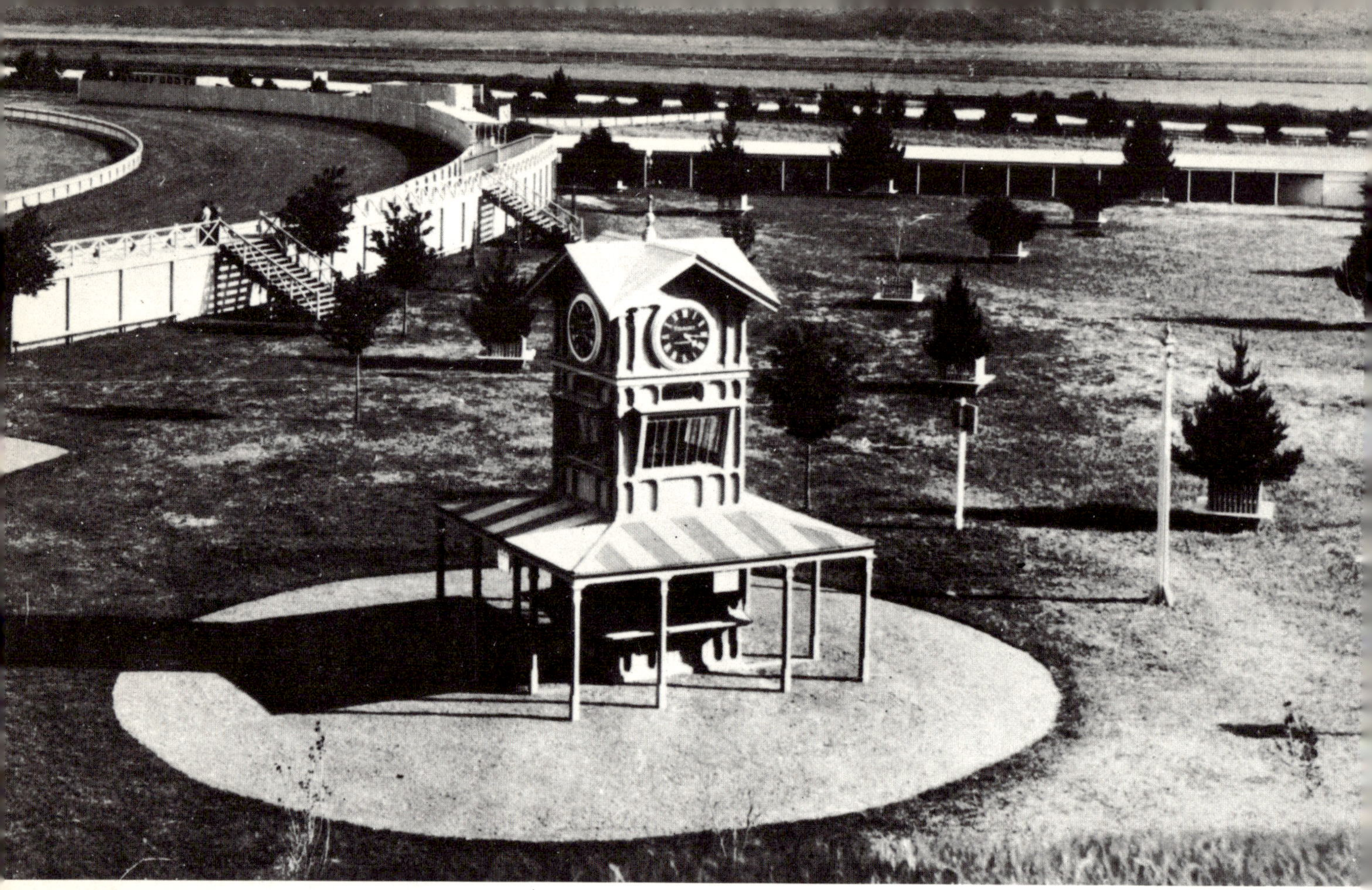

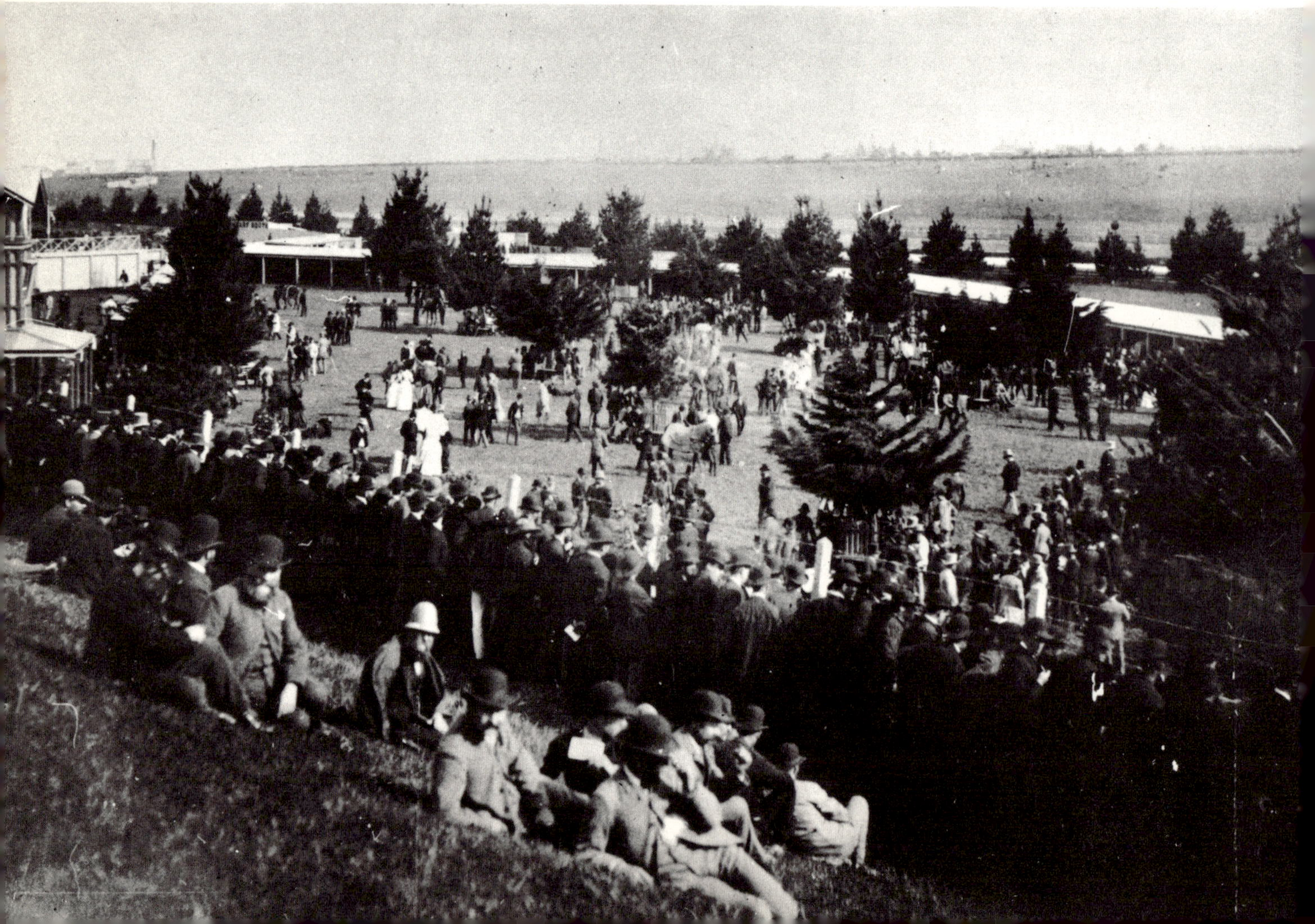

top far left: The saddling paddock, Flemington in
1880. The river, lined with trees, may be seen in the
distance, past the horse stalls. R.C. Bagot, the
secretary of the V.R.C., had worked with dedication
to make the course an attractive and convenient place
for family entertainment. He died a year after
this photograph was taken, handing on his position to
his friend Henry Byron Moore.

far left: The saddling paddock at Flemington on a
race day in 1885, its fence lined with onlookers.

left: An interesting advertisement of the 1890s—
inserted by Mr A.W. Steel 'the well-known Victorian
aristocratic tout'.

top: An advertisement for a sale to be conducted by
auctioneers at Kirk's Bazaar, the great Melbourne
horse market which had become a meeting place for
horse fanciers and those wishing to bet on forthcoming
races.

above: The drawing of a family sweep, a popular
method of allowing a taste of excitement to everyone.
Cup Day 1881.

5. EXPANSION

5. EXPANSION

Carbine was a superb bay with a noble head, born in New Zealand in 1885, a sleek handsome horse of exceptional courage and intelligence.   He was bred by the New Zealand Stud Company and raced as a two-year-old in New Zealand for Mr D. O'Brien.   After he had won every one of his first five races he was sold to Mr Donald Wallace, who brought him to Australia and put him in the hands of a master trainer—the former jockey, Walter Hickenbotham.   Quite apart from the magnificent record he built, there was in Carbine that indefinable trait only champion horses carry, a hauteur which suggests the horse realizes his rare quality.

He raced thirty-three times for twenty-three wins. The only race in which he was out of a place was when he went lame.   His three-year-old record included wins in the V.R.C. Champion Stakes, the A.J.C. Sydney Cup, and the A.J.C. All-Aged Stakes, but it was in his fourth and fifth years when he carried enormous weights that he emerged as a great racehorse. In the 1889 Melbourne Cup, with 10 st, he produced one of his best efforts to run second to Bravo despite a split heel.   This injury worried him from that time until he finished racing, which made his subsequent record all the more impressive.

As a five-year-old in 1890 Carbine started eleven times for ten wins, among them the Melbourne Cup with 10 st 5 lb, the biggest weight ever carried to victory in the race.   This was a memorable race, not only for Carbine but for the V.R.C. which surprised racegoers everywhere by putting up £10,000 over and above the sweepstakes contributed by owners.   This bold move made the Cup one of the world's richest races.   Carbine had to beat the biggest field in the history of the race, with thirty-nine facing the starter. He also carried the burden of being the favourite.   At a time when the working wage was £2 a week his stable backed him to win £30,000.   The public ignored his huge weight and his failure the previous year by backing him for £100,000 more.

pages 104-105 : A dour crowd of bowler-hatted gentlemen survey the scene at the races in the 1890s.

left : An elegant crowd on the lawn at Flemington watch the running of the Melbourne Cup.

Craftily ridden by Bob Ramage, who kept him close to the leaders, Carbine swooped to the lead in the straight and ran to the line with exciting long strides to win easily by two and a half lengths. The crowd, who knew Carbine as 'Old Jack' went delirious with joy and produced what is still regarded as the greatest reception ever for a Melbourne Cup winner. Owner Donald Wallace threw his arms around Carbine's neck, and trainer Hickenbotham danced with glee, handing out hairs from Carbine's tail to the ladies. Carbine refused to follow his groom out of the saddling paddock until the last of the applause had ended. His time for the two miles, 3 min 28¼ sec, was a race record.

Carbine's next race was the Sydney Cup, already one of the colony's most important races, and it was in this race that his split heel cost Carbine a place. The winner was Highborn, which carried 9 st 3 lb but had previously been unable to beat Carbine in the Melbourne Cup, with only 6 st 8 lb. Trainer Hickenbotham showed his devotion to a genuine champion by sitting up all night after the Sydney Cup, painstakingly treating the injury instead of attending Sydney Cup celebrations. Carbine was scratched from all races in the remainder of that season, but returned some months later to win six weight-for-age races. Then he was retired to the stud.

For some reason an impression has lingered that Carbine by Musket from Mersey, both of which were imported, was a flop at stud in Australia. This is false. He sired winners of more than 200 Australian races in four years at Lerderberg Stud, Victoria, including A.J.C. Derby winners Charge and Amberite, which also won the Caulfield Cup. His owner Donald Wallace was then compelled to sell Carbine following heavy losses in the banks crash of the early 1890s. Carbine was sold to the Duke of Portland in 1895 for 13,000 guineas and sent to England as sire at the Duke's Welbeck Abbey Stud. In all four stud seasons in Australia he undertook moderate programmes. In his first season, for instance, he was mated with only three mares. When his sale was finalized, they walked Carbine from Lederberg Stud to Bacchus Marsh railway station, with people from miles around lining

above : Walter Hickenbotham the trainer of Carbine. Hickenbotham, a former jockey, also trained the great stayer Trafalgar.

top right : Carbine, the great New Zealand stallion, repeatedly carried enormous weights to victory during his racing career. He raced thirty-three times for twenty-three wins, and missed a place only once— when he went lame. La Trobe

right : A brush made of Carbine's tail. The horse's strapper, Joseph Poynan, had the brush made when Carbine was sent to England. It is now in the possession of the Australian Jockey Club in Sydney.

the route. To this day the legend persists that a hair from Carbine's tail was something from which virtue stemmed.

At Welbeck Abbey Carbine sired Spearmint, winner of the English Derby, a tremendous boost for Australian bloodstock, and established a line of Derby winners which lasted for three generations. Carbine's grandson, Spion Kop, and his great-grandson Felstead also won the English Derby. When he first saw Carbine the Duke of Portland said, 'The pictures that have appeared of him in English newspapers are the most atrocious libels. I doubt if I have ever seen a better countenance on a racehorse. I could not have chosen a more suitable-looking horse to mate with my St Simon mares.'

By his performance on the track, the hero-worship he aroused among all classes of racing followers, and his success at stud, Carbine ranks with Phar Lap as the finest racehorse produced in Australia and New Zealand. He did more than Phar Lap, who never had a chance at stud, to improve our reputation in bloodstock breeding, and some believe that considering the weights he carried his race record stands alone. Curiously, at Welbeck Abbey he was given the second-choice mares. The best went to St Simon.

Confronted with intense competition from the south, the A.J.C. in Sydney tried hard to build up the prestige of races in its calendar. The year after the V.R.C. was founded the A.J.C. introduced the Epsom Handicap. The first Epsom went to the chestnut Dundee, who ran the mile in 1 min 53 sec. This race was decided on the same day as the renamed Australian Derby Stakes, which later became the A.J.C. Derby. The Derby Stakes winner was the mare Clove. The first Epsom carried stakes of £4 from each runner, with fifty sovereigns added by the club. The Derby Stakes was a sweepstakes of thirty sovereigns for each of thirty-eight subscribers, although some of these scratched.

By then country centres, newly-formed race clubs

right : Riders and horses return after a race at Randwick in the 1890s. A.J.C.

and the owners of out-of-town horses of merit looked to the A.J.C. for leadership on all New South Wales racing problems.   There were plenty of them and the club was fortunate that in this era of the squatter, when great expansion occurred in Australian racing, it had administrators of the calibre of Deas Thompson, the club chairman.   It was Deas Thompson, accompanied by committeemen A. Thompson, S. Jenner, S.C. Burt and C. Martyn, who in June 1859 first staked out the Randwick course with the help of surveyor C. Langley.   Four years later the crown granted the Randwick course to trustees of the A.J.C. for an annual rental of one black peppercorn.   The rental has never been collected.

A big triumph for the A.J.C. was the manner in which other race clubs in the state fell into line with its procedures.   Many country clubs in fact advertized that the conditions of their races would follow A.J.C. rules.   It was a period in which good horses travelled by sea a lot and covered big mileage on the road between meetings.   Travellers in Cobb & Co. coaches became accustomed to encountering racehorses and their grooms on the road.

A major headache arose in securing a uniform birthday for all horses.   The A.J.C. advocated 1 August, and in November 1859 held a public meeting to discuss this age rule.   The A.J.C. committee recommended a standard weight-for-age scale based on the 1 August birthday, but some country race clubs tried to attract good fields by framing conditions under which ages were taken from 1 January.   Gradually breeders saw the big advantage of a uniform age rule and from 1860 on most mares were mated in the spring to ensure they foaled after the following 1 August.   In 1861 the first big crop of foals was born to the 1 August rule.   From 1865 similar weight-for-age scales of weights to that proposed by the A.J.C. were adopted by the major clubs in all states.

The clubs followed the English Jockey Club very closely in naming their principal races.   The St Legers in each state came from the St Leger run at Doncaster, England, from 1776, and the Oaks' and Derbies from the Epsom races, which began in 1780.   Craven Plates and Craven Stakes sprung up, named after Lord

above : An old newspaper photograph showing riders returning to the saddling paddock at Randwick after the running of the Epsom Handicap. The first Epsom was run in 1865, and was won by the chestnut Dundee.

right : Thomas Watson, the official A.J.C. starter from 1889 till 1904.

top right : A race card for the Randwick spring meeting of 1861. The 1860s were years of expansion for the A.J.C. as it introduced new events and extended its influence over other New South Wales race clubs. A major triumph was the general acceptance of its proposal to make the uniform birthday for all horses 1 August. A.J.C.

far right : A.J.C. member's tickets : 1895, (open) and 1910. Faced with severe competition from the V.R.C., the A.J.C. worked continually to boost the prestige of its events and improve conditions at its meetings. A.J.C.

RANDWICK SPRING MEETING, 1861.

"BELL'S LIFE"  RACE CARD.

PUBLISHED BY AUTHORITY OF AUSTRALIAN J. CLUB.

PATRON—SIR JOHN YOUNG, BART., K.C.B., G.C.M.G.

STEWARDS:—Hon. E. Deas Thomson, Esq., C.B.; Alfred Cheeke, Esq.; George Rowley, Esq.; William McQuade, Esq.; Richard Jones, Esq. JUDGE:—John Lackey, Esq., M.L.A. STARTER:—W. McQuade, Esq. HON. CLERK OF THE COURSE:—W. G. Henfrey, Esq. HON. SEC.:—S. C. Burt, Esq.

FIRST DAY.

First Race, to start at a quarter-past 1 o'clock.

The —— STAKES of 5 sovs each, with £50 added; weight for age; once round; the winner to be sold by auction after the race for £75, any surplus realized by the sale of the animal above that sum to go to the race fund; if entered not to be sold, to carry 7lbs extra. Entrance £2 10s.

1. Mr J. Driscoll's b g PLANET, aged, 9st 5lb ....scarlet jacket and blue cap.
2. Mr I. Gorrick's CRINOLINE, 5 yrs, 9st ....black jacket and green cap.
3. Mr W. Town's ch c TRANSIT, 4 yrs, 9st 5lb, (not to be sold) ....red jacket and black cap.
4. Mr T. Ivory's chm FLYING DOE, 5 yrs, 9st 7lb, (not to be sold) ... magenta, blue sleeves, straw cap.
5. Mr W. Eaton's b g MAROON, aged, 9st 5lb ....black jacket and white cap.
6. Mr T. Benman's ch g YOUNG VENO, 4 yrs, 8st 9lb.................green and white jacket, red cap

Second Race, to start at a quarter to 2 o'clock.

The AUSTRALIAN PLATE of 120 sovs, with a sweep of 5 sovs added, for all horses, weight for age; twice round; the second horse to receive the sweepstakes. Entrance 6 sovs.

1. Mr J. Tait's ch g TARTAR, 6 yrs ....yellow jacket, black cap.
2. Mr E. J. Bailey's b g SHEET ANCHOR, aged ....white, red spots and cap.
3. Mr W. Town ns b g SHAMROCK, aged ....black jacket and white cap.

Third Race, to start at a quarter-past 3 o'clock.

The DERBY STAKES of 5 sovs each, with 100 sovs added; for three year old colts 8st 10lbs, and fillies 8st 5lbs; the second horse to receive twenty-five sovs; one mile and a half. Entrance 5 sovs. N.B.—No allowance to geldings.

1. Mr S. Jenner ns b c KYOGLE, by William Tell,—Cassandra.............blue jacket and yellow cap.
2. Mr Ryan's b c THE BABE, by New Warrior .... magenta, blue sleeves, black cap
3. Mr T. Lamond ns ch c POTENTATE, by Molyneux—Governess ....all black.

Fourth Race, to start at 4 o'clock.

The SQUATTERS' PURSE of 2 sovs each, with 50 sovs added, for all horses that have never won a prize exceeding 30 sovs at the time of entrance; once round and a distance; weight for age; second horse to receive 10 sovs. Entrance £2 10s.

1. Mr J. Tait's ch g TARTAR, aged ....yellow jacket, black cap.
2. Mr J. Ryan's LUCRETIA, 4 yrs ....black jacket, pink cap.
3. Mr W. Eaton's ch n EUGENIE, 5 yrs ....black jacket, white cap.
4. Mr F. M. Doyle's ch h WARRIOR, 5 yrs ....tartan, and black cap.
5. Mr R. Graham's b c ALDERMAN, 3 yrs ....pink jacket, white scarf, black cap.
6. Mr G. Waldron's c g ERIN-GO-BRAGH, 5 yrs ....red white and blue jacket, black cap.
7. Mr W. Hall's b m JENNY LIND, 5 yrs ....blue jacket and cap.
8. Mr H. McDermott's ch m IRISH KATE, aged.................................scarlet jacket, pink cap.
9. Mr H. Martineer's b c EUCALYPTUS, 4 yrs.................green jacket and white cap.
10. Mr T. Ivory's FENELLA, 5 yrs ....magenta, blue sleeves, straw cap.
11. Mr T. Lee's ch g SNIP, aged ....magenta cap and jacket.
12. Mr B. Richards' MAG ON THE WING, 4 yrs ....all white.
13. Mr E. H. Weston's ch g CORNSTALK, aged.................red jacket, black scarf and cap.
14. Mr W. Eaton's b g MAROON, aged.................................black jacket and white cap
15. Mr T. Lamond's br g RIFLEMAN, 5 yrs.................................all black.
16. Mr T. Ivory's ch c MARQUIS, 4 yrs ....blue body, red sleeves, straw cap.

Fifth Race, to start at a quarter to 5 o'clock.

The FREE HANDICAP of 3 sovs each, in case of acceptance, with 100 sovs added from the fund, for all horses, to be handicapped by the Committee; second horse to receive £15 from the stakes; one mile and a half. Entrance free.

1. Mr Ogg's b g SHAMROCK, aged, 9st 5lb ....

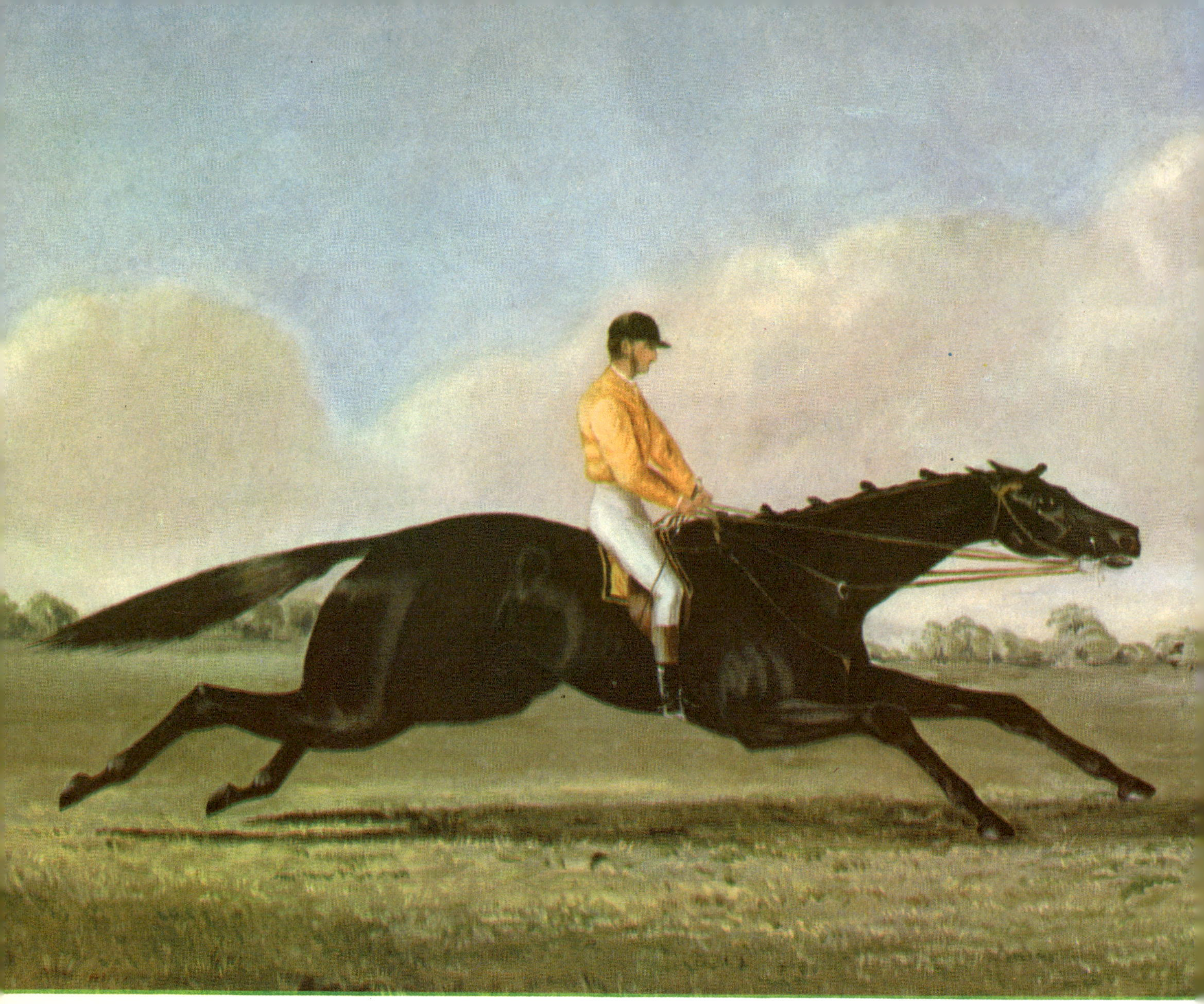

top left : The Barb, a brave, fast horse that thrilled the public and was almost unbeatable in weight-for-age races. Owned by John Tait, The Barb won the 1866 Melbourne Cup from Exile with Falcon, another Tait horse, third. *A.J.C.*

left : The Burke and Wills Expedition: The First Day's Order of March by W. Strutt. The news that the explorers had perished cast the city of Melbourne into gloom six days before the first Melbourne Cup. *La Trobe*

above : Archer—the winner of the first two Melbourne Cups, painted by Fred Woodhouse. This painting of the horse which holds such an important place in Australian racing history is owned by Mr. J.M. Royds of Sydney.

right : The Burke and Wills monolith passing through Collins Street, Melbourne in 1884. The monolith, to be made into a memorial to the explorers, weighed thirty-six tons. *La Trobe*

Craven, who had been a member of the English Jockey Club when the Craven Stakes began in England in 1771. Important events introduced by the A.J.C. in 1866 were the Doncaster Handicap, the Metropolitan Handicap, the Sydney Cup and the Champagne Stakes. Of these four big events, all of which have grown in importance ever since, three took their names from English races. The first Sydney Cup was worth £444 and a trophy worth £150. The winner of the first Metropolitan, Bylong, collected £400 in stake money.

Gradually the common sense of administrators prevailed and the turmoil of many early race meetings disappeared. The army lost its grip on the sport, and with rapid pastoral development major breeding properties appeared which gave great stimulus to racing. But no other clubs were prepared to emulate the courage of the V.R.C. in offering £10,000 in addition to the sweepstakes for the 1890 and 1892 Melbourne Cups.

At the time of Carbine's magnificent Melbourne Cup win the Australian economy had begun to slump. Wheat and wool prices plumetted. The goldrushes petered out. In Melbourne, completion of the tramway system threw hundreds out of work. A major shipping strike in 1890 created further financial strain on the nation. Early in the 1890s banks had to contend with constant withdrawals which compelled many to close their doors. Prize money dropped dramatically for major races all over Australia. From £10,000 in Carbine's year, 1890, the money put up by the V.R.C. for the Melbourne Cup fell to £3,000 in 1894. Book-makers' prices also dropped and with it their popularity, and this in turn proved of great benefit to the sweep-stakes.

The attraction of sweepstakes was that for an outlay of only a few shillings ticket buyers had the chance of drawing a runner in the big race, the joy of having it run for a fortune, and perhaps winning that fortune. The biggest sweepstake of them all was Tattersall's. Taking a 'ticket in Tatts' quickly became a national institution. And the man who founded Tatts and masterminded its astonishing success was George Adams, son of a Hertfordshire farmer who migrated to

top left: The lawn at Randwick in the late nineteenth century. The course was staked out in July 1859, and four years later the crown granted it to the A.J.C. for the annual rental of one black peppercorn. A.J.C.

far left: A stone marks Carbine's grave on the Duke of Portland's estate in England. It reads: Carbine, 1885-1914, Musket—Mersey, Melbourne Cup 1890. A.J.C.

left: Bylong, the winner of the first Metropolitan Handicap, which was run at Randwick in 1866. Bylong collected £400 in stake money. In the same year the A.J.C. introduced the Doncaster, the Sydney Cup and the Champagne Stakes.

above: Policemen patrol the Randwick course in the 1890s ensuring that peace and good manners prevail. A.J.C.

opposite page, left: Scenes at the Brunette Downs
picnic races, Victoria—blue sky, wide open spaces,
beautiful horses and sunshine.

above: Victorian Race Meeting near Sunbury by G.
Rowe, painted in 1856. Mitchell

Australia in 1855 when George was sixteen. Adams drifted from goldfields in Queensland to sheep stations in outback New South Wales to becoming licensee of the Steam Packet Inn at Kiama on the south coast of New South Wales. Among his customers were cattle and sheep men who when they went to Sydney met at O'Briens hotel, the Mayor Inn and later Tattersall's.

The truth of how Adams acquired Tattersall's, which was a full day's coach run from his inn at Kiama, is clouded. One version is that Tattersall's was bought for him by close friends who considered Adams was wasted in the bush and ignored his pleas that he could not afford the place. At any event Adams moved to Tattersall's where he soon became aware of the close interest clients paid to a small sweep run in the hotel's 'Tin Bar'. He took over the organizing of the sweep initially to foster trade, but the sweep quickly became his main enterprise. It was so popular that the politicians moved in on Adams, who fled to Queensland. There had never been the slightest hint of dishonesty in the running of the Adams sweeps and this was a major reason for their popularity.

New South Wales and Queensland—not yet united by Federation—prohibited the delivery of mail containing sweep tickets, and this drove Adams to Tasmania. He had, in fact, been invited to go there to help solve the tricky problem of disposing of the Bank of Van Diemen's Land. This bank had been in difficulty long before the bank crash in 1892. Adams mopped up the problem with a sweep of 300,000 tickets at £1, with the first prize the bank site on valuable Hobart land. It was an attractive proposition for such a small outlay and the bank received far more for the site under Adams' scheme than they would have got at auction. At least one hard-pressed stud owner followed suit by disposing of his property in the same way.

Adams' success in disposing of the Bank of Van Diemen's Land, his charm and obvious business acumen, brought him important contacts among Tasmanian parliamentarians. In 1896, he organized a sweep from Hobart on the Anniversary Handicap run at Randwick. For this he sold 25,000 tickets at 5s apiece,

above: Photographed in 1900 at a Poster Ball in Sydney.

top right: The tenth 'war service funds' consultation at Tattersall's. The organization was endangered after Federation in 1901 because other states were jealous of the money it attracted to Tasmania, and for many years the postal department would not carry mail addressed to Tattersall's.

right: Re-allotting marbles after the drawing of a Tattersall's lottery.

far right: After the race. The flag of the Tasmanian Racing Club flies above the grandstand as hundreds of spectators move homeward. At the end of the nineteenth century, the eyes of the nation were often focused on Tasmania, the adopted home of the enormous Tattersall's Sweep. T.R.C.

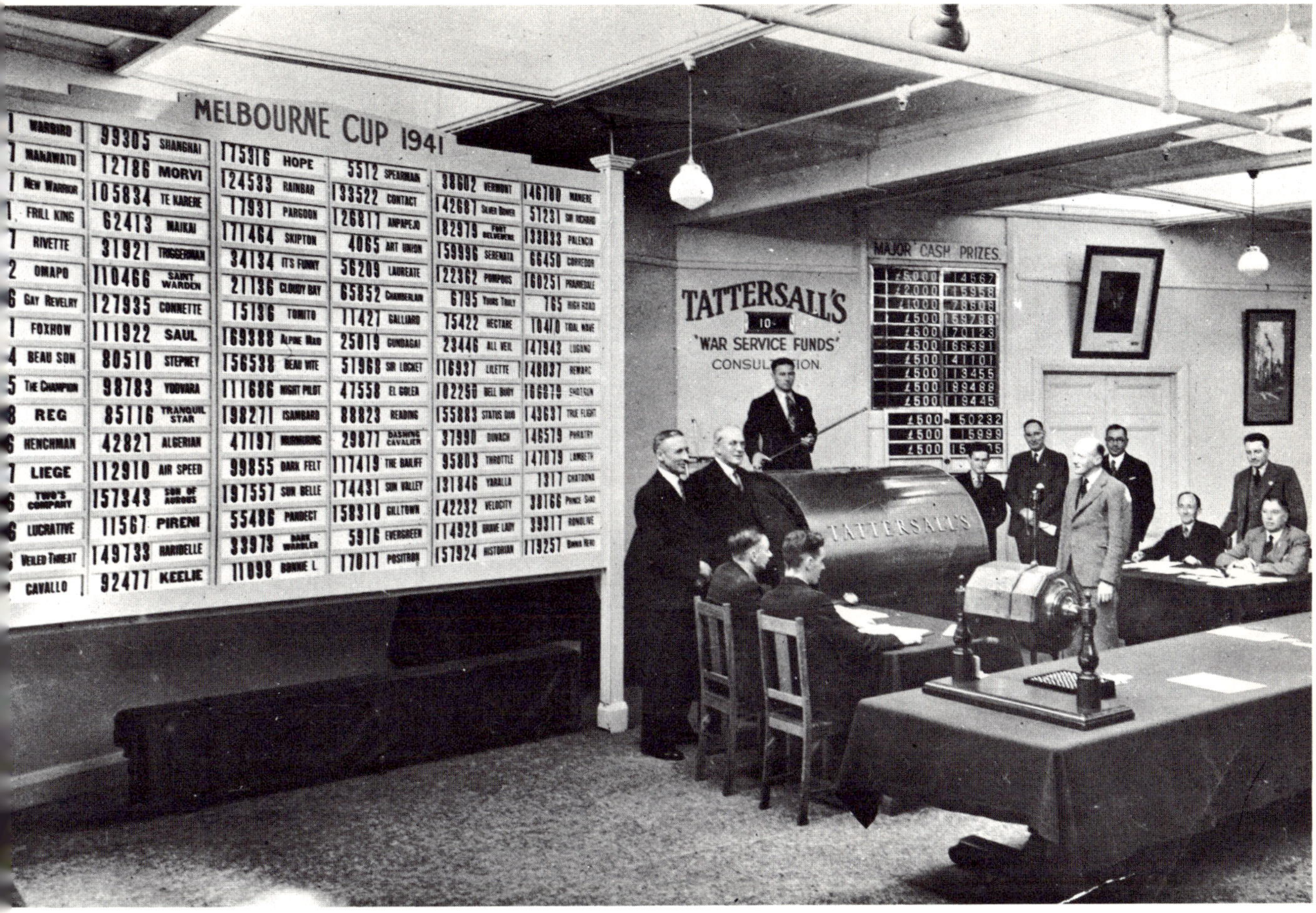
MELBOURNE CUP 1941
TATTERSALL'S
'WAR SERVICE FUNDS'
MAJOR CASH PRIZES
TATTERSALL'S

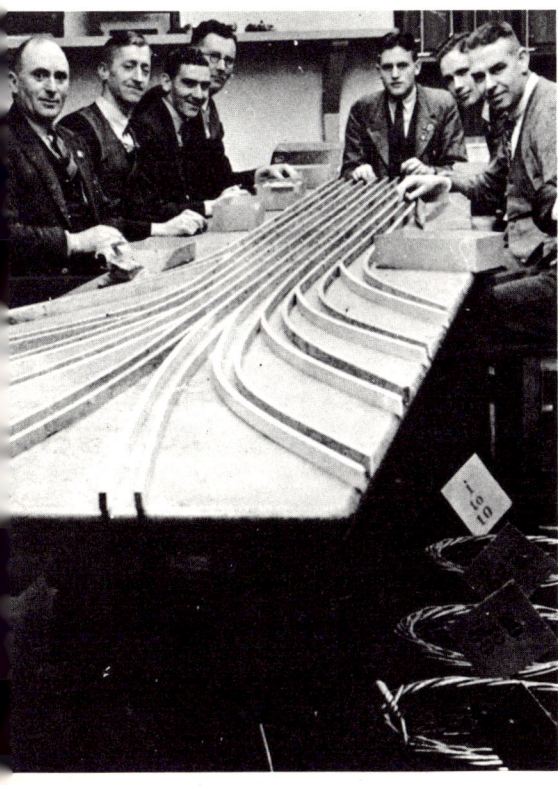

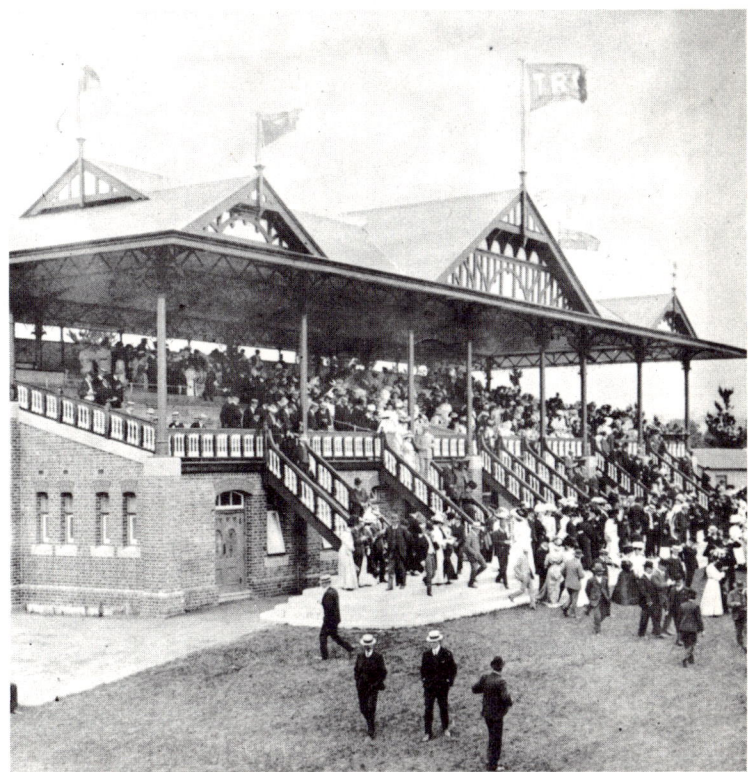

far left: 'Tatts' became a household name, with an aura of luck, success and excitement—as this old advertisement for Tatts cigarettes demonstrates. Famous Australian racehorses—Carbine, Ajax, Gloaming, Peter Pan, Phar Lap and many more surround the happy lady in the centre. Swan Hill Folk Museum

left: Bookies are still an important part of the racing scene in Australia, adding a colour and flair to the racetracks. Here a punter places a bet at Caulfield, Victoria. Victorian Tourist Authority

above: A scene at the Melbourne Cup in the 1880s. La Trobe

with a first prize of £900. The following year the Tasmanian parliament approved the licensing of a Tasmanian lottery. From then on Adams ran his Tattersall's sweeps from Tasmania under government control and had to lodge £10,000 as proof of his good faith with the Tasmanian treasurer. This all opened the way to big things in sweepstakes.

Adams' 1890 Tattersall's sweep on the Melbourne Cup was broken into three parts, one of 100,000 shares at £1 each and two of 100,000 shares at 5s each. In the midst of depression he acquired buildings and extensively enlarged his premises. Since those days the average Australian racegoer has dreamed of winning Tatts, perhaps even more than of owning a Melbourne Cup winner. Federation brought a serious threat to Tatts from states jealous of the money it attracted to Tasmania. The first Federal Parliament banned its postal department from carrying mail addressed to Tattersall's or George Adams. Overnight notices appeared in shop windows across the nation bearing the words 'Mailing To Hobart Daily' and other slogans readily understood by customers. Kiosks and barber shops all over Tasmania acted as collection agents for mainland mail.

Finally in 1930 the Federal Government repealed the ban on mail sent to Tatts and Adams' Hobart office (he had died in 1904 at sixty-five). By then all states had realized the revenue potential of lotteries and sweeps. In 1931, the New South Wales Government introduced lotteries which it has administered itself for the benefit of hospitals—and an Opera House—and Queensland opened its Golden Casket. It became clear that the Victorian Government was determined to channel Tattersall's money back into the state for the benefit of Victorian hospitals. The trustees of George Adams's estate therefore negotiated a deal whereby Tattersall's was operated legally in Victoria and the Government received 31 per cent of the takings. This has so far yielded more than $100,000,000 for Victorian hospitals.

Apart from the enormous Tattersalls sweep, hundreds of smaller sweeps sprang up in every corner of the nation. There had been a half-holiday in Melbourne on Cup day since the fifth Cup in 1865, when

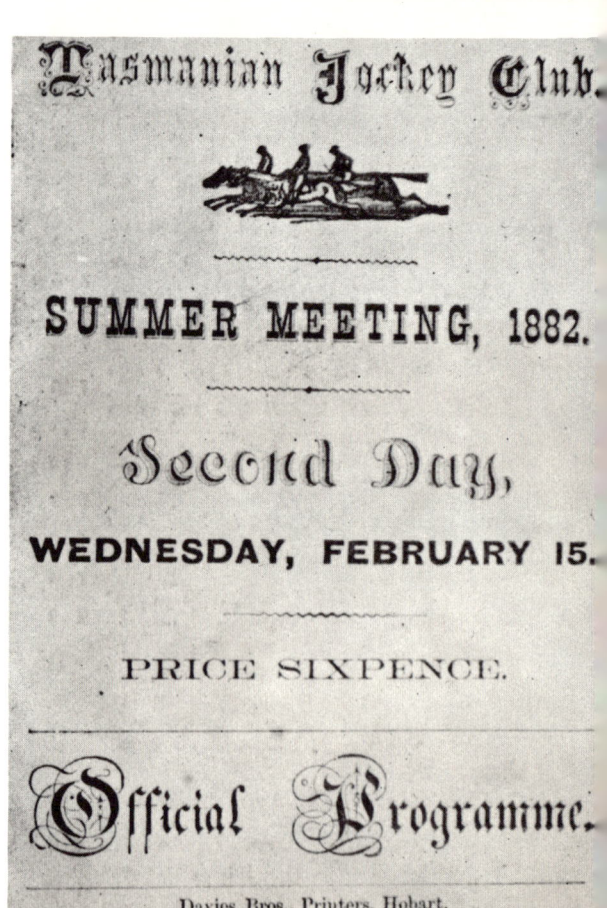

Tasmanian Jockey Club.

SUMMER MEETING, 1882.

Second Day,

WEDNESDAY, FEBRUARY 15.

PRICE SIXPENCE.

Official Programme.

Davies Bros., Printers, Hobart.

top left : The drawing of a £2,000 sweep on the *Melbourne Cup, 1876.* The sweeps, large and small, which are still held in offices, pubs, clubs and homes on Cup Day, give everyone a chance to taste the excitement of having a horse run in the big race.

far left : The cover of a Tasmanian Jockey Club racing programme for the summer meeting of 1882. The club was formed in Hobart in 1859, during a period of expansion in Tasmanian racing. The Tasmanian Turf Club was formed in the following year. *T.R.C.*

left : The Tasmanian crowd watches the running of the 1884 Hobart Cup, conducted annually by the T.R.C. First run in 1875, the race was originally over two miles, though the distance has now been cut to one and a half. *T.R.C.*

above : The scene at Elwick racecourse, Tasmania, on 7 December 1895, as the horses start for the first time from a mechanically raised barrier. Freed from the distraction of a human starter, the horses are able to make a clean getaway. *T.R.C.*

125

Cup Day at Flemington—still the most exciting day of the year for Australian racegoers. Flowers, brass bands, magnificent clothes and champion thoroughbreds are still as much a part of the great carnival as they were in the 1860s. V.R.C., Victorian Tourist Authority

the public service and banks stopped work. The next
year business houses closed, too, and from 1877 Cup
day was acknowledged as a public holiday in the
Government Gazette. Melbourne Cup historian Lee
Bernstein suggests that Federation came from a
meeting of state leaders in an amicable mood at Cup
time. The craze for sweeps in offices, pubs, clubs,
kitchens, ships, trains, and even among commuters in
buses gave the rest of the nation the small excuse it
needed to stop work like its Melbourne contemporaries.

With the country struggling against depression the
club showed a loss of £2,000 for the 1891-1892 season
but its foresight in making the Cup the world's richest
handicap race paid off in 1892 when, despite heavy
rain for almost a fortnight before Cup day, a crowd of
67,000 turned up. The noted starter George Watson
took twenty minutes to get this Cup field away because
of mud and slush. The spectators were soaked and
unable to distinguish the jockeys' colours through the
mud. There was a bad fall, with horses hurdling the
fallen horse Pilot Boy, and the race was won by a 50
to 1 milkman's horse, Glenloth. None of these
mishaps mattered. Everyone went home happy.

far left: A cartoon lampooning the A.J.C. committee's hopes to top the Melbourne Cup.

top left: Drawing a Cup sweep on the course in the 1870s. La Trobe

left: The finish for the V.R.C. Champion Stakes in 1876. This race was an annual event first organized by the V.R.C. in 1859, and one of the many great horses to win it was Carbine.

above: On the flat at Flemington in 1895, a group of gentlemen find a good vantage point—convenient, if a little crowded.

AUSTRALIAN NEWS

337.   MELBOURNE, SATURDAY, NOVEMBER 10, 1883.   PRICE { WITH TWO SUPPLEMENTS } 1s.

top left : In the tea room at the V.R.C. spring meeting in 1883. To the left behind the counter ladies preside over large urns, while the gentlefolk take refreshment amid the ferns and potted palms.

left : The staff of Tattersalls, photographed in about 1910.

above : Racing at Flemington in 1890. Note the advertizing sign on the hill in the distance. At the left of the photograph a gallant gentleman holds his lady up for a better view.

top right : The Assyrian, bred in 1877, winner of the Hobart Cup, the Randwick Autumn Stakes, the S.A.J.C. Derby and the 1882 Melbourne Cup. T.R.C.

right : The crowd views the favourite before the V.R.C. Derby of 1895, which was to be won by Wallace, one of the best sons of Carbine. Wallace was to prove an outstanding sire, getting a huge number of winners, including Trafalgar and Lady Wallace.

6. THE TURN OF THE CENTURY

In 1890, a nineteen-year-old Melbourne boot-clicker who had begun work in a woodyard invested all his savings, £50, on Carbine in the Melbourne Cup, backing the horse early at long odds. Carbine's win gave the lad, John Wren, the start which led to a multi-million fortune and powerful political influence in Australia. The day after Carbine won young Wren went to a race meeting where Melbourne's Elsternwick Park now stands and made further winning bets.

By 1893 Wren had sufficient capital to start his own form of illegal totalisator in the Melbourne suburb of Collingwood. This was a method of betting in which all wagers on a race were totalled and divided among those selecting the winning horse, in proportion to the amounts of their wagers. Wren took 10 per cent of the total bet in each race for himself, far less than the operators of today's legal totes. Melbourne people gave him their patronage in great numbers—some betting in threepences—because they regarded Wren's tote as honestly conducted.

The illegal tote operators were subjected to frequent police raids and prosecutions. These raids always proved highly effective in closing down Wren's rival totes but for some reason police could not catch Wren or find witnesses ready to testify about his operations.

Proprietary racing, which had begun in Australia in January 1884, when a syndicate organized a meeting at Sydney's Canterbury Park, had flourished. This form of racing hurt country race clubs—notably in Hawkesbury New South Wales—which lost the patronage of city folk unwilling to travel big distances when local meetings were available. In Melbourne, Wren and his associate Ben Nathan, whose fortune was built in selling furniture, acquired three proprietary courses, Fitzroy, Richmond and Ascot, and set about eliminating the malpractice for which proprietary clubs were noted. They formed the Victoria Trotting

pages 132 – 133: A pleasant afternoon tea in the carriage paddock at Flemington in 1901.

left : A bit of a gossip over lunch for this trio photographed at the Melbourne Cup in 1903. That year Lord Cardigan, ridden by Norman Godby, won the great event before a crowd of 95,000 people.

and Racing Association, appointed able officials and reduced programmes to provide greater safety than they had had when up to seventeen races were run in a day.

By the turn of the century the success of proprietary racing was well established. Apart from Wren's three Melbourne courses, Warwick Farm, Rosehill and Moorefield were all successes in Sydney, thanks to the shrewdness of the businessmen who formed the controlling syndicates. These unregistered clubs were not bound to race under Jockey Club rules and this enabled them to introduce pony races, one of the most colourful forms of horse racing Australia has known. The ponies were easier to get and cheaper to feed. They provided an exciting brand of racing for informally-dressed hard-bitten regular punters who were out of place at the meetings staged by the race clubs dominated by powerful owners and breeders. The form of the ponies was not as predictable as those of thoroughbreds and every race became a battle of wits between riders, ponies and punters.

The ponies were divided into grades according to their height—14 hands, 14.1 hands and 14.2 hands (a hand is four inches) and the syndicates which conducted their races usually added races for horses of any height. Pony racing attracted a rich and flamboyant gallery of characters. The nineteen-stone owner and trainer Grafter Kingsley landed some huge coups on them, especially on the ponies High Disdain and Dreblah. Most famous of the pony bookies was Rufe Naylor, who made and lost fortunes on them. The most prominent pony trainer was 'Baron' Bob Skelton, who at one time had seventy-two ponies in his stable.

Skelton trained one of the best ponies, Precious Dust, to win ten straight races. On one programme Skelton's ponies won eight races. Pony meetings with between ten and fifteen races were common and some had as many as seventeen. Ernie 'Jerky Jack' Henry rode 100 winners in each of three consecutive racing

right : An off-the-course tote in a Bourke Street Club in 1872. Illegal totes such as this one were constantly raided and prosecuted, but they were very popular and continued to do business until legislation in 1906 closed the last loophole in the law and forced their disappearance.

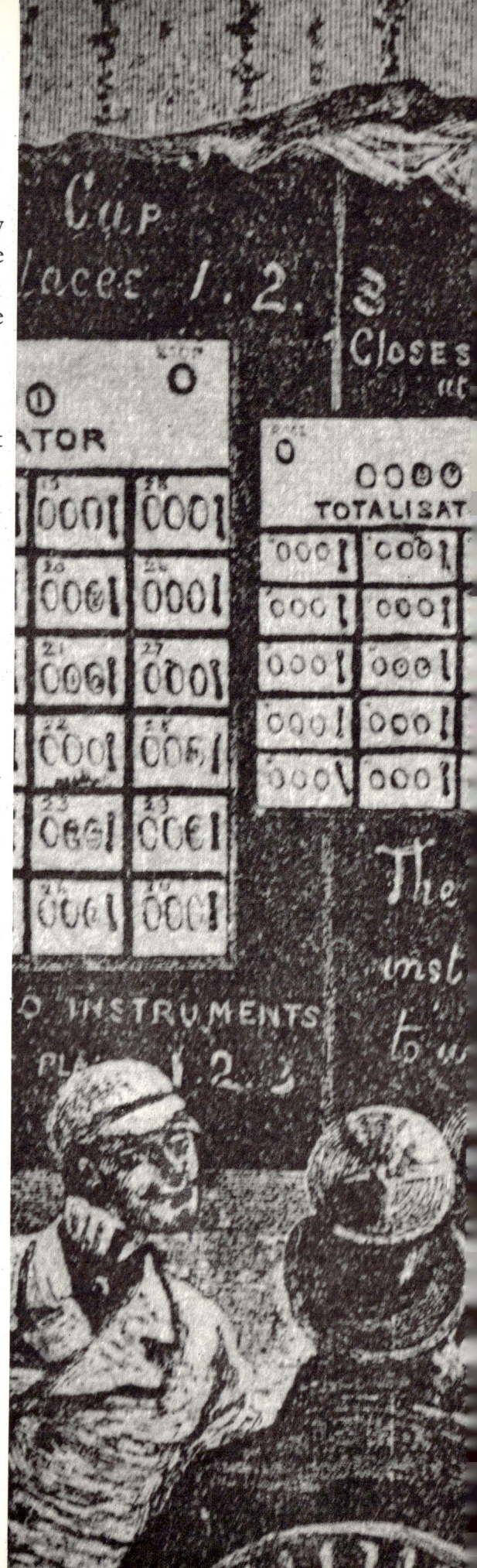

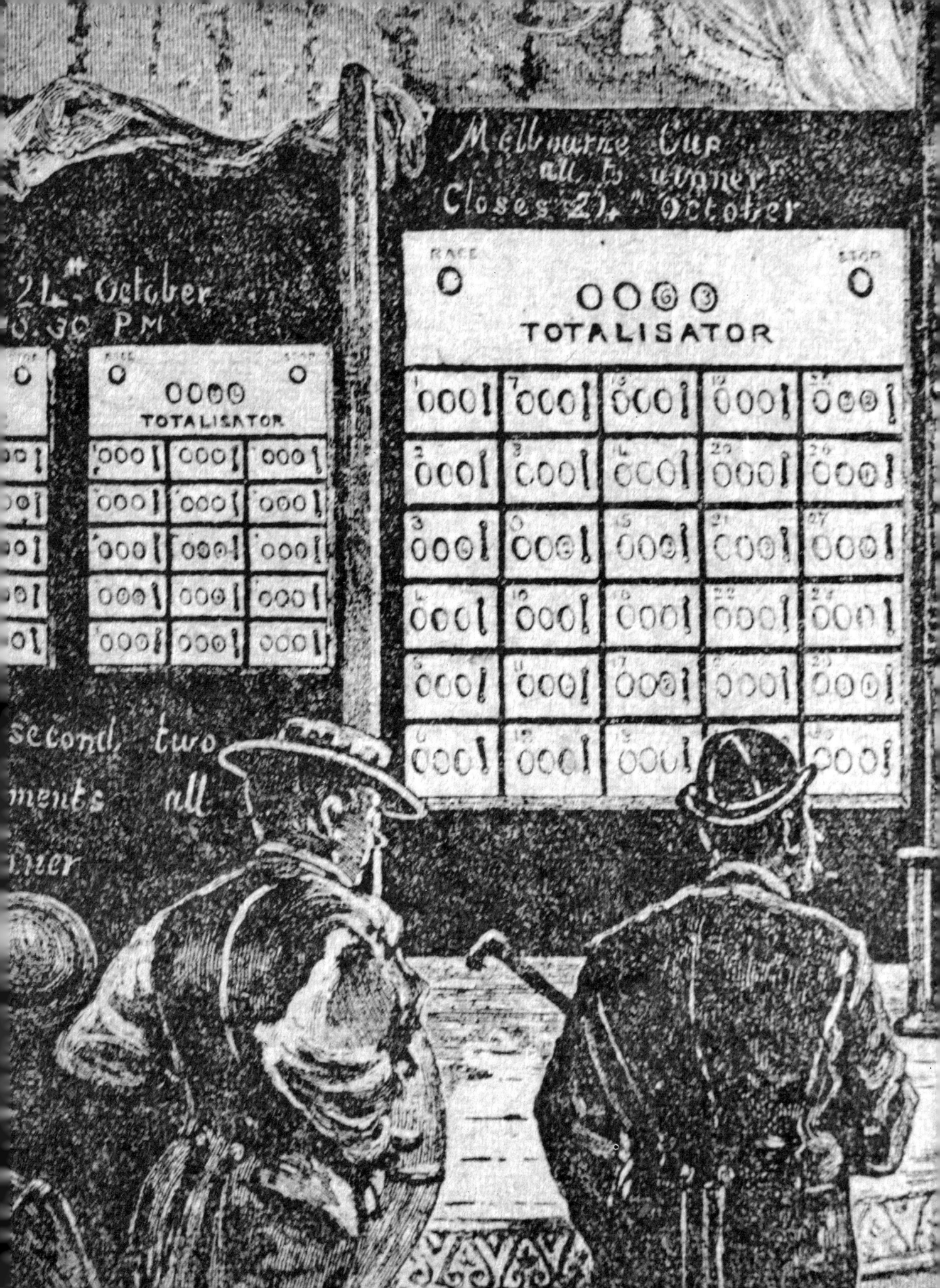

seasons, many of them for Skelton. One year when the pony trainers organized a strike which Skelton opposed, he helped break the strike by nominating enough ponies from his own stable to complete the programme.

Strangely enough, pony racing gave heavier jockeys, whose weight prevented them getting regular rides under Jockey Club rules, more opportunities. One of these was the colourful Alby Callinan, who spent hours every day in sweatboxes before he switched to ponies. Callinan told how in one pony race his mount had returned from a long spell and was not given a winning chance by its trainer. When the favourite ran off the course, Callinan's mount was left in the front with no challengers. After he had won easily Callinan told the trainer the horse must have been fitter than expected. 'Like hell it was,' the trainer replied, 'There just weren't any other triers in the race'. Alby Callinan's brother Steve won the 1897 Melbourne Cup on Gaulus.

Pony racing continued until the Depression when the race clubs granted an amnesty to all owners, trainers, jockeys, and thoroughbred horses who had appeared at pony meetings. With its disappearance characters like bookie Andy Kerr, 'the Coogee Bunyip', died out. Kerr once bet £100 to a cigarette to entice punters to bet with him on the ponies. Many of the pony race riding stars subsequently became top-class jockeys under Jockey Club rules.

Among the new celebrities that appeared on the Australian turf at the time of John Wren was James Scobie. He had been known as an accomplished cross-country rider around his hometown of Arrarat, was a fine steeplechase rider, and a winning rider on the flat. But it was as a trainer that Scobie became nationally famous. In 1900, four of Scobie's horses won three Derbies and three major Cups. Militades won the South Australian Derby, Malster won the A.J.C. and V.R.C. Derbies, and was second in the Melbourne Cup. Clean Sweep won the Moonee Valley Cup and Melbourne Cup and Paul Pry won the Williamstown Cup.

Clean Sweep had been picked out by Scobie as a yearling. Scobie paid only 90 guineas for him and then sold the horse to one of his clients, F.T. Forrest.

top left : Bob Lewis was one of the last great Australian jockeys to ride in the old manner, upright in the saddle. This style is demonstrated in the old engraving above. Note the long stirrups and reins.

centre left : The straight at Warwick Farm in the 1890s. Warwick Farm was one of the proprietary courses which had great success in Sydney, as had Fitzroy, Richmond and Ascot in Melbourne. Proprietary clubs were not bound by Jockey Club rules, and this enabled them to stage pony races, always colourful and exciting events. A.J.C.

left : The old homestead stables at Warwick Farm photographed at the turn of the century, by which time proprietary racing was well established. A.J.C.

above : The official stand and scratching tower at Warwick Farm, photographed at the turn of the century. A.J.C.

Both Clean Sweep and Malster started at 20 to 1 in the Melbourne Cup, strange odds considering Malster had won two Derbies, and Clean Sweep won the Cup by a length and a half. Malster made amends by winning the Flying Stakes on Oaks Day and the C.B. Fisher Plate on the last day of the Cup meeting to establish himself as the last outstanding horse of the old century. He later was a great success at stud.

Scobie's stable jockey was a superb horseman, Bob Lewis, whose successes for Scobie included six Victoria Derbies. Lewis who was born at Clunes, Victoria, in 1878, won his first race, a pony event, at fourteen. He developed a strong personal friendship with Scobie and went far beyond the scope of the normal jockey in trying to help Scobie's horses win. In the days before starting stalls were generally adopted Lewis reasoned that young horses were insufficiently trained in starting from a barrier. Often he would take a batch of yearlings out on to a track and school them in barrier behaviour.

Lewis was one of the last outstanding riders of the old school, the men who rode upright in the saddle with long reins and stirrups. Apart from his six V.R.C. Derbies for Scobie, he won it twice more for other trainers. He also won ten V.R.C. St Legers, nine Ascot Vale Stakes and in 1970 still had the best Melbourne Cup riding record. Lewis rode thirty-eight times in the Melbourne Cup, for four wins, four seconds and a third. Next best were Darby Munro, Bill McLachlan, Jack Purtell, and Jim Johnson, who each rode three Melbourne Cup winners.

Australians Tot Flood and James Barden were the first jockeys in the world to use the crouched riding seat in which the rider sits well forward on the horse's shoulders and neck, with shortened leathers and reins. This position gives the mount more freedom to use the back legs from which most speed comes. However, it was the striking success of the American Tod Sloan, first in the United States and later in England, which gave this riding style world recognition and led to its general adoption. Many racegoers referred to it as the 'Tod Sloan crouch'. A succession of dashing jockeys apprenticed to Australian Dick Wootton at Epsom, England, achieved marked success riding

George Perry, the anti-swank crank, was observed holding a racing pony at a suburban racecourse the other day, while another man brushed the "animile" down. Rumor hath it that George has blossomed forth as a horsey man, and intends to "follow the game." Bad Bill was so overcome on hearing this that he perpetrated the following red-eyed atrocity, which he has artfully disguised as a "pome":—

Behold here old George Perry, the anti-
   swankey bloke,
He's gone in for pony racing and has actually
   got a moke.
It stands 14.2, they tell me, when standing in
   its socks,
And since it started racing it has broken
   several clocks.
It had a "go" one day last week and should
   have won the race,
But the other horses went too fast and it didn't
   get a place.
But George is not discouraged; he still will
   train his moke,
And plunge on it when'er it starts until the
   Ring is broke.

He feeds it on dog biscuits, and gives it water
   pure
To wet its little bingey, so all persons may be
   sure
That when it starts in any race the other prads
   must fly
To beat the moke that never wets with beer
   its noble eye.
Last week George took his pony out to have a
   trial "go"
(The object being, of course, to get the bulge
   on Ikey Mo).
He sent his steed o'er half a mile (to the distance I will swear),
It cut it out in half an hour, and never turned

This pony's turned poor George's brain, at
   least it would seem so
For I have heard that he intends to ape old
   Ikey Mo.
He's going to buy a betting book, a bag, and
   pencil, too,
And lay the odds at Kensington like other
   bookies do.
Denouncing rum's a paying game, but still
   there is more tin
To be annexed by betting 'gainst the prads
   "not out to win."
So, as George is after shekels, the rumor may
   be true
That he's going to take on betting and give up
   reviling "brew."

For 20 years or more Old George, with all his
   might and main,
Has dealt it out to Hebe from his place in the
   Domain.
'Tis sad to think, then, that we will not see
   him any more
Ripping up the reputations of the barmaids
   with his jaw,
And tearing up the characters of men who deal
   in "lap,"
While using language that is blue and full of
   vim and snap.
So let us bid "Old Water Spout" a sad, tho'
   fond good-bye,
And may the prads he bets against ne'er catch

top far left: This photograph of Mel Schumacher on the Melbourne Cup winner of 1958, Baystone, shows that stirrups are today worn very short. The crouched style was not really approved of when it first appeared, and in 1924 George Lambton said of it 'You cannot like it. It has spoilt much of the beauty of race riding, but it has come to stay—and we must make the best of it'. McQuillan

top left: An old newspaper photograph, illustrating an article on the 'Tod Sloan Crouch'. The caption reads: 'Hood, a very short stirrup Australian artist, on Marvel Loch. Hood fairly represents the American Style.'

left: Young horses prepare to leap forward as the rope barrier rises. These were the days before starting stalls were adopted.

above: A newspaper sketch and a 'pome' by 'Bad Bill' concerning George Perry, a popular figure in New South Wales, well-known for his speeches in the Domain. Perry had apparently turned his attention to pony racing at this time.

crouched over their horses' withers. The greatest of these was Dick's son Frank, who became the youngest jockey in the world to ride a winner when he won in South Africa at the age of nine years ten months.

Overseas the reputation of Australian horses for durability was growing, helped by the success of Carbine's progeny and the incredible toughness of two horses, Chesney and Kiora, in surviving the wreck of S.S. *Thermopylae* near Capetown in 1899. The *Thermopylae* ran aground in mammoth seas and after the passengers had been rescued in lifeboats a police constable bravely swam out to the wreck to try and save Chesney and Kiora. Despite the heavy seas he got Chesney ashore in a tremendous swim but Kiora was given up. Next day Kiora was found alive on a piece of rocky coastline miles from where the *Thermopylae* went down, having swum through those huge seas for at least ten hours.

A further boost for our horses came in the 1900 English season when the Australian horse Merman won the Ascot Gold Cup, the Goodwood Cup and the Jockey Club Cup. Earlier the Australian horse Kirkham had finished unplaced in the 1890 English Derby and the Australian mare Mons Meg had won the 1891 Ascot Gold Vase, and both had made good impressions. Kirkham remained in England to sire a Grand National Steeplechase winner. Both Kirkham and Mons Meg were bred by James White at his stud, Kirkham, at Camden, New South Wales.

Mares played prominent roles in Australian racing at the start of this century, building a reputation for courage which has since distinguished a long line of horses of this sex. Carbine's daughter La Carabine won the 1900 Sydney Cup and Australian Cup in plucky style. She also won the Champion Stakes in 1901 and 1902, and over a career which brought her fifteen wins, won racegoers' admiration for refusing to give up in tight finishes despite big weights.

The mare which really captured public imagination, however, was the Victorian-bred Wakeful, an ideally-named lady by Trenton from Insomnia. Wakeful was owned by one of Australia's best-known owners, C.L. Macdonald, who had been manager of St Albans stables for several years. He did not race Wakeful

above : The reputation for toughness gained by Australian horses grew after Chesney and Kiora survived a shipwreck in huge seas near Capetown in 1899. Twenty-three years before, the steamship City of Melbourne had been caught in a storm near Jervis Bay, and of the eleven valuable racehorses on board, nine were drowned. This engraving of the disaster appeared in an Australasian Sketcher of 1876.

top right : The start of the V.R.C. Derby in 1898 from a rope barrier.

right : La Carabine—the plucky daughter of Carbine. La Carabine carried big weights to victory, as had her famous father, winning fifteen races in all, including the Australian and Sydney Cups of 1900.

far right : Wakeful, the champion Victorian mare whose outstanding record prompted the newspapers to call her 'The First Lady of the Turf'. She began racing at four years old and missed a place only three times, starting forty-four times for twenty-five wins, twelve seconds and four thirds. Herald and Weekly Times

until she was four, but in her third start Wakeful brilliantly won the 1901 Oakleigh Plate. She followed this by winning Newmarket Handicap and the Doncaster Handicap at Randwick in the record time of 1 min 39¾ sec.

Turf writers labelled her 'The First Lady of The Turf' and from then on even non-racegoers followed this gallant mare's performances. She won the Caulfield Stakes, but in the Caulfield Cup, in which she started favourite, she slipped slightly when leading and lost by half a head to Hymettus after a stirring struggle. The Melbourne Cup that year was won by Wakeful's stablemate Revenue. Wakeful was fifth. But after finishing second on Oaks Day in the Flying Stakes Wakeful was a place-getter at her next twenty-nine starts.

She won every one of her four Sydney races in the autumn of 1902, running a record time in the Sydney Cup with 9 st 7 lb. In the spring in Melbourne she won the Caulfield Stakes, the Eclipse Stakes, the Melbourne Stakes, the C.B. Fisher Plate and the Champion Stakes. By then Wakeful was a national institution, but her owner refused to start her in the Melbourne Cup because she had been allotted 10 st 5 lb. This caused a tremendous controversy among Wakeful's supporters. The 1902 Melbourne Cup field was one of the weakest on record and most experienced racegoers believed that Wakeful could have conceded the winner, The Victory, 21 lb and beaten him. 'The Melbourne Cup was thrown away', wrote Maurice Cavanough and Meurig Davies in their book, *Cup Day*.

Gladsome, bred in New Zealand in 1900, was a mare whose record in this period rivalled that of Wakeful. Gladsome won twenty-four races in all, twenty-one of them in Australia, and lost two others through disqualifications. Gladsome ran third to Australia's best horse, the 1903 Melbourne Cup winner Lord Cardigan, in the 1904 A.J.C. Plate. Melbourne bookmaker Sol Green bought her on the strength of this run and from then on she did most of her racing in Victoria. Like Wakeful, Gladsome was widely admired for her great heart.

By this time the country had recovered from the

top left : One of the most prominent jockeys of this period—Jim Barden, whose tremendous record of wins prompted this newspaper article to acclaim him as 'Australia's First Horseman'. His most famous mount was the great mare Wakeful.

left : A pleasant spring scene on the lawn at Elwick Racecourse, Tasmania in 1906. T.R.C.

top : The finish of the Newmarket Handicap, 1903. The widely-spaced field and the appearance of the jockeys, sitting almost upright in the saddle, make the pace look somewhat leisurely to a modern eye. La Trobe

above : The weighing-in paddock at Randwick at the turn of the century. Racing had by this time become big business—betting was heavy, both on the course and in the suburban hideaways of the illegal off-the-course bookies—and racing administrators became increasingly watchful, to ensure that honesty prevailed and the public was not cheated. A.J.C.

failure of the banks and big betting became a feature of our race meetings. Off-the-course illegal bookmakers flourished. Indeed the vast sums of money invested in horse racing added importance to the work of racing club administrators, who had to ensure that every race was conducted with absolute integrity and that wrongdoers were quickly punished. Here Australian racing was lucky at a crucial stage of its development in discovering men of the calibre of Adrian Knox, a leader of the Sydney bar and M.L.A. for Woollahra. Many of today's important procedures began during his long term in office as an A.J.C. committeeman and chairman. Stipendary stewards, assisted and paid by the A.J.C. were appointed to control the sport in each racing district, a system of uniform naming of horses was adopted, and provident funds were initiated for jockeys who fell on bad times. In 1906, important new races, the A.J.C. Breeders' Plate and the A.J.C. Gimcrack Stakes were introduced.

Importation of New Zealand horses to Australia was increasing. In 1905, for example, the New Zealand breeder Mr G.G. Stead, who had been sending horses to Australia since 1879, sent over four horses, Isolt, Sun God, Nightfall and Noctuiform. They won eight races in four days at Randwick and in the A.J.C. Derby Noctuiform and Sun God were first and second. The performance of the four horses in winning £7,650 at this Randwick meeting enabled Mr Stead to become the leading owner in Australia, the first time a New Zealander had achieved this distinction.

At the Sydney Easter yearling sales of 1905 Sir Hugh Denison paid 500 guineas for a colt by Positano named Poseidon. This sale gave a modest profit to Messrs W. and F.A. Moses, of the prosperous Arrowfield Stud in the Hunter Valley. They had paid 400 guineas for the mare Jacinth and a foal at foot, Poseidon, at the dispersal of R.H. Dangar's Neotsfield Stud in 1904. When Poseidon won only one race from six starts as a two-year-old, it looked as if the Moses had

right : The sale ring at Randwick early in this century.

been wise in selling him.

However, as a three and four-year-old Poseidon built a remarkable record, winning eighteen times from twenty-six starts. In all of his wins he was heavily backed by a Chinese market gardener from the Sydney suburb of Canterbury, Jimmy Ah Poon. Jimmy somehow had the good sense not to back Poseidon in races in which the horse finished second. Jimmy Ah Poon could not pronounce Poseidon's name and used to ask bookmakers, 'What price Possumum'? So Jimmy became known as 'Louis the Possum' and proceeded to win a fortune—estimated by some turf writers at £35,000—on Poseidon.

Sir Hugh Denison also backed Poseidon for the V.R.C. Derby-Melbourne Cup double and when the horse won the Cup by three lengths Sol Green had to pay out £100,000 to Sir Hugh. Jimmy Ah Poon continued to back Poseidon with uncanny discrimination and did not invest a penny when Poseidon lost the Champion Stakes. At the end of that season Jimmy Ah Poon disappeared from the Australian racing scene and was never sighted again on our race-tracks. Some said he had returned to China to live out his life in the luxury Poseidon had brought him.

No other horse has matched Poseidon's three-year-old record. His eleven wins that year included the two Derbies, the Caulfield Cup, Melbourne Cup, and both the A.J.C. and V.R.C. St Legers. This in a year of outstanding horses in which he had to overcome powerful opposition. His four-year-old efforts were not quite dramatic, though he won the Caulfield Cup for the second successive year. Altogether Poseidon won nineteen races and £19,946 in stakes.

Unperturbed over his heavy drubbing in Poseidon's Melbourne Cup, Sol Green made another trip to Europe the following year and bought the mare Tragedy Queen, which had a foal at foot that had been sired by the English Derby winner Persimmon. This subsequently became Comedy King, a horse that was to have a strong influence on Australian bloodstock breeding.

top : The betting ring at Randwick in the early 1900s. Big betting was a feature of racing in Australia at this time, as the country shook off the last traces of the depression which had blighted the 1890s. A.J.C.

above : Sir Adrian Knox, Chief Justice of the High Court of Australia from 1919 to 1930. During his term of office as A.J.C. committee-man (1896-1919) and chairman (1906-1919) many of the important procedures of racing today began, including uniform naming of horses, the appointment of stipendary stewards for each racing district, and the establishment of provident funds for jockeys. A.J.C.

top right : Stud matrons in New Zealand. New Zealand-bred horses were starting to make a big impact on racing in Australia at the turn of the century, and this influence was to grow. Windsor Photography

right : Gaulus wins the 1897 Melbourne Cup by half a head from Grafter. Gaulus was ridden by Steve Callinan, and came in at odds of 40 to 1. La Trobe

top left : James Scobie, best known as a trainer, began his career as a jockey, and was a particularly fine steeplechase rider. This photograph shows the running of the V.R.C. Grand National Steeplechase in 1899. La Trobe

left : Acrasia passes the post to win the 1904 Melbourne Cup from a large field of thirty-four. Racing the two miles in 3 min 28.25 sec, Acrasia beat the previous year's winner, Lord Cardigan, by three-quarters of a length. La Trobe

above : Brightly-coloured umbrellas protect complexions at Flemington in 1900. This year brought national fame to trainer James Scobie— four of his horses won three Derbies, the Moonee Valley Cup, the Melbourne Cup and the Williams-town Cup.

right : Lord Cardigan, brother of Poseidon, and winner of the 1903 Melbourne Cup, with his jockey Norman Godby. Lord Cardigan, was sired by Positano, an imported stallion by St Simon, and his dam was by Trenton. The brown colt won the race from twenty-three other runners.

*top left : A bad fall over a jump in the 1898 Grand
National Steeplechase. The falling horse is Beaver.
La Trobe*

*centre left : Entering the straight in the Caulfield Cup
of 21 October 1905. La Trobe*

*left : Excitement at the finish of the Victoria Derby at
Flemington in 1898. La Trobe*

*above : A family afternoon tea on the flat at
Flemington in 1901.*

*right : The Illustrated Australian News of 2
December 1895 shows a scene at the V.R.C. Derby of
that year and a portrait of Wallace, the winner.
Wallace was one of Carbine's sons, and proved to be
not only a good racehorse, but an outstanding sire,
getting winners of six V.R.C. Derbies, two Melbourne
Cups, four A.J.C. St Legers, six V.R.C. St Legers
and many more. His progeny won 949 races between
them with £246,145 in prize money.*

Wallace
Winner of
the Derby.

7. THE EDWARDIAN AGE

7. THE EDWARDIAN AGE

The Edwardian age saw a big increase in skullduggery in most Australian sports, and racing did not escape. In pugilism, professional footrunning and cycling, reports of fixed bouts and races were common. Racing offered crooks potentially higher rewards than other sports, however, and despite the diligence of stewards the ingenuity of the law-breakers frequently shocked racegoers.

After the favourite Revenue defeated San Fran in the 1901 Melbourne Cup it was discovered that a tunnel had been cut under the room containing the scales on which jockeys were weighed. Blankets, bottles and food were found in the tunnel, with a set of weights. Apparently it had been planned to send San Fran out for the big race with considerably less than his allotted 9 st 7 lb and thus give him a better chance of beating Revenue, to whom he conceded 25 lb. Somehow signals between the person in the tunnel and his accomplice in the weighing-in room went wrong and San Fran lost by half a length. The effort of carrying 9 st 7 lb over two miles was so great that San Fran could not race again.

The culprits were never publicly named because of a lack of evidence that would stand up in court. Suspensions were handed out over the next few years to those believed to have been involved in the tunnel digging. This Australian tradition for resourcefulness in cheating has endured on many courses.

At the start of this century the magnificent English thoroughbred St Simon, who had once won the Ascot Gold Cup by twenty lengths, was the sire with the biggest influence on breeding throughout the world. His progeny won more than a million dollars in prize money at a time when stakes were far smaller than today's. One of his most brilliant sons was Persimmon, sire of Comedy King, which almost from the time he arrived in Australia in the *Afric* started to win races in both Melbourne and Sydney.

pages 154-155 : Picnickers on the Flemington hill enjoy a pleasant lunch under the tree on Derby Day, 1905.

left : At Flemington in 1909, Lord Dudley (left) and industrialist and coal magnate John Brown (in bowler hat). John Brown was the owner of Prince Foote 1909 winner of the V.R.C. and A.J.C. Derbies and St Legers, and the Melbourne Cup. Prince Foote's dame and sire were both imported by Mr Brown, who used the pseudonym 'J. Baron' when racing his horses.

There was quality in everything Comedy King attempted, and it was no surprise when he won the fiftieth Melbourne Cup in 1910 in a stirring finish, from Trafalgar and Apple Pie. The crew of the *Afric*, which by coincidence was berthed in Melbourne at the time, won heavily when Comedy King became the first imported horse to win the Cup. Immediately the result was known, they decked their ship in bunting.

Sol Green's success as an owner had proved ample compensation for the setback he had suffered as a bookie when Poseidon took the Cup. Comedy King was ridden by W.H. McLachlan who had also won the Cup the previous year. McLachlan subsequently became the first Australian to ride for the Royal Family. This victory was the highspot of a sustained duel between Comedy King and Trafalgar. In the Cup Trafalgar came with up from near the rear of the field with a breathtaking run in the straight but Comedy King held him off by a half head. Trafalgar was a son of the outstanding Australian sire Wallace but Comedy King beat him eight times.

Comedy King went to stud at Norman Falkiner's property, Noorilim, in Victoria, and like his great ancestor proceeded to exert a powerful influence on bloodlines. He was twice Australia's leading sire and remained among our top sires for many seasons. His best son was Artilleryman, winner of the 1919 Melbourne Cup.

Comedy King established Noorilim as one of our finest studs, rivalling the St Albans Stud at Geelong, the reputation of which had been boosted by Wakeful, Mr R. Hunter's Northwood Park Stud, near Seymour, and Henry Phillips's Bryan O'Lynn Stud near Warrnambool. These studs and others such as Canning Downs, Alma Vale and Lyndhurst on the rich Darling Downs, and the studs in the Hunter Valley of New South Wales enabled the eastern states to produce more than three-quarters of the nation's thoroughbreds. Best known of the South Australian studs were the establishments run by ancestors of James Hurtle

right : A Sydney Mail photograph of the great chestnut stayer, Trafalgar, with his jockey, J. Pike. During his racing career Trafalgar won twenty-three races, amassing over £11,000 in winnings, a huge total for that time.

Fisher and George Angas, and Morphetville stud, which came out of the partnership between Sir Thomas Elder and R. Barr Smith.

Australia sent a total of 16,357 horses to the South African war of 1899-1902, tough, hardy mounts which had to withstand severe punishment and carry big loads every day. Douglas Barrie has recorded that one unit travelled more than 4,000 miles all over Transvaal, including some forced marches of seventy-five miles overnight, with few losses in horse-flesh. After the South African war thoroughbreds were given a bigger role in the breeding of light-horse mounts and when the first world war began Australia became one of the Allies' main sources of reliable horses. The Australian *Official War History* for the first war stresses that 'the thoroughbred element' in Australian remounts made them invaluable in operations requiring stamina and spirit. Barrie has calculated that 121,324 first-class horses were sent overseas during this war, most to Egypt, 39,348 to the A.I.F., and 81,976 to India. They participated in the greatest—and the last—cavalry exploits in the history of warfare, enduring immense hardship as the Allies advanced up the Sinai Desert into the Palestinian Plain.

'Almost without exception', Barrie says, 'the horses of the Anzac Division were got by thoroughbred sires. Their stamina and courage was superb. Where baser-bred horses lost the will and strength to go on, the walers even when distressingly wasted from lack of water and food continued alert and dependable. The Australian Light Horseman soon found that to have a good horse evacuated sick meant that someone else would acquire him. This lesson learnt, the Light Horsemen would go to any lengths to avoid having his charger declared unfit for duty.'

The walers, which took their name from the country of their evolution, New South Wales, came from all states, from the colder Tasmanian bush, from the forests of Gippsland, from the Darling Downs and Maranoa, from the Kimberleys, and all over Australia. Many were the sons and daughters of Cup winners, some of them Stud Book horses and winners of big races. 'What a bargain they were in horse-flesh', Barrie adds.

above : The English horse Prince Palatine, whose father was the great sire Persimmon. Persimmon also got Comedy King, an outstanding racehorse and one of Australia's most influential sires.

top right : Mares and foals at a stud in the Hunter River district, New South Wales, late in the nineteenth century. The white faces and legs of these horses proclaim the strain of Adieu (Imp.) by Blair Athol, winner of the English Derby and St Leger and four times leading English sire.

right : Samuel Hordern, (later Sir Samuel), a Sydney businessman and stud-owner. He was responsible for bringing several good horses to Australia, and had success in breeding and buying winners.

far right : The famous racing mare Maltine, with her first-born foal, a filly by the imported stallion Flavus. During her racing career, Maltine, bred in 1904, won many important races including the A.U.C. Craven Plate, and Metropolitan Handicap, the latter being also won by her daughter Jocelyn.

The military histories show that the Australian horses were far superior to camels in the desert, for they could travel just as far at a faster pace. For heavily-loaded cavalrymen these thoroughbreds also had the advantage of instinctively progressing from a walk into an easy, flowing canter whereas the traditional cavalryman's charger went from a walk to a trot, increasing the noise of the troop's movement and adding to the strain on the rider.

The first world war also saw a spectacular exploit by one of Australia's finest race riders, Brownie Carslake, who like many of the Light Horsemen who performed so well in Egypt had learned to ride at bush meetings. Carslake was interned in Austria in 1914 but escaped to Rumania in a railway engine, dressed as a fireman. Back in England his success made him legendary. He was particularly noted for his surging finishing bursts. Carslake won all the English classics except the Derby, including two St Legers. His ashes were scattered on the Rowley Mile track at Newmarket, his favourite course, at the point where he used to start his thrilling finishing runs.

The period leading up to the first world war saw a steady increase in prize money for Australian races. The A.J.C. offered a total of £40,435 in 1904-1905 but by the 1914-1915 season this had grown to £97,345. This period also saw a big advance in the prestige of major races conducted in capitals apart from Melbourne and Sydney. An energetic race club committee had opened Helena Vale racecourse in Perth in 1898 and not long afterwards the old Burswood course near Perth was remodelled and reopened as Belmont Park. By 1911 there were eighty-seven race clubs in Western Australia, and the South Australian Derby was beginning to attract entries from eastern states. In Tasmania, the Tasmanian Turf Club at Launceston and the Tasmanian Racing Club at Hobart had strengthened their positions as leaders of the sport. It had become the habit of owners of good horses in the west and in Tasmania to send them to the eastern states for big races, but invariably they found it very hard to win against horses bred in the east.

Further evidence of Australia's rising reputation in racing came in the 1909-1911 English racing seasons.

top : A view of Randwick in the early 1900s. From the turn of the century until the first world war, prize-money for Australian races gradually increased. The A.J.C. for example offered a total of £40,435 in the 1904-1905 season, but by 1815 this total had risen to £97,345. A.J.C.

above : The St Leger enclosure at Randwick early in this century. The scratching tower may be seen at the extreme left of the photograph. In the betting ring in the foreground, bookmakers stand on their little platforms surrounded by clusters of punters. A.J.C.

top right : Elwick racecourse in 1906. The Tasmanian Racing Club had by this time assured its position as leader of the sport in the capital, basing itself at Elwick, while the Tasmanian Turf Club retained its supremacy in the north at the Mowbray course, Launceston. T.R.C.

right : An impressive array of Tasmanian trophies, photographed at Elwick racecourse. The trophies have all been won at the course.

Frank Wootton became the first Australian to win the English jockeys' premiership. His feat of taking it out three years in a row has never been matched by any of his countrymen. Wootton's best total of wins for a season was in 1910 when he rode 187 winners.

At home the Australian Government had moved to correct faults in the laws governing off-course totes. Legislation introduced in 1906 effectively closed the last loophole, and the John Wren tote and others went out of existence. But by then Wren was a wealthy man. He had gone into boxing promotion in 1905 and his proprietary racecourses were flourishing. In 1906 his horse Murmur won the Caulfield Cup. Bookmakers provided a chance for the wealthy punters to place their bets and brought colourful personalities to the tracks, but the appeal to the small punter of the totalisator did not escape the race clubs.

In 1913, George Julius (later Sir George) introduced the world's first automatic totalisator at Ellerslie, New Zealand. He spent years making improvements to the machine, and in September 1917, at a Randwick meeting, his tote was used for the first time on an Australian course. The Julius tote was the first successful machine of its kind and was exported all over the world. Today it operates in twenty-eight countries. New types very much faster and more versatile than those in use in Australia have recently been installed in America and in Hong Kong by the Julius company, Automatic Totalisators. One big step forward in tote betting was the introduction of an automatic odds-computing device in 1932.

Julius was a highly gifted engineer, and his machine quickly won preference over the pari-mutuel tote system developed in France in the 1860s. The weakness of the pari-mutuel system was that it involved a large army of clerks and accountants and was therefore expensive to operate. With Julius's tote, pre-printed and serially-numbered tickets were handed to investors by clerks but the rest of the operation was automatic. The automatic tote transmitted every investment to the appropriate pools, made deductions for government taxation, and instantly adjusted the odds displayed on public indicators.

Originally Australian tote pools were divided among

top left : After the running of the Hobart Cup, one of Tasmania's most important racing events, at Elwick racecourse in 1906. T.R.C.

left : A view of Morphetville course on Adelaide Cup Day in about 1900. At left stands the scratching tower, and behind it, a carriage park, in the centre stands the board showing totalisator results—the tote having been first used at Morphetville in December 1879. A Julius automatic totalisator was installed at the course in 1921. S.A.J.C.

top : Trentham, New Zealand on a winter's day, showing the totalisator board. Windsor Photography

Mr James Wilson, owner of St Alban's Stud at Geelong, Victoria, in the late nineteenth century, photographed in 1885. St Alban's is one of the most successful Australian studs, and has been the home of many great horses—Trenton, Enfield (the sire of Melbourne Cup winner Rimfire), Sirius, Gay Lothario (sire of Tranquil Star) and Wakeful, to name a few.

the holders of tickets on the first three place-getters. When there were fewer than eight starters the pool of money invested paid only two dividends, and when there were less than five starters only one prize was paid. From this win-and-place tote betting has developed a wide variety of pools for doubles, trebles and quinellas. Julius's company has also produced a mobile tote which can be taken from one course to another in a caravan, providing tote betting for country race clubs which could not afford installation of permanent totes.

The growth in tote betting on our race meetings has been staggering. In 1935, the Commonwealth collected £4,370,000 in taxes on tote betting. Twenty years later government tax was £31,481,000. The total of off-course and on-course totalisator betting on the Cup day meeting at Flemington in 1968 was $2,825,935 in Victoria. New South Wales tote investment that day were $2,051,533—a total for the two states of $4,877,468. As the tote also operated in other states, the total tote investment all around the nation probably exceeded $5,000,000 for a single day!

From the earliest days of Australian racing picnic race meetings have been a feature of rural life. Originally these meetings provided an opportunity for different properties to match their best horses against one another. They were ridden by amateurs and weights carried were consequently far greater than at race meetings under Jockey Club rules. Country people travelled hundreds of miles for these annual gatherings, some of which continued for several days and were accompanied by wild celebrations.

The advent of the motor car meant that cars largely replaced horses in much farm and station transport work, except perhaps on the very big cattle properties. Picnic meetings continued as the highlight of the rural year but the horses were usually bought especially for racing. A rule was introduced which stipulated that all entrants had to be placed in one paddock for some weeks prior to the meetings to ensure an equal standard of feeding, a vital factor in performance of any racehorse.

The enormous cattle properties of Queensland and the Northern Territory continued to use big teams of

BETTING BY MACHINERY.

THE GREAT TOTALISATOR.

Cutting Out Dishonesty.

FACTS THAT THE PUBLIC SHOULD KNOW.

Fair Odds, Bigger Prizes, Revenue for Hospitals.

The totalisator machine is in use in all the Australian States (except New South Wales and Victoria), and in New Zealand. Residents of this State who have been fortunate enough to travel have seen the machine working, but the great majority of racegoers know it only by name. In the absence of a general knowledge of the advantages of the machine, all kinds of misconceptions have been formed, and many honest people have been led to believe that the totalisator is a fiendish invention of the devil. There is already a strong influence in New South Wales and Victoria in favor of the machine, and it is only necessary for it to be better known to come into general use.

top left : These cartoons under the heading 'What the totalisator doesn't know', appeared in the Sydney Sun of 25 January 1914.

left : Totalisator boards showing the betting odds attract the crowd at a meeting at Elwick, Tasmania early in this century. T.R.C.

above : The introduction to an article which appeared in the Sydney Sun of 25 January 1914. As the article points out, there were many popular misconceptions formed about 'betting by machinery', at that time, but doubts were eventually dispelled, and with the introduction of the automatic Julius tote in 1917, the advantages of the system became obvious.

horses despite the motor car, and it is there that the real spirit and atmosphere of the Australian picnics remain strongest. The picnics at Brunette Downs in the Territory and at Laura on Cape York have become national institutions, rivalled only by one or two picnics in the south such as the Bong Bong picnics.

One of the most important races of the Edwardian era was a three-miler, the Australiasian Champion Stakes. The race originated in Victoria in 1859 as the Champion Stakes, was run at Randwick in 1860, and at Ipswich, Queensland in 1861. After rotating for some years around the states, it eventually became part of the V.R.C. Autumn Carnival. Some great horses competed in this race, including Carbine's daughter La Carabine, which won it two years running (1901 and 1902), Wakeful, which won in 1903, and Trafalgar, which emulated La Carabine by winning the race in successive years, 1911 and 1912. The Australasian Champion Stakes was the longest important flat race run in Australia, though it never challenged the popularity of the Melbourne Cup. It was abandoned after Carlita won the fifty-eighth running of the race at Flemington in March 1915.

above: 'Jack hears of a certainty'—a sketch which appeared in The Australasian in 1905. The sailor is receiving a hot tip for the 1905 Melbourne Cup, which was to be won in record time by Blue Spec.

right: Fruit vendors on the hill at Flemington early in this century.

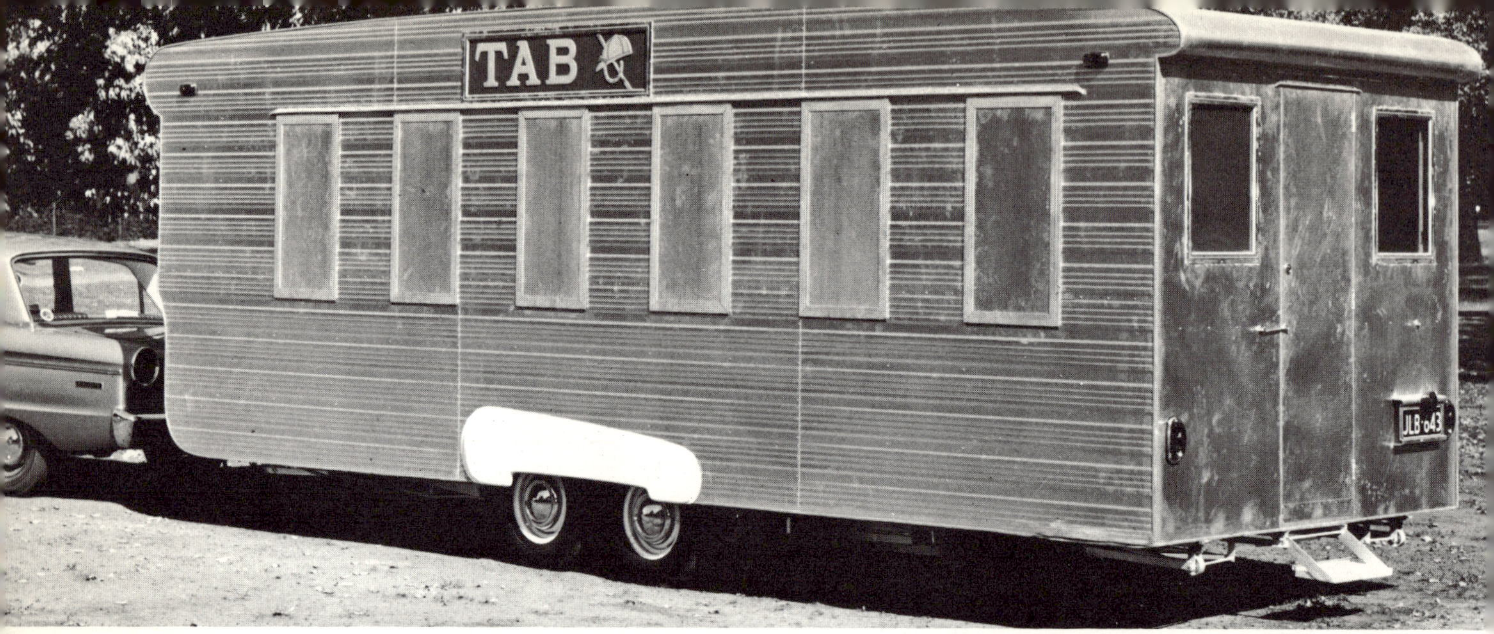
TAB

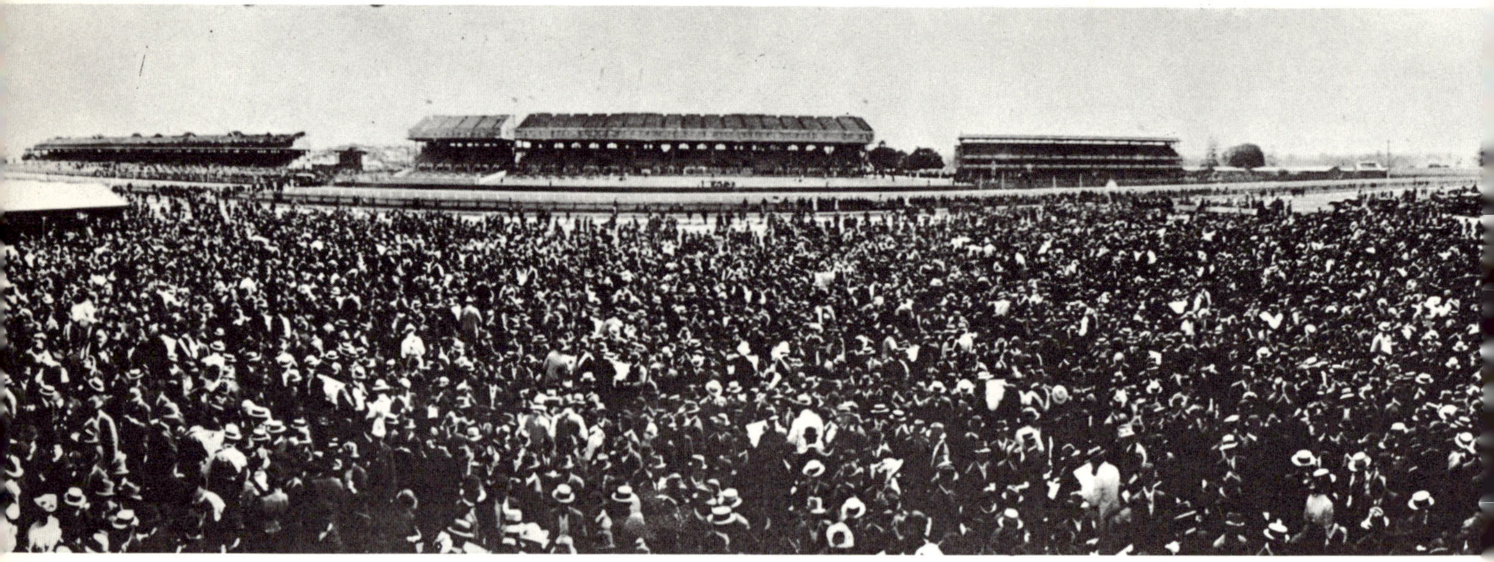

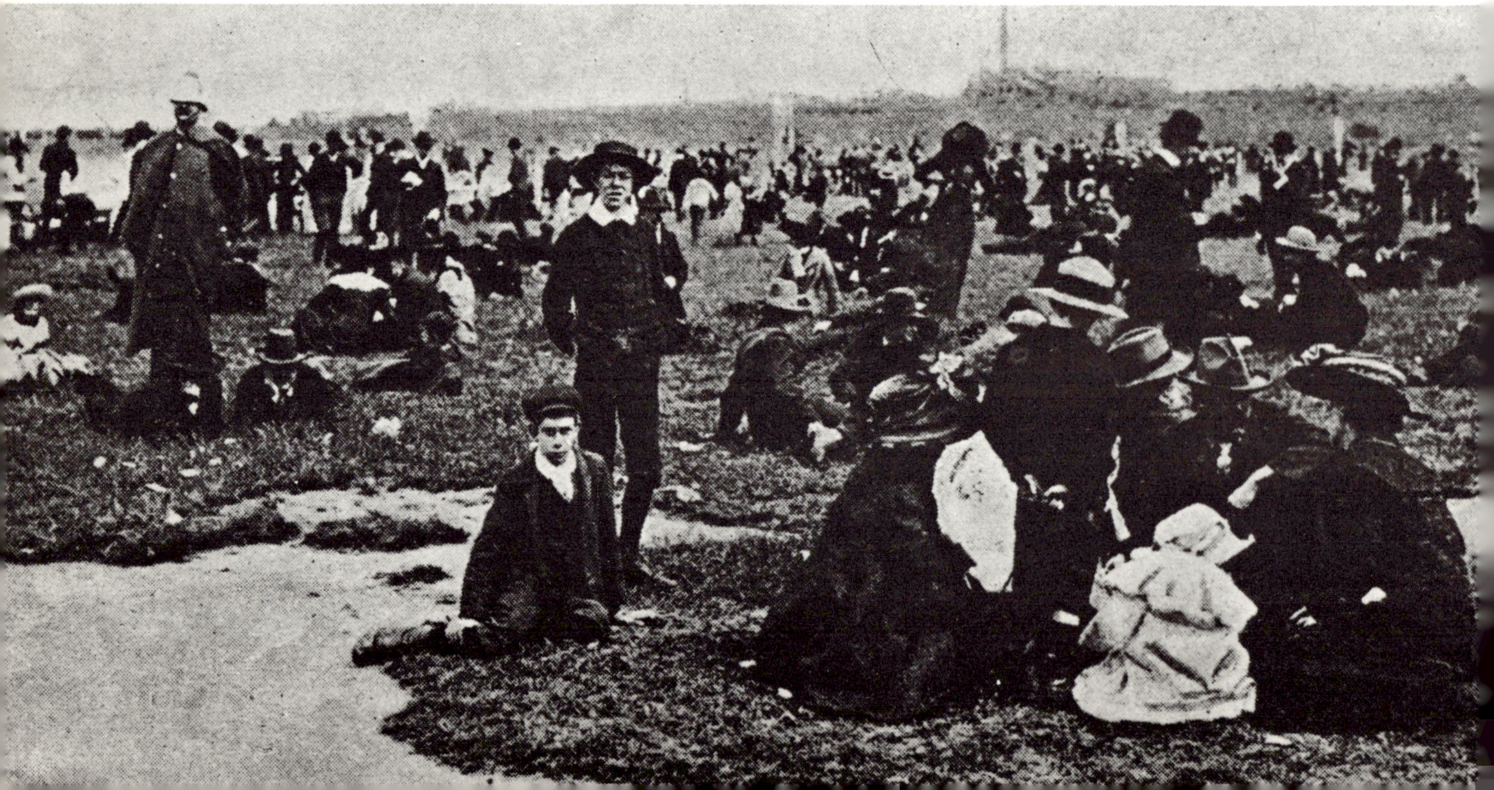

top left : One of the later developments of the Julius company was a mobile tote which enabled small country tracks to provide totalisator facilities without installing a permanent tote. This T.A.B. caravan is used on racecourses for selling daily doubles.

centre left : The flat at Randwick in the early 1900s, the betting ring in the foreground crowded with punters and bookies doing business. A.J.C.

left : Between races on the flat at Flemington, 1906, groups sit and lie on the grass, watched over by the ponderous policeman at the left of the photograph.

above : Picnic racing at Kyneton, Victoria. One of the most pleasant country courses in Victoria.

top right : A snapshot taken at the Melbourne Cup of 1915—wartime. Eighty-eight thousand people, many of them servicemen, watched Patrobus win the Cup by half a neck from Westcourt. Patrobus was a son of Wallace, and thus grandson of Carbine.

right : Trafalgar after his retirement in 1913.

top far left : Racing fashion in 1910—hats were enormous!

top left : The silver cup presented by Mr G.G. Stead of New Zealand, to the winner of the 1906 A.J.C. Craven Plate. The Craven Plate is run over one and a half miles, and famous winners include : The Barb, Carbine, Wakeful, Poseidon, Cetigne, Gloaming (three times) and Phar Lap.

left : Ninety thousand people pack Flemington race-course to watch Blue Spec streak past the post in record time to win the Melbourne Cup of 1905. Blue Spec, ridden by F. Bullock, ran the two miles in 3 min. 27.5 sec., carrying 8 st. and beating the second horse, Scot Free by three-quarters of a length.

above : At the Victoria Derby, in 1912, two attractive ladies of the Edwardian era watch events.

8. A SPORT OF THE PEOPLE

8. A SPORT OF THE PEOPLE

Early settlers transplanted the rules and customs of English flat racing to Australia without very much difficulty. Hurdling and steeplechasing proved more troublesome. In England jumping races conducted by hunt clubs on their own courses took over in the winter when cold and muddy conditions made flat racing impractical. But in Australia there were not enough jumping race fans to sustain hunt clubs and the weather remained favourable to flat racing throughout the year.

Initially, all states conducted races over the jumps, but today this form of racing survives in only three states and only as part of programmes in which the main features are flat races. Despite their lack of numbers, however, Australian horses and jockeys have fashioned a splendid record over the jumps.

Thiefcatcher was the first recorded winner of an Australian hurdle race. He won the first race over the five-mile course between Botany and Coogee in 1832. Thiefcatcher was owned by Edward (later Sir Edward) Deas Thomson, who became Chief Secretary and was Chairman of the A.J.C. for twenty years. Thiefcatcher overtook Tam O'Shanter, which had led from the start, to win by a neck. This race took the field of seven over scrub-lined hills and several vast jumps. A week later Tam O'Shanter reversed this defeat by winning a steeplechase at Barwon Park in what is now the suburb of St Peters.

The Cumberland Hunt Club was formed in New South Wales in 1838, and foxhunting flourished at that time in Tasmania. Races over jumps spread to Bathurst, New South Wales, and in Melbourne a race over jumps 4 ft high was part of the first meeting at Batman's Hill in 1838. The first Hunters' Stakes run at New Town, Tasmania, ended with the entire field disqualified for 'clouting' or striking an obstacle. The race was declared void. Brisbane had its first

top left : *An oil painting of Carbine in his stall by A.C. Havell. The painting hangs in the committee room of the Australian Jockey Club.*

far left : *Exercising a racehorse. From 'The Henry Aitken Scrapbook and Sketches' in the Mitchell Library*

left : *A 19th century English country race meeting.*

above : *The scene hasn't changed much at the races today. The clothes may be different but the faces and feelings are very much the same. Victorian Tourist Authority*

179

race over the jumps in 1843, when a hack hurdle over two miles was run at Cooper's Plains.

The colder weather in Victoria apparently encouraged growth of the sport there, and it spread to several country centres. A Great Western Steeplechase was run at Coleraine in western Victoria in the 1860s, and in 1872 the Warrnambool Winter Steeplechase meeting was inaugurated. Many of the administrators of these early steeplechase meetings rode regularly to hounds and in cross-country chases.

The early steeplechase horses had to be tough. The hurdle race conducted in 1841 at Sydney's Sandy racecourse was over three miles and nine big fences. All thirteen starters had to carry 11 st 9 lb. The field in a race called the Hawesbury Stakes in 1844 had to cover three miles of brooks, fences and stone walls at Mr J. Abercrombie's Five Dock estate. Six years later the winner of that race, Highflyer, won all three three-mile heats with 12st in the Coppin Cup in Adelaide.

In October 1868, the poet Adam Lindsay Gordon rode three steeplechase winners in one afternoon at Flemington. He won the Melbourne Hunt Club Cup on Babbler, then rode his own horse Viking to win the Metropolitan Steeplechase, and capped it all by winning the Selling Steeplechase on Cadger. Each race was over three miles. Despite his hat-trick Gordon was grief-stricken as his win on Cadger in the Selling Steeplechase meant that he had to sell the horse to the highest bidder. Cadger went for £40, which Gordon regarded as small compensation for the loss of such a game horse even though he was desperate for money.

In these formative years of Australian hurdling it was common for well-known horses in flat races to occasionally start in jumping events. Indeed the versatility of some of these early horses was remarkable. Malua, a horse which won at distances from three and a half furlongs to three and a quarter miles, including the 1884 Melbourne Cup, the Oakleigh Plate, the Newmarket Handicap, Adelaide Cup, Melbourne Stakes (later the L.K.S. McKinnon Stakes), and the Geelong Cup, also won the V.R.C. Grand National Hurdle in 1888. Malua, a son of St Albans, also proved a success as a sire as his son Malvolio won the

top: Viking, Adam Lindsay Gordon's favourite steeplechaser, takes a jump. Gordon rode Viking in the Metropolitan, the second of his three steeplechase wins in one afternoon at Flemington in 1868. La Trope

above: The hunt—an English tradition which did not transplant well in Australia.

top right: A ladies' coursing meeting, illustrated in The Australasian Sketcher of 30 September 1876. Hunting was never as popular in Australia as it was in England, though clubs such as the Cumberland Hunt Club, formed in New South Wales in 1838, did exist, and foxhunting was popular in Tasmania.

right: Riders take the third jump during a steeplechase at Newtown, New South Wales, early in the nineteenth century. Early race meetings in all states often featured steeplechase events, but today only Victoria, Tasmania, and South Australia conduct races over the jumps.

top left: Poseidon, whose three-year-old record has never been matched by any other Australian race-horse. In that year, 1906, he won the two Derbies, the Caulfield Cup, the Melbourne Cup, and both the A.J.C. and V.R.C. St. Legers. *A.J.C.*

far left: From 1860 it was generally accepted that the birthday of all horses should be 1 August. This decision marked the end of years of confusion and dissent, and from this time mares were mated in the spring to ensure that they foaled after the following 1 August. Pictured is a four-week-old colt with its mother, the champion brood mare Misty Anne. *V.R.C.*

left, centre left: Lady jockeys at the country racecourse.

above: The picnic races at Warrnambool, Victoria— a watercolour by Sir Daryl Lindsay. *Ballarat Art Gallery*

1891 Melbourne Cup, defying a rainstorm which put parts of Flemington 3 ft under water to win the first prize of $20,000 for his owner.

In winning the Newmarket, Malua's rider surprised spectators by taking his mount out on to the far outside of the track instead of hugging the rails as had previously been the riding custom. Jockeys in subsequent straight six furlong races at Flemington copied this idea and discovered that under certain conditions the outside or grandstand side of this wide track can be faster than the inside route. Ever since horses which take the outside course are said to be following 'Malua's track'.

The year after Malua's startling Grand National Hurdle win saw the emergence of Redleap, one of the finest horses over jumps ever produced in Australia. Redleap had superb jumping skill and rare pace between jumps. He won the 1889 V.R.C. Grand National Hurdle and took it again in 1892 with 11 st 12 lb. The same year he won the V.R.C. Grand National with a record weight of 13 st 2 lb.

Another famous Australian jumper was Jack Rice, a brown gelding born in 1909. Jack Rice, who was ridden in most of his races by Ted Moon, our leading rider over fences up to the start of the first world war, was not fast but he could stay at one pace over long distances. He became a favourite of racegoers because of his remarkable jumping with big weights. He repeatedly won carrying 12 or 13 st and during the first war Australian infantrymen began to use the phrase 'even Jack Rice couldn't jump it' to describe a big object. Jack Rice died after a fall in Melbourne in 1919 but the saying has endured.

In all its forms, racing in Australia in the two decades before and the decade after the first war became a sport of the people. When Parisian won the Melbourne Cup in 1911, 105,000 people watched, and this was the fifth time the Cup attendance had exceeded 100,000. R.C. Bagot had started this trend

right: Over a jump during a recent Flemington steeplechase. Victorian Tourist Authority.

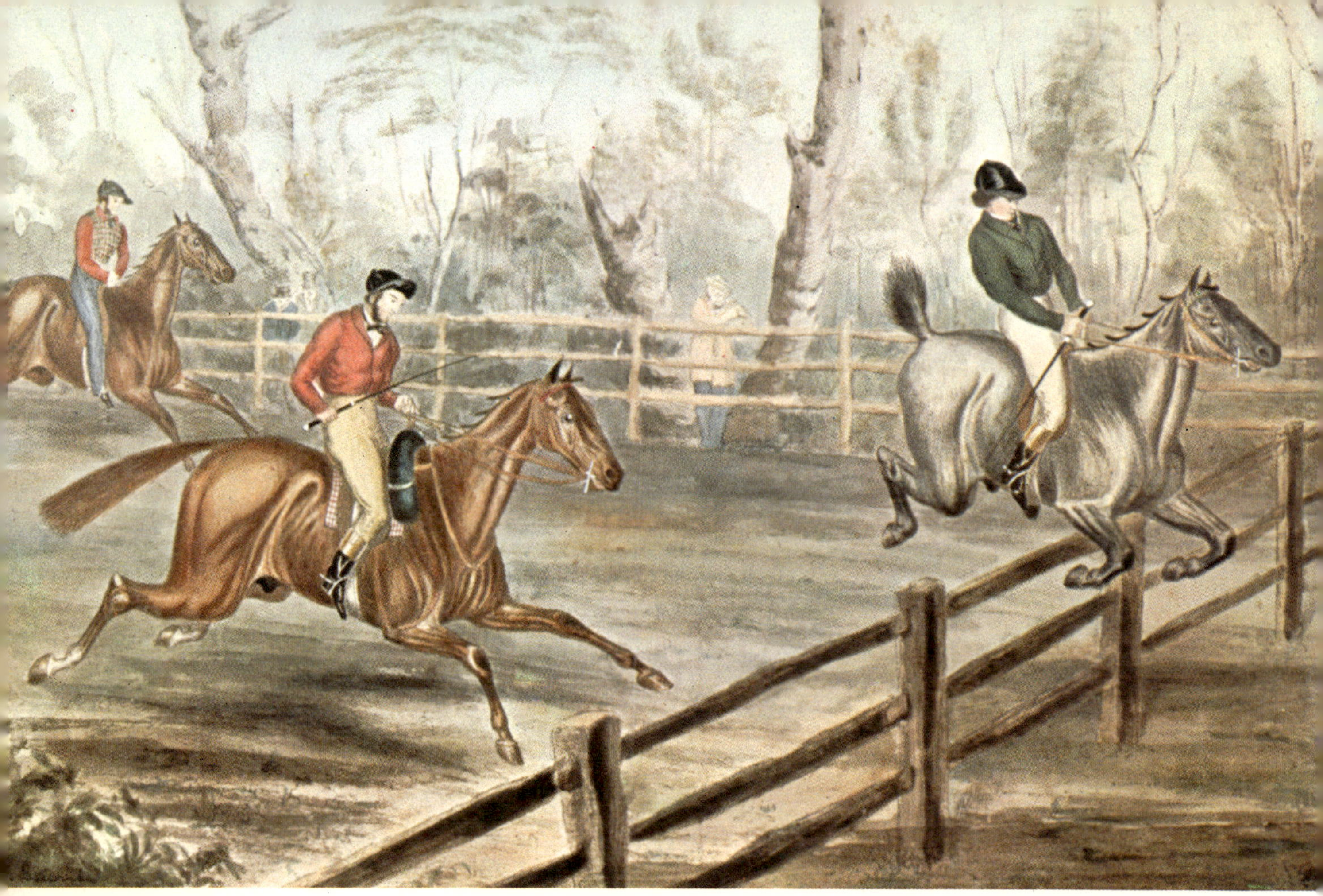

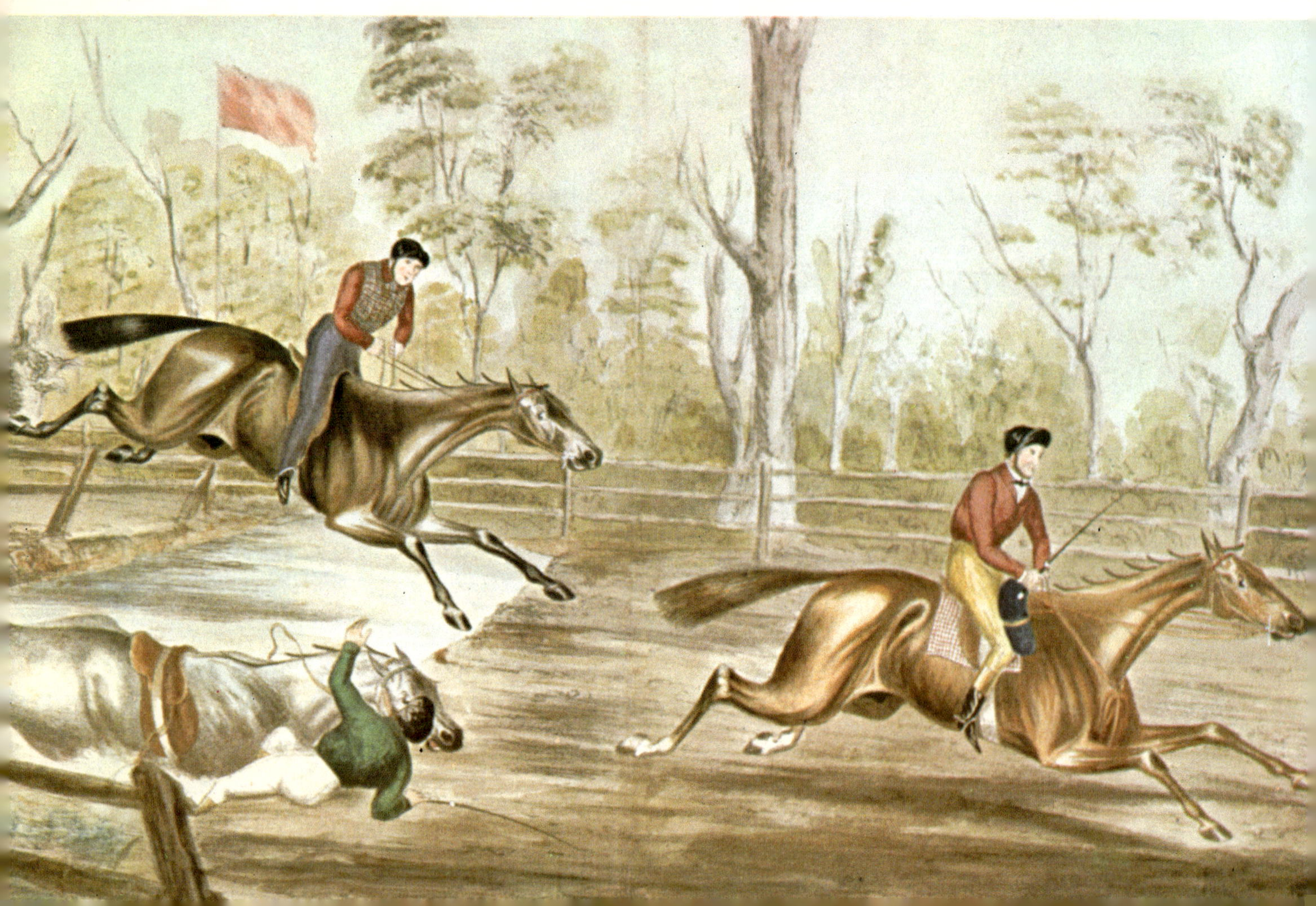

top left : The first leap of the Five-Dock Grand Steeplechase, 1844, by T. Balcomb. Mr Hely leads on Block, followed by Mr. Watt on Highflyer, with Mr Gorrick trailing on British Yeoman.

left : A change in fortune at the brook. Block takes a fall and Highflyer moves into the lead with British Yoeman gaining.

above : Block backs at the stone wall, and Highflyer just clips it as British Yoeman streaks ahead into the lead.

right : The finish—British Yoeman first, with a good lead from Highflyer and Block. Mitchell

towards attracting entire families to the races when he revolutionized facilities at Flemington. But he set standards which many administrators have found it very difficult to match. Since his time the Australian racegoer has demanded first-class facilities far removed from the primitive conditions which the ordinary public usually accept on English courses.

Maurice Cavanough, the Melbourne racing writer, has calculated that when Grand Flaneur won the 1880 Melbourne Cup before an audience of 100,000 it meant that more than one in three of Melbourne's population had gone to the races. The city's population was then 282,000. The strong appeal of the races was underlined by the newspapers which were quick to see circulation-boosting chances in enlarged racing coverage. Teams of reporters were put to work producing stories that might entertain or help the punters in their quest for winners.

This tradition has prevailed even when attendances have slumped and Australian newspapers retain a closer watch on track gallops, reversals of form, buying and selling of racehorses and on big money betting plunges than newspapers in any other country in the world. Certainly the liaison between racing reporters and turf administrators is closer in Australia than elsewhere in the world where racing has largely remained a sport for the privileged.

'When the Joe Blow Australian started to go to the races, he was not much impressed by the classics', Cavanough wrote once. 'For him the disadvantage of this type of race was that it did not offer him much chance to get rich. Because all runners are weighted equally in a classic, the best horse should win, barring accidents real or contrived. Bookmakers are as well aware as punters about which is the best horse in a race and consequently they offer only meagre prices about the probable classic winner.'

The view that classics seldom offer punters the get-rich-quick chance that handicap races do is generally accepted by all Australian racing experts. It explains the popularity of handicap events in Australia and shows why the Metropolitan, the Doncaster, the Epsom, the Sydney Cup, Caulfield Cup and Melbourne Cup have always meant more to our racegoers

above : Mr Vincent Dowling, a great advocate of steeplechasing, photographed in 1878. An active A.J.C. committee member for many years, Mr Dowling took over from George Watson as official starter for the club. A.J.C.

top right : A record crowd gathers to watch the running of the 1911 V.A.T.C. Caulfield Cup. The Sydney Mail in which this photograph appeared notes that 'the weather was ideal and a capital day's sport resulted'.

right : Tom Hales on Grand Flaneur. Grand Flaneur began racing early in 1880, and won the Victoria Derby and the Melbourne Cup in the same year. He retired, unbeaten, to stud after his third year and was a successful sire, getting many winners. He was leading Australian sire in 1895. La Trobe

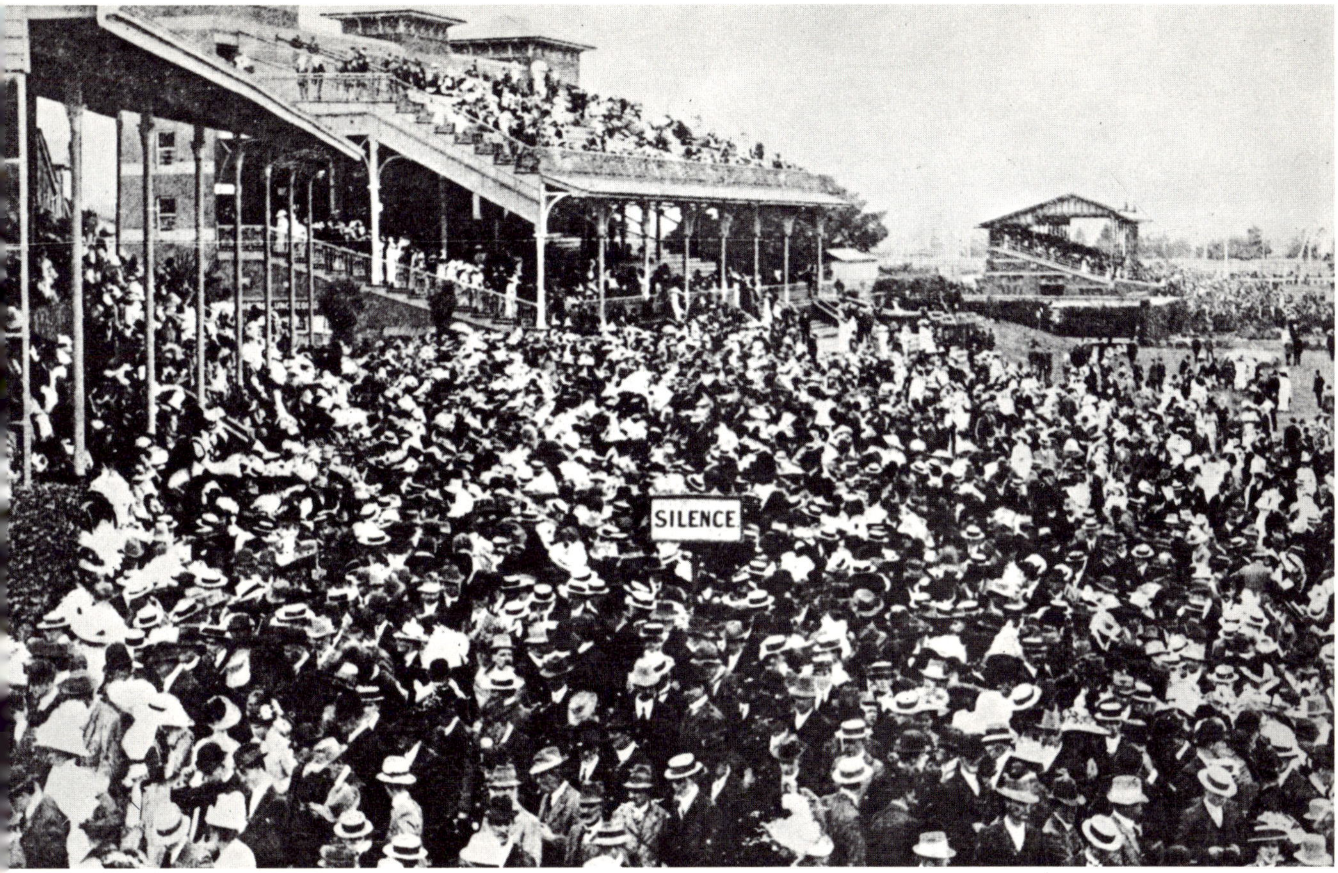
SILENCE

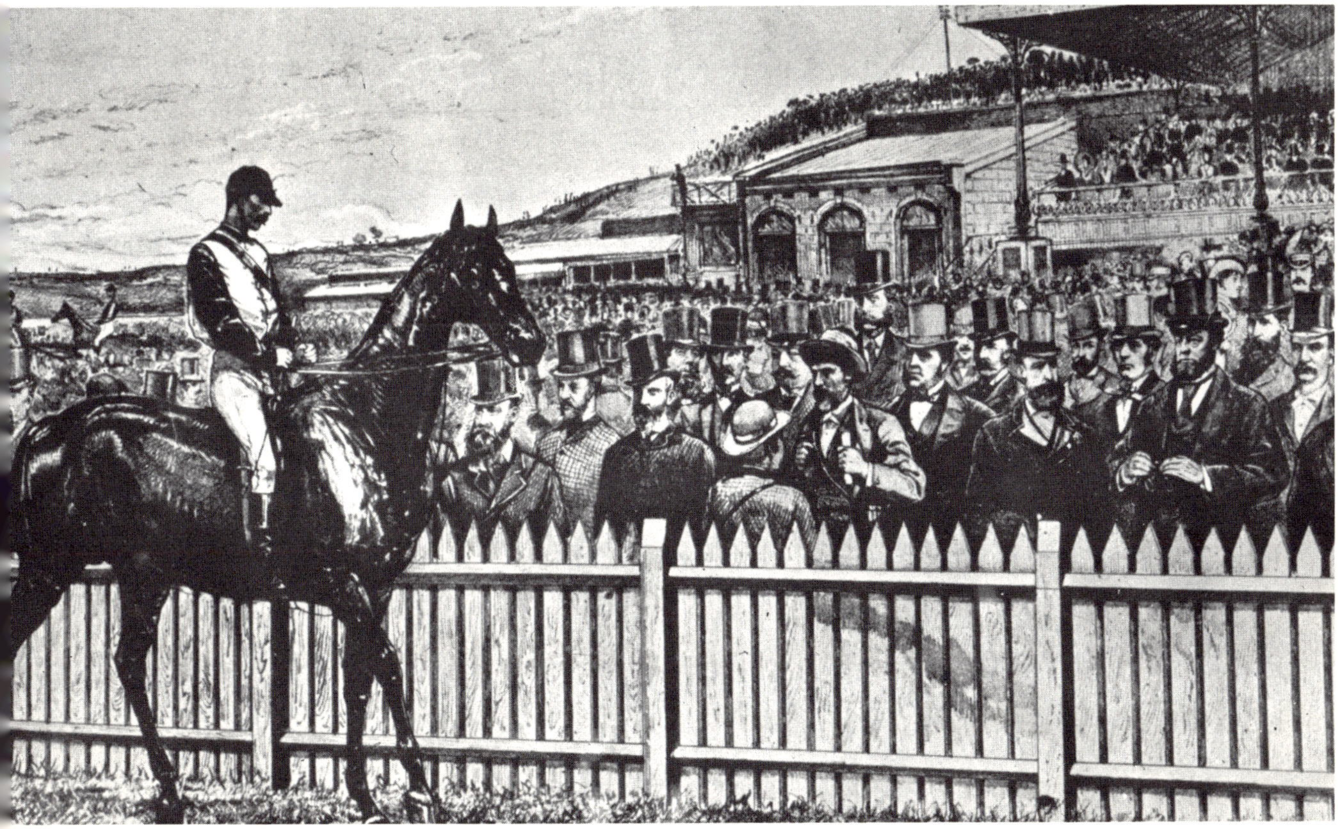

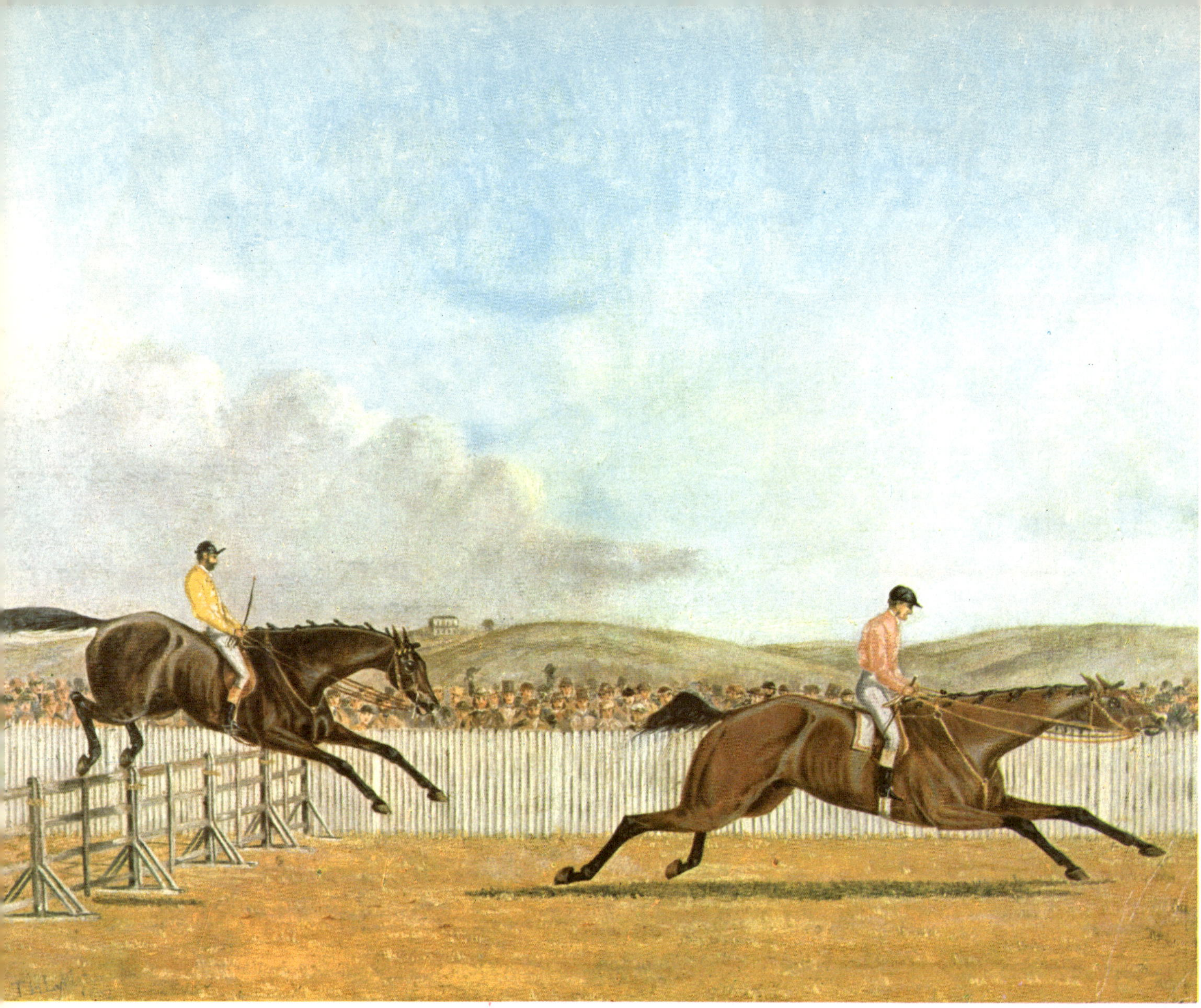

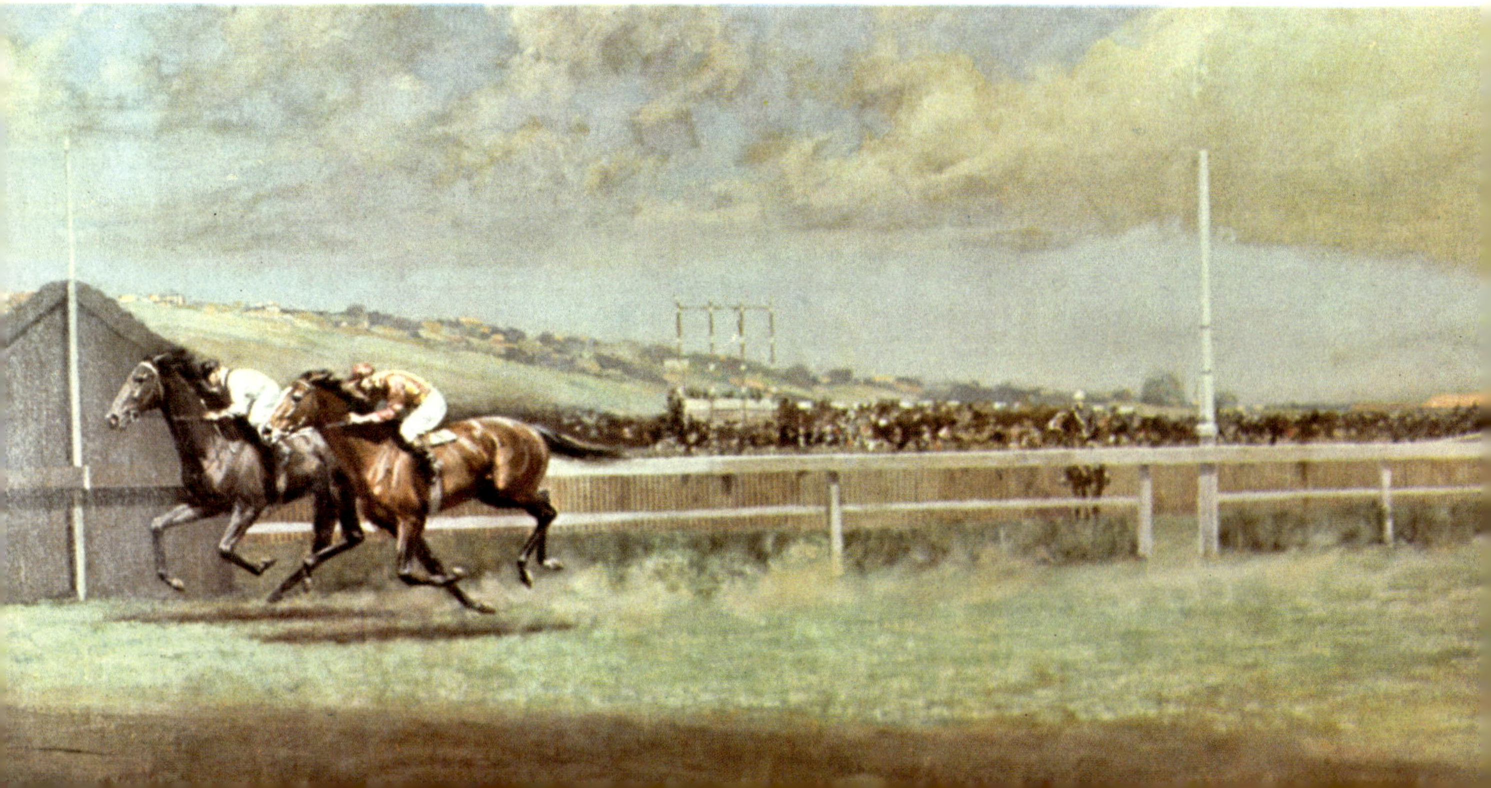

top far left : Adam Lindsay Gordon riding at Dowling Forest. in 1869. Gordon was well-known for his daring horsemanship, and his skill over the jumps was legendary. In October 1868, Gordon rode three steeplechase winners in one afternoon at Flemington. La Trobe

top left : The two sides of picnic racing—the excitement of the races, and the enjoyment of food, drink and company. These photographs were taken at the well-known Brunette Downs picnic, held annually in the Northern Territory.

left : The finish of the A.J.C. Spring Stakes of 1 October 1922, painted by Martin Stainforth. The winning horse was Beauford, a six-year-old gelding ridden by A.A. Wood. Next was Gloaming, and Speciality was third, followed by David, Furious, Wirraway and Violincello. A.J.C.

above : Phar Lap, with his gifted jockey Jim Pike.

191

than any of the local Oaks or Derbies. For they are all handicap races in which the handicapper attempts to adjust the weights carried so that the poorest runner in the field has a chance of beating the best-performed horses. And bookmakers' odds are invariably more appealing in handicap races than in classics.

Handicappers can err, of course, and they can be fooled by owners, trainers or jockeys who do not allow a horse to run at his best before big handicap weights are announced. But the Australian racegoer enjoys using his own judgment, and it adds spice to his quest for a big winning bet.

Despite the big turnover of the tote the place in which punters make these big bets, the betting ring, remains the hub of every Australian race meeting, whereas in many overseas countries bookmakers have been outlawed and all betting is done on the tote.

The bookmakers have responded to this attention by providing Australian racing with a fascinating array of spectacular personalities. Some regard them as a scourge on the sport and scorn bookies as 'people who live without working', but this ignores the extreme skill involved in making a book. Bookies like E.N. 'The Count' Abrahams who fielded on more than fifty Melbourne Cups, develop minds like computers that can judge to a penny the prices at which to back and lay a horse to win a percentage without risk of a loss. When Sol Green went to England each year he paid the cost of taking his family overseas by attending the calling of the card at Tattersall's on the night before the Derby, backing every runner in the race at prices which ensured he won handsomely whatever the outcome. And he did it without pen and paper.

Green was adept at picking out horses which ultimately would be heavily backed in big races when the fields were first announced. He would back them well himself at good odds so that when prices shortened as race day neared his profit was assured. His method was to carefully study the form of every horse in training, to keep up with form in all states, painstakingly studying reports of track gallops. At the track he bet with breathtaking speed but could still remain alert enough to detect big plunges on a horse just before the start of a race by skilled professional

top: Sol Green, the well-known bookmaker who lost £100,000 to Sir Hugh Denison when Poseidon took the 1906 Melbourne Cup. Green amassed a fortune as an owner after this time, one of his most notable successes being the importation of Comedy King in 1907. *Herald and Weekly Times*

above: An old newspaper cartoon—'Weights For Randwick'.

top right: Decorating the winner of the A.J.C. Derby, Cider, after a great race watched by 50,000 people.

top far right: The finish of the A.J.C. Doncaster Handicap, run at Randwick on 11 April 1914, and won by First Principal. *A.J.C.*

right: In the betting ring at Randwick in 1920 bookmakers do business beneath signs proclaiming their names. In many countries of the world, bookmakers have been outlawed, but they continue to lend colour and excitement to Australian racecourses. *A.J.C.*

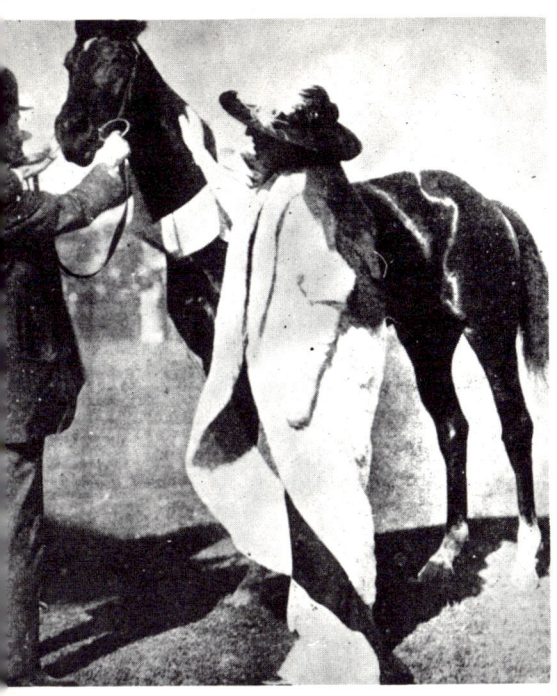

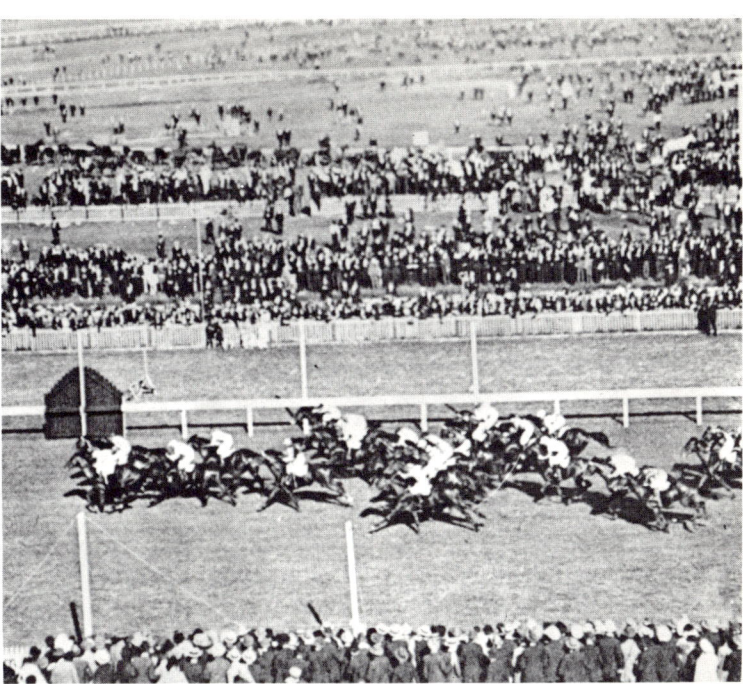

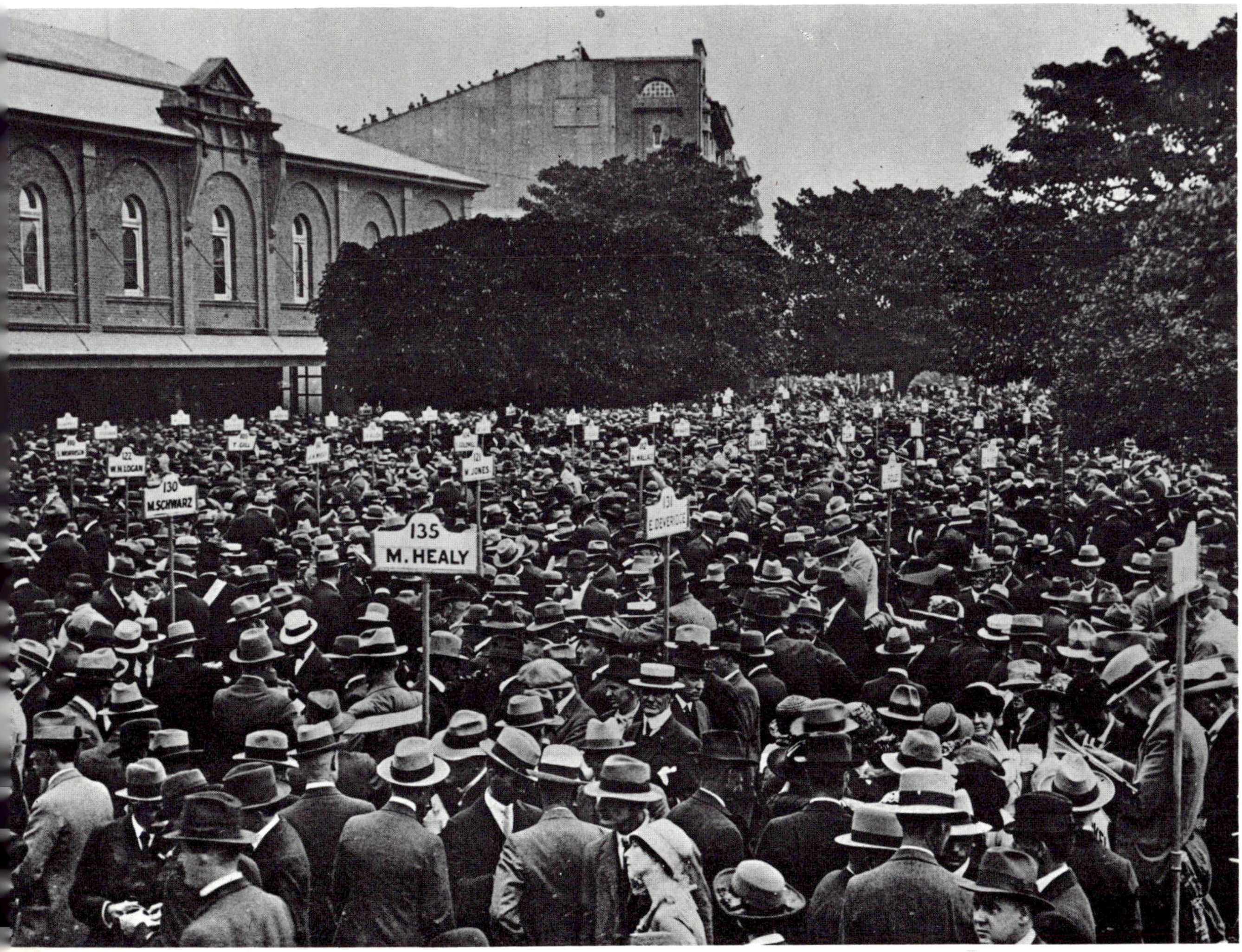
122
W.H. LOGAN
130
M.SCHWARZ
121
W. JONES
135
M. HEALY
131
E. DEVERIDGE

punters who deliberately wagered on other horses also, to fool the books and help boost the price on the real medium of their plunge.

Australian bookmakers are subjected to close scrutiny by the race clubs. They must satisfy the clubs that they have sufficient financial backing to hold a license and they are only permitted to bet at licensed racecourses. They pay annual license fees to the Government and fees to the clubs on whose courses they field. They also pay a turnover tax and stamp duty on all betting tickets. Off-the-course or starting price gambling is an offense in all states except Tasmania and Western Australia, where a form of betting shop operates successfully. Despite all the fees and the high upkeep of trained staff, leading bookmakers retain a showy affluence and are among the biggest donors to charities.

The newspapers' search for 'personality' horses with which to delight readers was richly rewarded just before the first world war by the appearance of Desert Gold. Born in 1912 in New Zealand, Desert Gold won every one of her five races as a two-year-old, and followed this by winning her next fourteen races. Racegoers were spellbound, wondering each time she appeared on the track whether her winning streak would continue. She won thirty-six races in all and by 1970 her record of nineteen straight wins had only been matched by one other horse, Gloaming.

The first horse to beat the mighty Desert Gold in Australia was Poitrel, who beat the mare at Randwick in 1918 in the A.J.C. Spring Stakes. Poitrel's courage made him a tremendous crowd-pleaser and at the age of six he culminated a fine career by winning the 1920 Melbourne Cup with 10 st, conceding 42 lb to the second and third horses. Poitrel was bred by the Moses brothers at Arrowfield, where he returned for stud duties.

The horse that finished fourth in Poitrel's Melbourne Cup, Eurythmic, is still regarded as the finest horse Western Australia has known. Eurythmic was

right: Outside the grandstand at the A.J.C. autumn meeting of 1920. Motor cars were of course very much in evidence by this time, although their housing was not yet the monumental problem it is today. A.J.C.

bred in New South Wales but did all his early racing in Western Australia for his owner Sir Ernest Lee Steere. He was sent east after winning all the main Western Australian races and won the Caulfield Stakes and Caulfield Cup. In the Melbourne Stakes he beat a hot field that included Poitrel for his eleventh straight win. This brought him a handicap of 9 st 4 lb for the Melbourne Cup won by Poitrel, but after that defeat he won eight races in a row, among them the 1921 Sydney Cup with 9 st 8 lb. In all, Eurythmic won thirty-one races, retiring at six years old with the then record Australian stake-winnings of £36,892.

Apparently sensing the average racing fan's disdain for English-type classic races, the A.J.C. revised the rules for its Derby in 1918 to permit geldings to run. The winner was Gloaming, which in a career which included fifty-seven wins and nine seconds from sixty-seven starts had one sequence of nineteen consecutive wins and thus equalled Desert Gold's Australian record. Many punters believe that Gloaming was New Zealand-bred, but he was born at the Melton Stud in Victoria. His owner, E.E. Clarke named him Celestial as he was by Welkin from Light, but when the horse came to Sydney to race this name was rejected and he was known thereafter as Gloaming.

Gloaming raced initially in Sydney, setting a record time in the Chelmsford Stakes and winning the A.J.C. Derby. Then he went to New Zealand where he had a great first season, losing only to Sasanoff in the New Zealand Cup and to Desert Gold in the G. Stead Memorial Stakes. His wins included the New Zealand Derby. He returned to Sydney to race in 1919, winning the first of three Craven Plates and beating a fine horse, Wolaroi, for the Rosehill Spring Stakes. By the time he arrived back in Australia in 1922 he was a legendary racehorse. But in his first start he was defeated by Beauford in the Chelmsford Stakes and this began a stirring duel with Beauford which ended in two wins each for the season.

Gloaming retired from racing in May 1925, going out after a memorable match race against The Hawk for the Ormond Gold Cup at Hastings. There were two other acceptors for the race but both scratched, leaving two champions with distinguished records in

top left : Eurythmic in action. This great horse won races over all distances, and on his retirement to stud in 1923 his winnings totalled £73,782, at that time an Australian record.

left : The crowd cranes from the stand to watch horses and jockeys on the lawn below at the A.J.C. autumn meeting at Randwick in 1920. This was the era of the 'personality' horse with newspapers taking a keen interest in racing events and racehorse form. A.J.C.

top : Eurythmic 'the finest horse Western Australia has known' and winner of thirty-one races. He raced exclusively in Western Australia as a two and three-year-old, and then moved to the east where he consolidated his reputation as a champion.

above : Poitrel, a courageous stallion bred in 1914, the winner of seventeen races including the Melbourne Cup (1920) carrying 10 st. Poitrel beat Desert Gold in the A.J.C. Spring Stakes of 1918, breaking the mare's winning streak which had extended to nineteen races in a row. Herald and Weekly Times

Australia to race for the Cup over their best distance, a mile, at level weights, 9 st 10 lb. The race attracted so much public interest the tote turnover for the day's racing more than doubled compared with the previous year.

After six furlongs The Hawk led by a length. The pace was on all the way. At the half-mile post, Gloaming was a head in front but The Hawk challenged bravely and they raced side by side over the last furlong until Gloaming edged ahead. The Hawk came again to a background of tremendous cheering but failed by just under a length to catch a great horse. Gloaming at the age of nine had won eight of his ten starts, and with 9 st 10 lb on his back he ran the mile to win the Ormond Gold Cup in 1 min 38.8 sec. No other horse has since equalled his record of wins on Australian race courses.

far left: This elegantly-attired pair featured in the *Sydney Mail* in 1911.

top left: Gloaming with an admirer, stage star Dorothy Brunton. On his retirement at nine years of age Gloaming boasted the magnificent record of fifty-seven wins and nine seconds from sixty-seven starts in New Zealand and Australia.

left: The 1920s and 30s were to see the climax of racing's popularity as a spectator sport in Australia—huge crowds, great jockeys and famous horses combined to give the sport an excitement hard to duplicate today. *A.J.C.*

top, above: Early morning training. Newspaper commentators today still keep a close watch on early morning gallops, to predict and judge form, just as their forerunners did at the turn of the century. Australian papers realized early the enormous news potential in racing and the huge numbers of Australians vitally interested in the sport ensured a return for extensive coverage. *McQuillan*

*top far left : The vice-regal procession up the straight
at Flemington in* 1911.

*top left : A rather dismal scene at the V.R.C. Derby
of* 1914, *with rain subduing fashions and spirits. The
war had begun, and the golden Edwardian era had
come to a close. Racing continued throughout the war
years, and race clubs contributed heavily to the war
effort. D.L. Bernstein notes that the V.R.C. alone
gave more than £*100,000.

*far left : Afternoon tea under the famous Flemington
elms in* 1913.

left : Fashion on the lawn at Randwick.

*above : More racing fashions—this time at the
Melbourne Cup of* 1913. *The big race, the last one to
be run in peace-time for several years, was won by
Posinatus, ridden by the jockey Shanahan. Shanahan
had also ridden the previous years's winner, Piastre.*

9. THE RACING TWENTIES

9. THE RACING TWENTIES

Early in 1924 well-known Victorian racehorse owners George Tye and Jack Corteen agreed to form a racing partnership with all the horses controlled by the partnership to be trained by C.T. Godby. The sole proviso in this merger of interests was that the brilliant colt Heroic should not be included in the partnership and should remain the sole property of Corteen.

Heroic was the most famous son of Valais, imported in 1919 by the Moses brothers to their stud Arrowfield, and in the view of many the finest sire ever imported into Australia. Valais dominated Australian bloodlines between the wars and his influence remains strong. His stock have won races from five furlongs to two miles and apart from Heroic he sired great horses in Manfred and Valicare.

In the spring of 1924, The Purser, a game old horse which was raced by the Tye-Corteen partnership ran a disappointing eleventh in the Coongy Handicap three days before the Caulfield Cup. The partnership had two starters in the Cup, Purser and The Monk, and trainer Godby announced that The Monk was the stable's first choice for the Cup and that Purser was an unlikely starter despite a fairly impressive record which included a Moonee Valley Gold Cup win.

This caused The Purser to drift in the betting on the Cup, which was over the same distance as the Coongy Handicap. At the course on Cup Day, however, The Purser was backed down from outsider's odds in a sensational, sustained betting spree. He won the race well and set a weight-carrying record with 9 st 5 lb. For the first time The Purser, a popular horse with race fans, received a hostile reception.

On the Tuesday after The Purser's win stewards opened a retrospective enquiry into the Caulfield Cup and decided that The Purser had not been allowed to do his best in the Coongy Handicap. They dis-

pages 202-203 : Phar Lap wins the 1930 Melbourne Cup in effortless style, defeating Second Wind by three lengths. The great horse's movements before the Cup had been shrouded in secrecy because of the shooting scare before the Melbourne Stakes. This race brought jockey Jim Pike his first Cup win. La Trobe

left : Phar Lap with his devoted attendant Tommy Woodcock, who cared for the great horse from the time he arrived at Telford's stables until his death in America in April 1932.

qualified George Tye and Jack Corteen, trainer Godby and jockey Hugh Cairns for one year. The disqualification meant that the nomination of Heroic, the nation's finest three-year-old and winner of £21,953, a record sum for his age at that time, could not be accepted for Australian races. Heroic had won the A.J.C. Derby brilliantly and was hot favourite for both the V.R.C. Derby and Melbourne Cup.

A transfer of ownership of Heroic to a New South Wales hotel proprietor was lodged with stewards who, alert to the danger of a dummy sale, refused to accept it. This temporarily ended Heroic's racing career and left rich pickings for his outstanding contemporaries Spearfelt and Windbag.

In 1926 Corteen sold Heroic to former cycling champion Charles B. Kellow for £16,800. Kellow had started his fortune by winning the 1902 Austral Wheel Race, sharing £25,000 with a backer. He spent his winnings launching himself into bicycle selling, and, when cars became popular, car selling. Prosperous in business, he turned to horse racing, buying top horses for Jack Holt to train for him. One of his first buys, Blue Cross, won two Standish Handicaps and a Newmarket Handicap.

Kellow's amazing rags-to-riches story continued when he coupled Heroic in the 1926 Newmarket with Pilliewinkle in the Australian Cup. They landed a double said to be worth £150,000 to Kellow. To commemorate this coup Kellow mated a mare named Herowinkie with Heroic, a union which produced Hall Mark, winner of all two and three-year-old classics in Sydney and Melbourne, including the two Derbies, the 1933 Melbourne Cup and the 1934 Doncaster. Heroic also sired Hua and Ajax and was our leading sire for seven seasons from 1932-1933 to 1938-1939. Flight, a legendary racehorse and brood mare, was Heroic's grand-daughter.

It is intriguing that despite his enforced spell from racing following the suspension of Tye and Corteen, Heroic still managed to finish ahead of both Windbag and Spearfelt in both stake money and races won. Heroic won twenty-one times and earned £38,062 in prize money, Windbag eighteen times and £35,939 Spearfelt eighteen times and £28,173. Both Windbag

above: Stewards at Caulfield racecourse, Victoria, keep a sharp watch on horses and riders from their special tower. V.R.C.

top right: Two great contemporaries—Manfred (first) and Heroic (second). Manfred was a brilliant performer, capable of astonishing speed, but he was unpredictable and inclined to be temperamental, and this lost him many races. Herald and Weekly Times

right: Hall Mark, an outstanding son of Heroic, winner of every two and three-year-old classic in Sydney and Melbourne. His Melbourne Cup win was an indication of his courage—he ran the two miles with a cracked heel. Herald and Weekly Times

far right: Heroic, a great racehorse and sire, was bred in 1921. He won twenty-one races and earned £38,062, retiring to stud in 1927. He was leading Australian sire for seven years, getting many outstanding winners including Hall Mark and Ajax. Herald and Weekly Times

and Spearfelt won the Melbourne Cup. All three horses did well at stud, though neither of the other two came close to matching Heroic's record.

Spearfelt's Melbourne Cup win in 1926 saw the climax of this race's popularity, with 118,877 people counted through the Flemington turnstiles. This remained for forty-three years the biggest crowd ever to attend an Australian sporting arena. The 1969 Victorian Football League grand-final between Richmond and Carlton drew 119,165 spectators, the first time the crowd for Spearfelt's Cup was exceeded.

The roaring twenties saw some impressive feats by Australian jockeys, now established as among the world's best race tacticians. One of the most praise-worthy was the handling of Manfred by Billy Duncan. Manfred won £28,830 in stakes but was a horse of such brilliance he would have far exceeded this sum had he not been prone to race tantrums. In the 1925 A.J.C. Derby he refused to start until the rest of the field had run 100 yards. Even when he started he had to be nursed from a trot to a canter and then to a gallop by Duncan.

Although the opposition included such fine horses as Amounis and Vaals, Manfred overtook them, and with the Randwick crowd roaring him on, gradually edged past Amounis into the lead. Duncan somehow coaxed a superb finishing burst from the horse and Manfred won, moving away from good horses in Petunia and Tibbie. Considering the start he had conceded the rest of the field Manfred's time of 2 min 35 sec was astonishing. A few weeks later in the V.R.C. Derby he behaved himself at the start and won over the same distance, a mile and a half, in 2 min 31.5 sec. In the Melbourne Cup Windbag had to run a race record time to beat Manfred, who the following year won the Caulfield Cup with 9 st 6 lb. Retired to the stud in South Australia Manfred sired many fine horses, including the Caulfield-Melbourne Cups winner The Trump.

right : Jockeys and horses at Randwick in the 1920s. The period between the wars marked a peak in the popularity of racing as a spectator sport, in Australia, and it was during this time that many of the greatest Australian jockeys were riding. A.J.C.

Just as Manfred formed a great partnership with Duncan so did Limerick with Maurice McCarten. Limerick, bred in New Zealand, at one stage won thirteen races in succession, and McCarten always said that he was the finest horse he rode. They won many big races together including three Chelmsford Stakes and a King's Cup with 9 st 5 lb from a strong field. Limerick was a gelding by Limond from Medley, a mare which also produced Ballymena, an A.J.C. Derby winner and like Limerick an outstanding performer in New Zealand.

One of Maurice McCarten's contemporaries was Arthur Edward 'Scobie' Breasley, who was born in Wagga in 1914 and began riding in picnic races at twelve years of age. Breasley rode his first big winner Cragford in the Metropolitan at Randwick at sixteen. He completed a great double for a teenager that day by also winning the last race. Then he was told that after an enquiry into the running of the Metropolitan stewards had disqualified him for two months for crossing too sharply in front of another horse on Cragford. Breasley returned to the saddle to build one of the best records ever achieved by an Australian jockey. Before he settled in England in 1950 he won five Caulfield Cups and two Sydney Cups.

The 1920s and 1930s were a vintage period for Australian horsemanship, with jockeys of the calibre of Jim Pike, Jim and Darby Munro, Billy Duncan, Fred Shean, Billy Cook, Jack Toohey, Breasley and McCarten consolidating the reputation for judgment of pace and all-round skill built by Tommy Hales, Bobbie Lewis, Bill McLachlan and other early riders. Indeed the competition for big race mounts among highly proficient local riders sometimes persuaded gifted jockeys to go overseas to take advantage of better opportunities. Among these were Rae 'Togo' Johnstone and Edgar Britt.

Jim Pike was rated the greatest of them all by some experts, a rider of superb balance who rode the mighty Phar Lap in most of his races. But Pike made fourteen attempts before riding his first Melbourne Cup winner—Phar Lap.

Phar Lap captivated even those who never went to the races, a thrilling big red horse with blistering speed

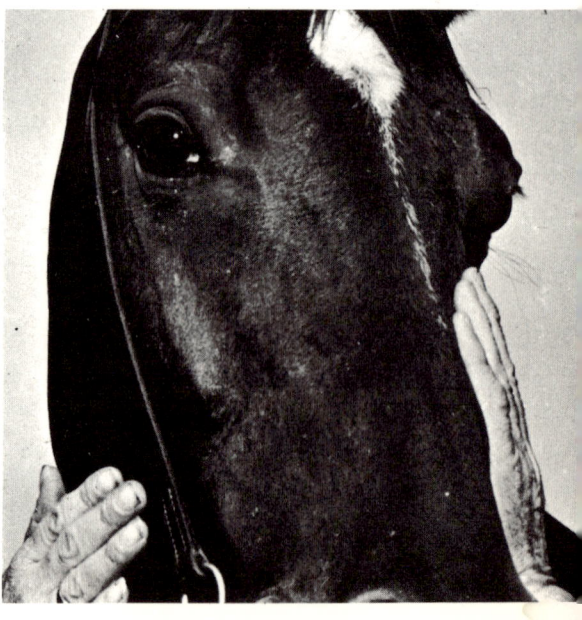

top left: Scobie Breasley, a jockey with an impressive record of wins in Australia, continued his success in England. Breasley had his first ride at a picnic race when he was twelve. *Age*

left: Maurice McCarten, with Todman. McCarten was perhaps best-known for his partnership with Limerick, the brown, New Zealand-bred gelding which at his peak beat all the best horses in Australia, including Heroic, Windbag and Valicare. *McQuillan*

above: Windbag, winner of the 1925 Melbourne Cup. This great stayer was bred in 1921 at the Kia-ora Stud in New South Wales. He beat many great horses including Spearfelt, Limerick and Manfred, and in his Melbourne Cup he set a record which was to remain unbroken for ten years. *Herald and Weekly Times*

and a great heart which had overcome humble origins. Phar Lap had brought only £168 when sold as a yearling at Trentham in New Zealand and the man who bought him, battling Sydney trainer Harry Telford, was so badly-off that he had to find a backer, David Davis, owner of a Sydney photographic studio, to put up the money. Telford had picked out the horse while reading the catalogue for the Trentham sales. Phar Lap was by Night Raid out of Entreaty and Telford noticed that Musket, sire of the mighty Carbine, appeared on both sides of the pedigree. But when Phar Lap arrived by sea from New Zealand Davis declared that he wouldn't spend money training such an ugly horse.

They named him Phar Lap after Telford had met a visitor from the Far East in Sydney and discovered that Pharlap was a Siamese word meaning 'to emit light from the sky.' Telford could not afford to buy Phar Lap from Davis, but agreed to lease him for three years to save Davis paying training fees. Davis was to collect a third of all prize money won by the horse. Telford had to pay entry fees for races and for Phar Lap's upkeep.

At first Phar Lap refused to work on the track, though he wolfed all his food. He was cared for by a stable lad, Aaron Treve 'Tommy' Woodcock, son of a Cobb & Co coach driver. Other trainers scoffed at Phar Lap's 'laziness' on the track, and only Telford and Woodcock defended him. They were seldom able to force Phar Lap to gallop beyond half pace, for his legs seemed too big and awkward for him to manage. To strengthen them Telford rode him for hours around the sandhills, dourly sticking to his faith in the horse's pedigree.

Phar Lap had his first start in a race in February 1929 and in his first four races did nothing to vindicate the faith shown in him by Telford and Woodcock. He won his fifth race, a six-furlong maiden at Rosehill and after a spell Telford decided to try him as a stayer. Phar Lap ran a close fourth to Limerick, Mollison and Winalot in the Warwick Farm Stakes over a mile, finishing so well that he was installed as fourth favourite for the A.J.C. Derby.

Telford had been telling his friend Jimmy Pike

top : A view of Wanganui racecourse in New Zealand. The 1920s and 30s saw the success in Australia of several New Zealand horses with good records in their own country. Limerick, often ridden by Maurice McCarten, was an example. Windsor Photography

left : Young apprentice jockeys of the 1950s receive a 'pep talk' at the A.J.C's school.

above : Australian jockeys are still among the finest in the world. This cartoon celebrates the International Stakes of 1961, attended by leading overseas jockeys, but won by Australian Roy Higgins. V.A.T.C.

about the big red colt, stressing that Pike should not book a ride in the Derby until they saw how Phar Lap shaped.   Pike was thirty-five, and behind him were great achievements on such horses as Strephon, Gothic, Whittier, The Hawk, Amounis, Fujisan and Heroic.   He disliked the idea of wasting for a Derby ride and in his first ride on Phar Lap in a Randwick trial he found the horse green and clumsy.

A fortnight after the Warwick Stakes Phar Lap finished second to Mollison in the nine-furlong Chelmsford Stakes.   Then he won the Rosehill Guineas in effortless style with Jim Munro in the saddle.   Never again did he start in a race other than as favourite or second favourite.   Pike took the ride in the Derby and a legendary combination began, Phar Lap winning by three and a half lengths in race record time of 2 min 31.2 sec.   In two years Pike rode Phar Lap thirty times for twenty-seven wins and two seconds.   Wherever Phar Lap went in that period Tommy Woodcock was close by and he was the only person Telford would allow to open Phar Lap's stall.

Pike was a jockey who seldom used the whip, a tall man for one of his calling, gaunt and pale from continual use of the sweat box.   He had very powerful hands and wrists and he rode Phar Lap on a fairly short rein perched well up on his neck so that Phar Lap could exploit the power in his hind legs.   He could not ride Phar Lap in the 1929 Melbourne Cup as he could get nowhere near the 7 st 6 lb Phar Lap carried.   Phar Lap started favourite in this race and led into the straight after behaving badly from the start for his new jockey Bobby Lewis.   In the run to the post Nightmarch won by three lengths from Paquito, with Phar Lap a length back third.

Telford turned Phar Lap out for a spell and three months in the paddock transformed Phar Lap from a big, gawky horse into an enormous, handsome animal. Motoring through the streets one day, on his way to ride him in the Melbourne Stakes, Jim Pike saw posters saying gangsters had tried to shoot Phar Lap. He dismissed it as imaginative reporting, but when he reached the course Tommy Woodcock confirmed the report.   He had been exercising the great horse when a car approached at speed.   A shotgun blazed away

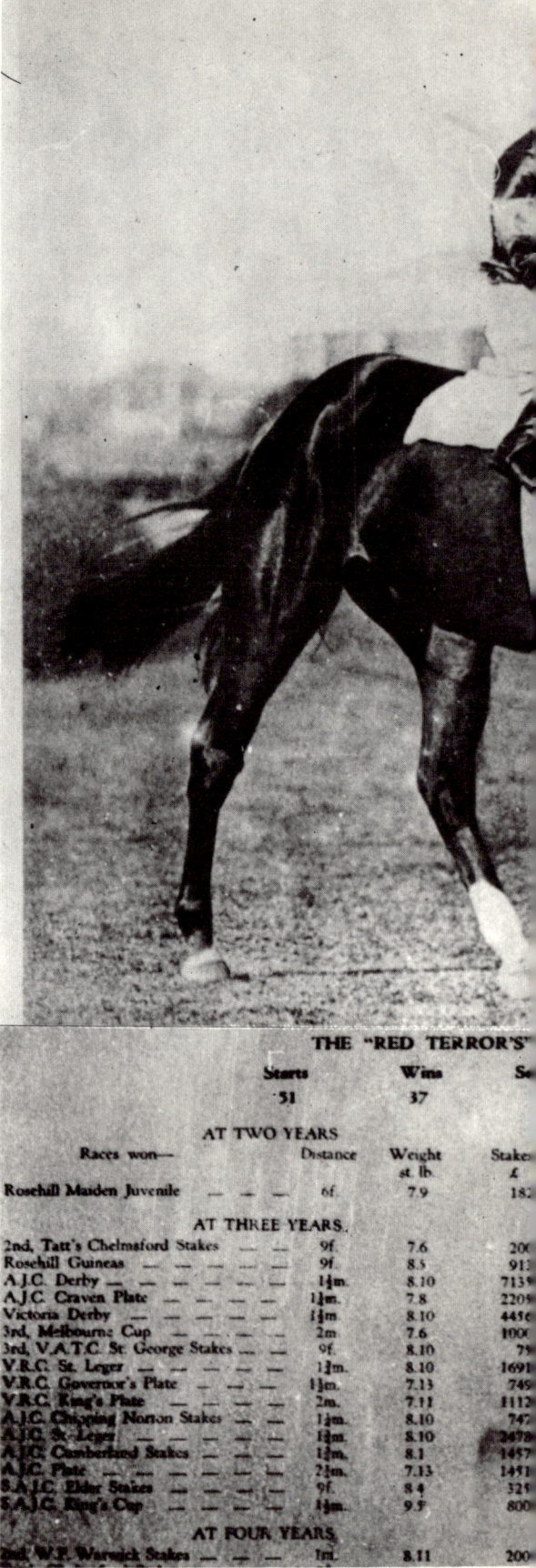

left : A newspaper photograph of Phar Lap headed 'Australasia's Wonder Horse', and listing 'The Red Terror's' great record. The 'lazy', 'ugly' bargain was now hailed as the greatest champion to run in Australia since Carbine.

above : Intense concentration is shown on the faces of these jockeys as their horses burst from the starting stalls. Australia has produced a long line of outstanding jockeys, some of whom have moved overseas to continue their success. McQuillan

from the car window, the bullets spattering into the fence behind Phar Lap. Phar Lap won the Melbourne Stakes that day in a canter and immediately Telford whisked the horse away with Tommy Woodcock, telling Pike to take care in case the gangsters tried for the jockey instead of the horse.

With three days to go before the Cup, Telford took Phar Lap, now quoted at 6 to 1 on for the big race, to St Albans Farm near Geelong, forty-odd miles from Melbourne. By then Phar Lap had won twenty-three races, usually starting at such short odds that Telford found him unbackable and raced him only for stakes won. The size and speed of the horse and repeated newspaper stories of impending attempts to nobble him gave him the biggest following an Australian horse has ever had.

On Cup Day 1930, the float carrying Phar Lap to Flemington seized as it left St Albans Farm, police motorcyclists in front and behind. There in teeming rain Telford and Woodcock and the escorting police took turns swinging the crank handle, with less than two hours to go before the Cup start. After half an hour the engine coughed to life and the float bucketed to Flemington, with Telford and Woodcock holding loaded pistols beside Phar Lap inside the float. They arrived with half an hour to spare and Phar Lap won the race by three lengths to give Jim Pike his first Cup win.

In the next fourteen days Phar Lap started four times for four wins, including £12,429 in prize money in one week. 'There could never be another horse like Phar Lap,' said Jim Pike. 'It's sacrilege really to ride some horses after once having been on the back of Phar Lap.' In February 1931, Telford's three year lease of Phar Lap expired and Davis accepted £4,000 from Telford for a half share in the horse. From then until his death fourteen months later Phar Lap won a further £20,000 in stakes.

After Phar Lap won the Melbourne Stakes for the second successive year as a five-year-old in 1931 he was made favourite for the Melbourne Cup for the third year in a row, an honour no other horse has earned. Pike warned Telford and Davis not to start him in the Melbourne Cup straight after the Mel-

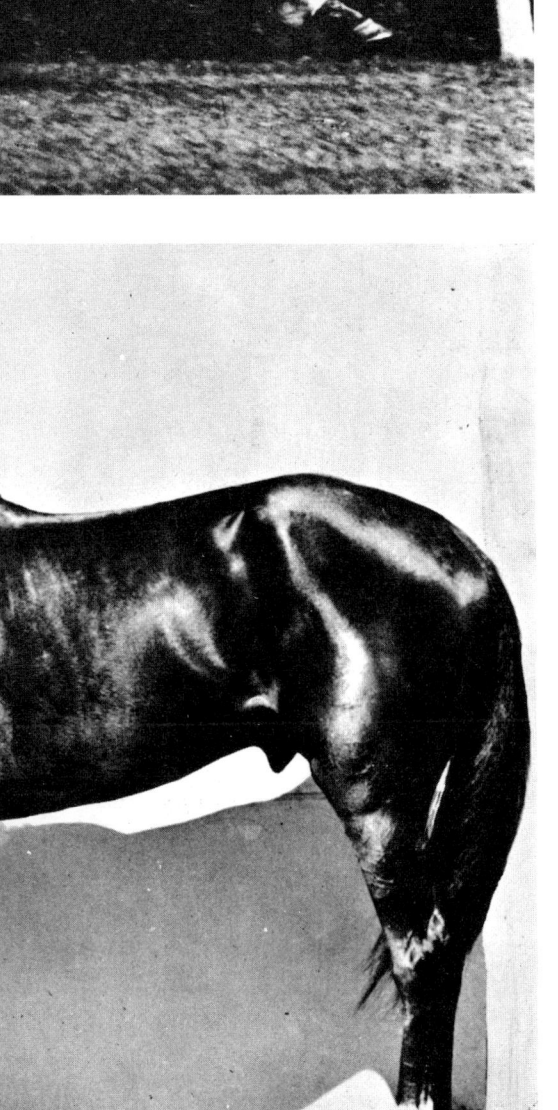

top left : *Phar Lap in action, showing the powerful muscles and giant stride which gave the big red horse his speed and staying power. Herald and Weekly Times*

left : *Phar Lap, the champion chestnut gelding who swept all before him in a tremendous racing career which included wins in almost all the weight-for-age races in Sydney and Melbourne. McQuillan*

above : *Jim Pike, the jockey who piloted the great Phar Lap to victory in most of his races. Pike was already a very successful jockey before he began riding Phar Lap, and was known for his magnificent balance and good hands. McQuillan*

bourne Stakes. Phar Lap had faltered in the last few strides of the Stakes and had only won by a few feet. Pike knew he was not sound to run in the Cup, but Telford argued that he could not scratch a horse that had won eight races in a row and was such a hot favourite. 'Nobody would believe me if I said he was unfit, Jim', Telford said.

The chairman of the V.R.C. told Davis in an interview before the Cup that he owed it to the public to run Phar Lap. Thousands of little punters had backed him. Racing was struggling against economic depression, with attendances declining at all courses. The V.R.C. had even been forced to reduce the Cup prize money to £5,200, the smallest in twenty-four years. Phar Lap could help the prestige of racing by taking his place at the barrier.

But Phar Lap's weight, 11 st 10 lb, proved too big a burden even for such a huge horse. Pike did not ride him out when he realized that he had no chance. The race was won by White Nose.

Mindful of the reduced purses in Australia, Davis took Phar Lap to America to run him in a handicap with an advertized first prize of $100,000. Before Phar Lap arrived to take his place in the field for this race, the Agua Caliente Handicap just inside the Mexican border at Tijuana, the prize had been cut to $20,626. Telford did not accompany Phar Lap to America because of a disagreement with Davis, and Tommy Woodcock was left to train the horse.

Not long before the race Phar Lap went lame. He had a split in his hoof. An emergency operation by an American veterinarian repaired the damage but Woodcock could not allow Phar Lap to gallop until three days before the race. Davis plunged heavily on Phar Lap and overnight his price dropped from 7 to 2 to 6 to 4. On the day of his American debut, 20 March 1932, Phar Lap was hot favourite at 6 to 5. He was near last soon after the race started but jockey Billy Elliott, who had travelled from Australia especially to ride the horse, moved him from last to first in a fantastic two-furlong spurt.

Just before the furlong post Phar Lap seemed to prop but Elliott let him go again and they swept to a two-length victory in the race record time of 2 min

top : The three-year-old Phar Lap wins the V.R.C. Derby in record time, from Carradale and Talsho. He had previously carried off the A.J.C. Derby, again in the fastest time then recorded for that race, 2 min 31¼ sec His Victorian Derby win chopped ¼ sec off the time set by Manfred, the previous record-holder.

above : Weanlings at the Sanders ajistment farm, New Zealand. Could one of these become another Phar Lap? Windsor Photography

right : Phar Lap wins the Agua Caliente Handicap, his first and only race after leaving Australia for America. He broke the race record, running the twelve furlongs in 2 min 2.8 sec He collected $20,626 for his win—a good sum, but nothing like the advertized prize of $100,000 which had tempted Davis to try his luck outside Australia. McQuillan

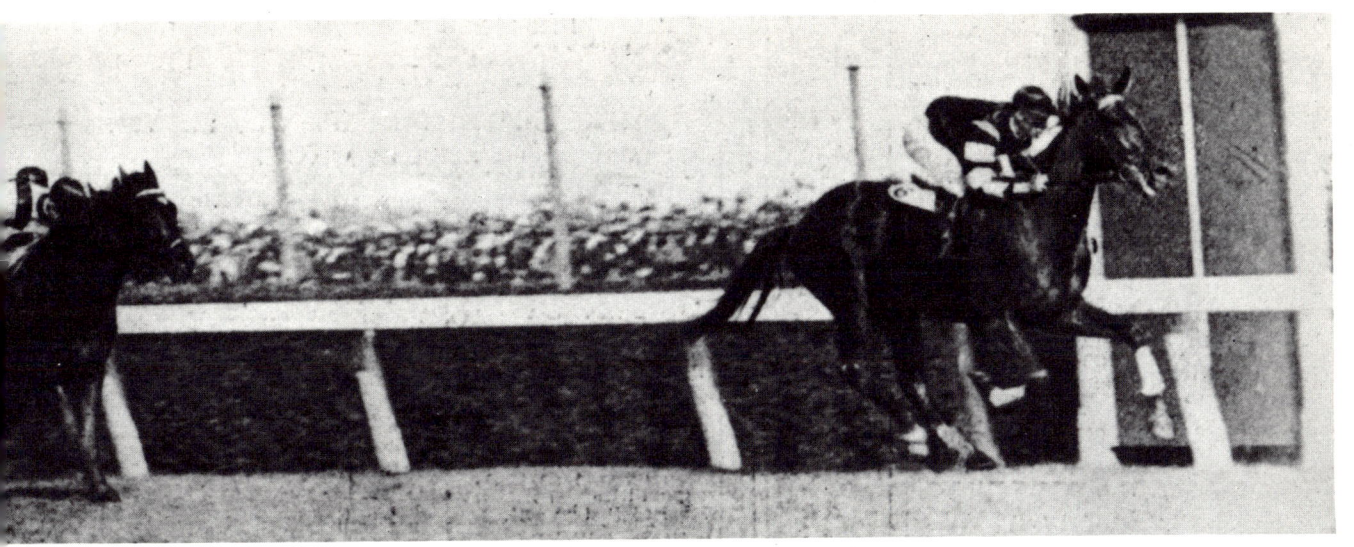

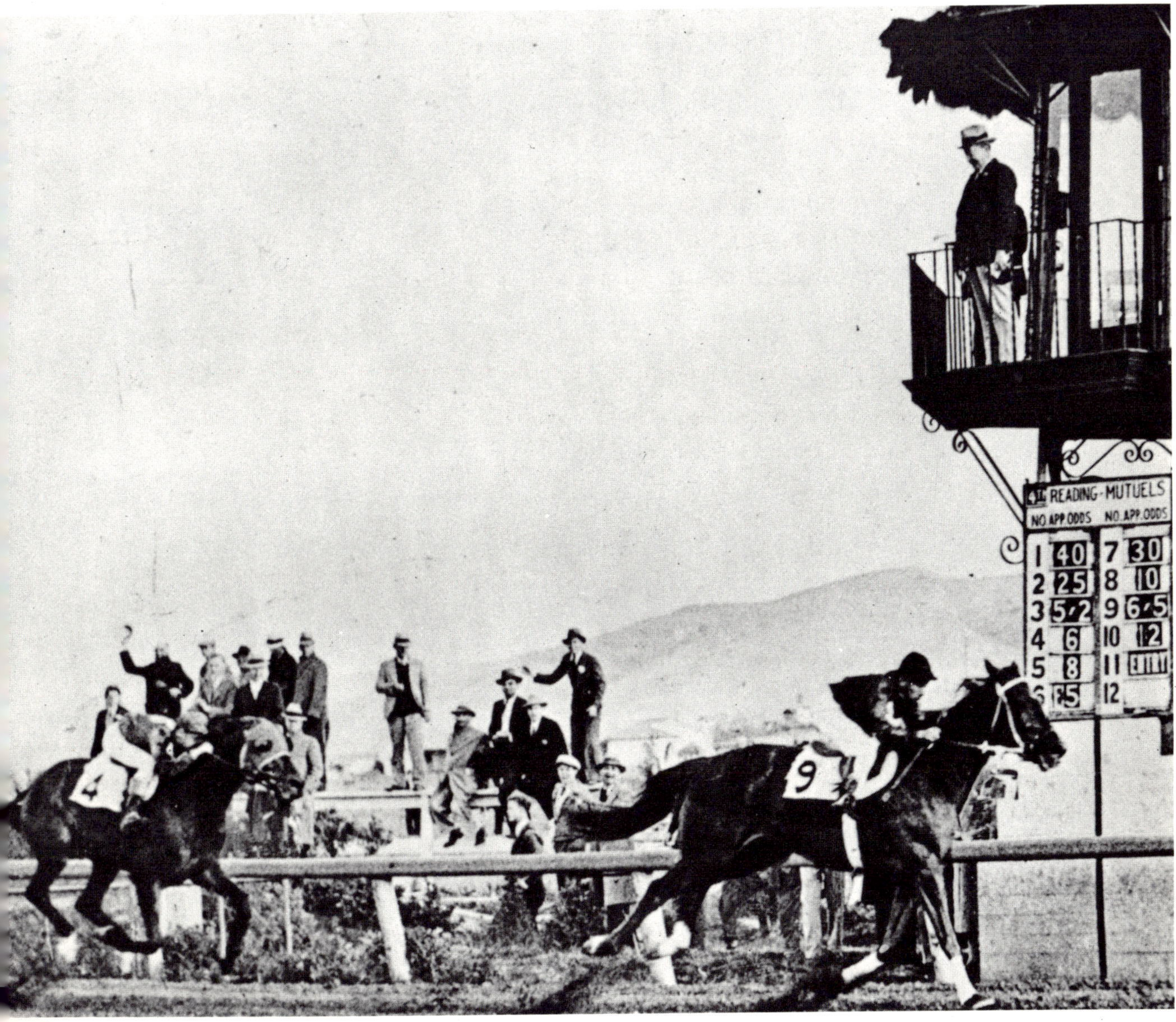
READING - MUTUELS
NO. APP. ODDS
NO. APP. ODDS
1 40
2 25
3 5-2
4 6
5 8
7 30
8 10
9 6-5
10 12
11
12
4
9

2.8 sec (for twelve furlongs).   At the presentation
ceremony, however, Phar Lap backed away from film
stars trying to place a garland of flowers around his
head, slipped sideways down some steps and injured a
tendon in his near foreleg.   America went wild with
excitement at the speed of this wonder horse from
Australia, but Woodcock and Davis knew he couldn't
run again until his legs were sound.

They sent Phar Lap to stables about twenty-five
miles from San Francisco owned by wealthy breeder
and owner Edward Perry.   There on 5 April 1932,
Phar Lap collapsed in his stall and died, and to this
day his death is unexplained.

At first it was thought that colic had killed the great
horse, but although many theories have been suggested
to explain Phar Lap's death, the mystery has never
been solved.   Rumours swept Australia that he had
been poisoned by American race gangs and his death
was coupled with that of Les Darcy at Memphis,
Tennessee, earlier in the century.   Some Americans
believed it was the feed that Davis and Woodcock
had brought from Australia especially for Phar Lap,
claiming that it had gone green and mouldy in the
heat.   Others said that the horse had eaten grass which
had been sprayed with a weed poisoner—the lining of
his stomach was badly perforated as if by an irritant
poison.   Caesar Masoero, who conducted a post-
mortem on Phar Lap, said, 'I believe the horse died
from some poison in the stomach.   Ordinary colic
could not have killed him in so short a time.'

In Australia there was disbelief when news of Phar
Lap's death arrived.   In America one radio station
called for a minute's silence from its listeners.   Phar
Lap's heart was brought back to Australia and installed
in the Institute of Anatomy in Canberra.   His heart
weighs 14 lb compared with the 6 lb heart of an Army
remount.   The hide was stripped from the great red
horse by one of America's most skilled taxidermists
and since 1938, when an overflow crowd attended, a
taxidermist's sculpture of Phar Lap has stood in

*right : Phar Lap, ridden by jockey Jim Pike with
whom the great horse formed a brilliant partnership.
Together they won twenty-seven races in two years.*

Melbourne Museum. Phar Lap's skeleton is in the Dominion Museum in Wellington, New Zealand. It was sent there and prepared for exhibition with funds donated by horse-lovers.

The mystery of Phar Lap's death can never be satisfactorily solved—too many of the principals in the tragedy are dead. But no other horse has ever been so deeply admired by so many Australians. Americans, too, grew to revere him, and all over America when he died amazing tributes appeared in print. The *New York Sun* published six stanzas of verse, the first of which read:

Where the thoroughbreds immortal
Graze in pasture ever green,
And steeds of song and story
Feel the touch of hands unseen,
There's a whinny in the distance
And a pawing at the gate,
As the big stout-hearted Phar Lap
Joins the Legions of the Great.

WHERE IS THE MAN WHO IS *not ready to mourn the* *movement enthralls; his bounding exuberance of unconquerable s* *who became a Natio*

WAS PHAR LAP
IN HIS PAD

Tragic End in U.S.A
Greatest Ra

WHY "RED TERROR"

DEAL! Phar Lap, Australasia's idol and

EVERY Australian—sportsman and non-sportsman—t *cast the fatal news. It cast gloom over this vast Con* *man—the birth place of this racing phenomenon.*

SPORTSMEN were flabbergasted by the news. Every m whether he was of the five shillings or £100 variety, into his throat.
TO *each and every one of them came the realisation* *by this wonder-horse.*

N more shall we see this equine giant with his seven - league strides thundering down the straights of Randwick and Flemington.
Never again will Australians be able to read

enabling a dividend to be decl
But what of the capital?
At one fell blow this has right off the slate. Compare what would have happened ha been allowed to remain in t his conquests.
A conservative estimate down Phar Lap's weight for earnings during the next years at £10,000 per annum.
Thus about £40,000 has tossed into the discard for sake of £5,000.

above : *Tooheys Ltd. says good-bye to Phar Lap.* *'The World's Greatest Horse'.*

right : *One of the newspaper reports which greeted the* *announcement of Phar Lap's death.*

222

ine Idol Dies in Exile

beloved *Phar Lap?* Who will not see nobility and gallant heart in every line of the magnificent animal's action? The very freedom and force of his ... y as he literally jumps past his opponents is sufficiently stirring to grip one's gaze for minutes on end. Yet .... pictures only .... mere images of a horse ... . pictures that paint his glorious memory with the vivid and tremendous action of his courageous life!

POISONED
OCK?

f Australia's
horse

N IN SILENCE

der horse! Dead!

ggered when the cableman broad- and the Dominion across the Tas-

o had wagered on this champion, e pangs of remorse steal chokingly

ever more would they be thrilled

This illustrates most forcibly that Phar Lap, in Australia, was regarded as a national property. Racing enthusiasts had the welfare of their idol at heart.

To-day he is an inanimate thing, an object of pity in the racing world.

THE CHAMPION AND HIS FAITHFUL ATTENDANT, Tommy Woodcock, taken just before their departure for America.

Phar Lap has been unlucky right throughout the piece. His end could not have been more tragical.

From the time he was knocked down to Telford at the New Zealand Yearling Sales of 1927, he has had a strenuous time. He was hawked about so that he could be raced on lease by Telford.

The wonderful chestnut raised Telford from a racecourse battler to a rich man. By the time his lease of the gelding had expired he was worth very many thousands of pounds. This transition is one of the most remarkable in the annals of the turf.

When Telford was racing Phar Lap on lease, he was very strenuously raced. It is testimony to the gelding's wonderful constitution that he answered the every call.

NEVER THE SAME
AFTER FUTURITY!

Jim Pike Tells How Gruelling Races Took Their Toll

CHAMPION SUFFERED INJURY

"I HAVE always held the opinion that Phar Lap was never the same after his Futurity Stakes run with 10.3 up," declares Jim Pike, who rode the champion in most of his races.

"NOBODY but Phar Lap and myself know what a hard race it was to win," he added. "I think he suffered an internal injury that afternoon."

GREAT horseman Jim Pike dropped this bombshell when chatting to "Truth" at his palatial home in Robertson-road, Centennial Park.

With a real sob in his voice Pike spoke of Phar Lap as he would of a lost relative, and said, "And to think I shall never throw a leg across him again."

"No horse I ever rode came within stones of Phar Lap. He was an absolute wonder.

"And what an intelligent fellow! On many occasions when I was riding him work at Randwick, he would prick his ears and slow down near the opening where Woodcock stood watch in hand with sugar and an apple in his pocket.

"The old horse knew that the little tit-bits were awaiting him, and I would

wide, and, though there were four or five horses inside us, I had to take the risk and leave it to Phar Lap.

"How he flew! Straining those mighty muscles of his to breaking point, the chestnut gradually mowed horse after horse down, until there was only Mystic Peak in front of us.

"Then, with one elastic bound, he headed Mystic Peak and won the ra...

"If there had been anything roman... about me, perhaps I would have ki... him. I certainly felt like it.

"But that race took toll of the cha... pion. He was never really the s... horse, but Phar Lap sick or well c... beat 'em all because he was Phar L...

"He had a heart like a lion and p... to the Futurity his constitution ... have been like an ox.

"The old horse was particularly fit... the day he won the Craven Plate in ... cord time, but what a changed an... he was the following Saturday when ...

Won 37 Races

A FIVE-YEAR-OLD chestnut ...

223

10. UPSETS

10. UPSETS

At Randwick in the spring of 1928 a colt called Prince Humphrey unwound a defiant finishing sprint to beat the favourite, Mollison, for the A.J.C. Derby. Prince Humphrey was splendidly ridden by one of Australia's greatest horsemen, Jimmy Munro, older brother of 'Darby'. The racebook described Prince Humphrey as a bay by Duke Humphrey (imp.) from Shepherd Princess, owned by the new Zealand sportsman, C.G. McIndoe, one of the prominent owners of the day, and trained by J.T. Jamieson.

Some weeks later Dick Tate, then living in Toowoomba, Queensland, chanced upon a magazine which carried a picture of Prince Humphrey. Tate had handled all horses bred at Woodlands Stud at Denman, New South Wales until its dispersal a few weeks before the Derby. One glance at the photograph told him that the colt in the magazine was not Prince Humphrey, for he knew that Prince Humphrey had white markings on his face and on each foot. There was no white at all on the horse in the photograph.

For some months Tate dismissed his discovery as a mistake by the magazine, but eventually his story reached a Sydney newspaper, which began an investigation. Eight months after the Derby the paper published the claim that Prince Humphrey had won a race for which he had never been entered! The paper declared that Prince Humphrey had been wrongly entered and that his correct pedigree was that under which another horse, Cragsman, had been registered. The story was hotly denied by the A.J.C. secretary and by McIndoe and H.R. McKenzie, of the Auckland Stud Company, which had sold McIndoe the colt.

Tate held to his view that the Derby winner was from Princess Hazel and not from Shepherd Princess and that somehow in the dispersal sale and shipment of the two colts to New Zealand they had become confused. The strong point against Tate's claim was that all horses bred in Australia carry identification numbers at all times and the colts could easily have been identified from these. Many race fans were also

pages 224-225 : The first jump at the Tasmanian Racing Club Brush Steeplechase, held at Elwick on 13 February 1926. Lockington, the eventual winner of the event, leads the field carrying 12 st. He is being ridden by F. Tupper. T.R.C.

left : Champion jockey Billy Cook on Pride of Egypt, winner of the 1955 A.J.C. and V.R.C. St Legers. Cook moved to England to ride successfully, but returned to Australia to become a well-known trainer. McQuillan doubtful that a man like Tate, who handled hundreds of horses as manager at Woodlands, could describe two of them so precisely two years after he had last seen them.

Tate stuck to his story despite official cries of poppycock, and at the peak of the controversy Frank Kitchener, who had worked with Tate at Woodlands, produced photographs of the two colts which proved Tate to be correct. Kitchener, an ardent amateur cameraman, had taken hundreds of pictures while he was at Woodlands. His photographs resulted in an official enquiry and two months later the keeper of the *Stud Book,* the late Loddon Yuille, admitted that a mistake had been made and that Prince Humphrey was in fact the Duke Humphrey-Princess Hazel colt and not the Duke Humphrey-Shepherd Princess colt.

No penalty was inflicted on McIndoe or his trainer and McIndoe was allowed to keep the Derby stake money. Apparently the A.J.C. considered it was just as much to blame as McIndoe for a mistake which would have been revealed if the numbers on the Derby winner's hind leg had been inspected. Only the Woodlands brand of an inverted V over B on the shoulder had been examined. And if the registration had been compared with the certificates of pedigree the error would have been found in the A.J.C. office.

A tightening of registration methods resulted from the Prince Humphrey case, and under the efficient system used these days a similar mistake could not occur. Prince Humphrey continued to race, but never again showed the form he had produced in the Derby. The hard race had finished him. But he remains Australian racing's most famous ring-in.

Prince Humphrey was not Jimmy Munro's only celebrated winner in 1928, for in that year he also won his second Melbourne Cup on Statesman. He was a brilliant rider who did very well in England. This has often been forgotten, however, and Jim has been overshadowed by his brother, David Hugh Munro, otherwise known as 'Demon Darby'. Jim was

right : Soggy going on a wet track. It was on such a track that Darby Munro rode Peter Pan to victory on Melbourne Cup Day, 1934, cleverly making use of the normally unfavourable outside barrier position to keep the horse on the firmer outside track. McQuillan

not as spectacular as Darby—few riders have been—but he had consummate skill in coaxing the best from a horse.

Darby Munro rode three Melbourne Cup winners and five A.J.C. and V.R.C. Derby winners. One of his most notable rides was on Peter Pan in the 1934 Melbourne Cup. Peter Pan carried 9 st 4 lb and on a sodden, muddy track drew the normally unfavourable outside barrier position. During the race Munro cleverly kept his horse on the outside well away from the rails, realizing that the going was firmer out there. A furlong and a half from the post he took Peter Pan into the lead and despite the top weight he strode home almost nonchalantly to win by three lengths from Sarcherie and La Trobe.

This was Peter Pan's second Cup win in three years—he did not start in the 1933 Cup because of an attack of rheumatism—and his fifth win in five starts at Flemington. It was also compensation for Munro, who had missed the winning ride on Hall Mark in 1933 because he could not make the Cup weight of 7 st 8 lb. The ride had been given to the young Sydney apprentice J. O'Sullivan who had ridden Hall Mark with exceptional skill to hold off late finishes by Shadow King, Topical and Gaine Carrington, which dead-heated for third.

Peter Pan was bred at the homestead in Singleton, New South Wales, where his owner R.R. Dangar was born. He was a long, loose-limbed colt by the English horse Pantheon from the unraced mare, Alwina. Dangar was so impressed with Peter Pan as a yearling that he decided not to sell him but to race him himself.

Peter Pan was a highly photogenic horse with light chestnut colouring and a flamboyant silvery mane and tail. He just could not keep out of the news. As a two-year-old he trod on a nail and almost died from the subsequent infection. Then his jockey, Andy Knox, was sacked when his riding of the colt displeased Dangar and trainer Frank McGrath. In the 1932 Melbourne Cup Peter Pan was bumped so severely that he almost fell, but luckily a second bump propped him back on his feet and, brilliantly ridden by Billy Duncan, he recovered to win by a neck. Ironically Andy Knox was on the second horse, Yarramba.

top left : Hall Mark wins the 1933 Melbourne Cup, holding off Gaine Carrington, Topical, and Shadow King which were to dead-heat for third. Herald and Weekly Times

centre left : Darby Munro wins the 1934 Melbourne Cup on Peter Pan, triumphing over a soggy track, an unfavourable barrier position and a big weight, 9 st. 4lb. Herald and Weekly Times

left : Peter Pan, a beautiful light chestnut with a silvery tail and mane. He was a great horse, often compared with Phar Lap both because of his racing ability, and because of the fact that he never seemed to be out of the news. Herald and Weekly Times

above : Darby Munro, one of the most spectacular jockeys Australia has known. He won three Melbourne Cups, on Peter Pan (1934), Sirius (1944) and Russia (1946), and rode five A.J.C. and V.R.C. Derby winners. His brother Jim was also a gifted jockey, although Darby's fame kept him in the shade. McQuillan

Racegoers of the time repeatedly compared Peter Pan to Phar Lap, and he certainly had the same flair for trouble. In the 1933 Rawson Stakes in Sydney he caught a barrier strand in his mouth and finished last. Just before the 1935 Melbourne Cup an official of the Royal Society for the Prevention of Cruelty to Animals called on Dangar asking if he could inspect Peter Pan. He had been told the horse was lame. Dangar was understandably furious at this, though in the Cup with 10 st 6 lb Peter Pan was only a shadow of the great racehorse he had been. Retired to stud Peter Pan broke a leg in his paddock and had to be shot, a tragic end, just as Phar Lap's had been.

Despite the presence of great horses like Hall Mark, Peter Pan, High Caste, Beaulivre and Beau Vite, the 1930s saw the start of racing's decline as a major spectator Australian sport. There were colourful personalities to watch in rival sports such as Don Bradman, Jack Crawford, Jimmy Carlton, Haydn Bunton, Dick Reynolds, Noel Ryan and Dave Brown, and the organization of these sports had improved. Commercial radio had won great support and many people preferred to stay at home, listen to race broadcasts and bet with the local illegal Starting Price (S.P.) bookies or with the bookies' runners who obligingly called at the door between races.

A new breed of race broadcasters emerged, men who could describe a race at a furious pace, repeatedly identifying and placing every horse. To most Australians these men were the greatest race broadcasters in the world, men with a flair for quips and colourful phrases. Nobody minded the garbled syntax or the appalling enunciation even though adherents to the polished diction of the B.B.C. were horrified.

The popularity of the illegal S.P. bookies in the 1930s was a national phenomenon. In every city on race days men with silver coins jangling in their pockets could be seen darting in and out of houses and up and down lanes, shoving scribbled bets into their pockets and reporting back to base just before races started. Police made sporadic attempts to catch the S.P. operators but the cockatoos or look-out men manning vantage points on verandahs or forks in the streets invariably tipped off their base before raids occurred.

AUSTRALIAN JOCKEY CLUB
1930
DATES FOR RACING FIXTURES

1930.			1930.	
January.			**July.**	
Tattersall's Club	(New Year's Day) Wednesday, 1st		Canterbury Park Racing Club	Saturday, 5th
Australian Jockey Club (Warwick Farm Races)	Saturday, 4th		Rosehill Racing Club	12th
Canterbury Park Racing Club	11th		Moorefield Racing Club	19th
Moorefield Racing Club	18th		Canterbury Park Racing Club	26th
Australian Jockey Club	24th			
Australian Jockey Club	Anniversary Day, Monday, 27th		**August.**	
			Australian Jockey Club (Warwick Farm Races)	Saturday, 2nd
February.			Moorefield Racing Club (Bank Holiday) Monday, 4th	
Rosehill Racing Club	Saturday, 1st		Canterbury Park Racing Club	Saturday, 9th
Canterbury Park Racing Club	8th		Rosehill Racing Club	16th
Australian Jockey Club (Warwick Farm Races)	15th		Rosehill Racing Club	23rd
Rosehill Racing Club	22nd		Australian Jockey Club (Warwick Farm Races)	30th
March.			**September.**	
Moorefield Racing Club	Saturday, 1st		Canterbury Park Racing Club	Saturday, 6th
Canterbury Park Racing Club	8th		Tattersall's Club	13th
Moorefield Racing Club	15th		Rosehill Racing Club	20th
Hawkesbury Racing Club	22nd		Hawkesbury Racing Club	27th
Rosehill Racing Club	29th			
			October.	
April.			Australian Jockey Club	Saturday, 4th
Rosehill Racing Club	Saturday, 5th		Australian Jockey Club (Eight Hours Day) Monday, 6th	
Australian Jockey Club (Warwick Farm Races)	12th		Australian Jockey Club	Wednesday, 8th
Australian Jockey Club	19th		Australian Jockey Club	Saturday, 11th
Australian Jockey Club (Easter Monday) 21st			City Tattersall's Club	18th
Australian Jockey Club	Wednesday, 23rd		Canterbury Park Racing Club	25th
Australian Jockey Club	Saturday, 26th		Rosehill Racing Club	Wednesday, 29th
May.			**November.**	
City Tattersall's Club	Saturday, 3rd		Rosehill Racing Club	Saturday, 1st
Rosehill Racing Club	10th		Moorefield Racing Club	8th
Tattersall's Club	17th		Australian Jockey Club	15th
Moorefield Racing Club	24th		Australian Jockey Club (Warwick Farm Races)	22nd
Australian Jockey Club (Warwick Farm Races)	31st		Moorefield Racing Club	29th
June.			**December.**	
Canterbury Park Racing Club	Saturday, 7th		Australian Jockey Club (Warwick Farm Races) Wednesday, 3rd	
Australian Jockey Club (King's Birthday) Monday, 9th			Australian Jockey Club (Warwick Farm Races) Saturday, 6th	
Australian Jockey Club	Saturday 14th		Rosehill Racing Club	13th
Rosehill Racing Club	21st		Australian Jockey Club	20th
Moorefield Racing Club	28th		Australian Jockey Club (Boxing Day) Friday, 26th	
			Tattersall's Club	Saturday 27th

SYNOPSIS OF MEETINGS.

Australian Jockey Club (at Randwick)	15	Moorefield Racing Club	9
Australian Jockey Club (at Warwick Farm)	9	Tattersall's Club	4
Rosehill Racing Club	13	City Tattersall's Club	2
Canterbury Park Racing Club	9	Hawkesbury Racing Club	2

IMPORTANT NOTICE.

1. Meetings of the Australian Jockey Club at Warwick Farm, and Rosehill, Moorefield and Canterbury Park Racing Clubs are exempted from the operation of Rule 61, so far as regards races of a distance of one mile and a quarter or over. The amounts payable for entering and starting in any race at such meetings (other than Sweepstakes) shall not exceed Ten Shillings (10/-) in all.

2. At every Registered Meeting held within a radius of 43 miles from the G.P.O., Sydney, there shall be on each day at least three races on the flat run at a distance of not less than one mile, unless the programme includes a Hurdle Race and a race for Two-year-olds, or consists of not more than five races, and includes either a Hurdle Race or Steeplechase, when there shall be at least two such races on the flat. Of such races one which shall be open to all horses and shall not be a Selling Race), shall be run at a distance of not less than one mile and a quarter.

3. At every Registered Meeting held during the months of May, June, July, August and September, within the Metropolitan Area (40 miles radius), Hawkesbury Racing Club excepted, the Programme shall include a Hurdle Race or Steeplechase.

4. These fixtures are subject to alteration by the Committee, and are issued on the understanding that the Clubs hold Race Meetings on the days allotted, weather permitting, and subject to any alteration that may be made by the Government for the keeping or celebration of particular holidays.

BY ORDER OF THE COMMITTEE

C. W. CROPPER, Sec. A.J.C.

6 Bligh Street, Sydney.

*top left : Racing in Tasmania in the 1930s. Tasmania
shared with the rest of the nation the gradual decline
in course attendance which began at this time.
Important events still attracted large crowds, but
these did not continue to grow as population expanded.
T.R.C.*

*left : Ken Howard, betting London to a brick.
Howard is one of the best-known Australian race
commentators today, and goes annually to England to
call the English Derby. 2GB*

*above : An A.J.C. notice stating the dates for racing
fixtures in 1930. The final paragraphs list the
conditions under which races may be run. This
programme indicates the high degree of control and
organization which had entered the racing scene
between the wars. A.J.C.*

You could bet in threepences with these men and sit back in your own living room with a beer in your hand listening to the lively accounts of how your fancy ran.

One of the horses which caught the imagination of these stay-at-home punters was Ajax, the champion miler. Ajax ran up a string of eighteen successive wins between November 1937 and March 1939, and national interest was stirred. Would he beat the record of nineteen straight wins set by Desert Gold and Gloaming? Hundreds of thousands of silver-coin bets with that man up the lane said he would.

But Ajax was one off equalling the record. In mid-March 1939, he started in the Rawson Stakes at Rosehill at the astounding odds of 40 to 1 on and was beaten by Spear Chief. The post-mortems continued for months but probably the best explanation came from Ajax's jockey Harold Badger, who simply said that weeks of hard racing had wearied the horse.

Badger's view was borne out when Ajax returned after a brief spell and won two good races after the Rawson Stakes. His defeat in that race probably spoilt a sequence of twenty-one wins in a row, a mark that would have been virtually unbeatable. Badger rode Ajax in thirty of his thirty-six wins and in the process had some tense struggles with horses ridden by former New Zealander Maurice McCarten. The duel culminated in the Rawson Stakes loss to McCarten on Spear Chief.

Only three horses started in that memorable Rawson Stakes, Ajax, Spear Chief and Allunga, which led to the turn into the straight and then tired. Ajax, which had had a gruelling struggle to shake off Allunga, was left in front with still a long way to go. Those who watched the race through binoculars saw Maurice McCarten grinning all over his face as he realized Ajax was tiring and his own mount had plenty left. Timing his run perfectly McCaten swept past Ajax in the last few strides to win by half a length in 1 min 52.5 sec, a time which made it very clear Ajax had not been nobbled.

Ajax was by Heroic from the English mare Medmenham and was bred at Widden Stud, New South Wales, by A.W. Thompson and E.L. Baillieu, who raced him in partnership. He was foaled the night Peter Pan

above: Harold Badger being weighed on the jockey scale. One of Badger's most famous mounts was the champion Ajax. Together, Badger and Ajax won thirty races. Age

top right: The trophy is presented at the King's Cup meeting at Elwick Racecourse, Tasmania on 3 February 1932. T.R.C.

right: The magnificent chestnut Ajax, son of Heroic. Ajax held the sporting public spellbound as he won time after time to gain eighteen successive wins. The record, held by Desert Gold and Gloaming, was nineteen straight wins, but a weary Ajax missed equalling their score when he lost the Rawson Stakes in mid-March 1939. Herald and Weekly Times

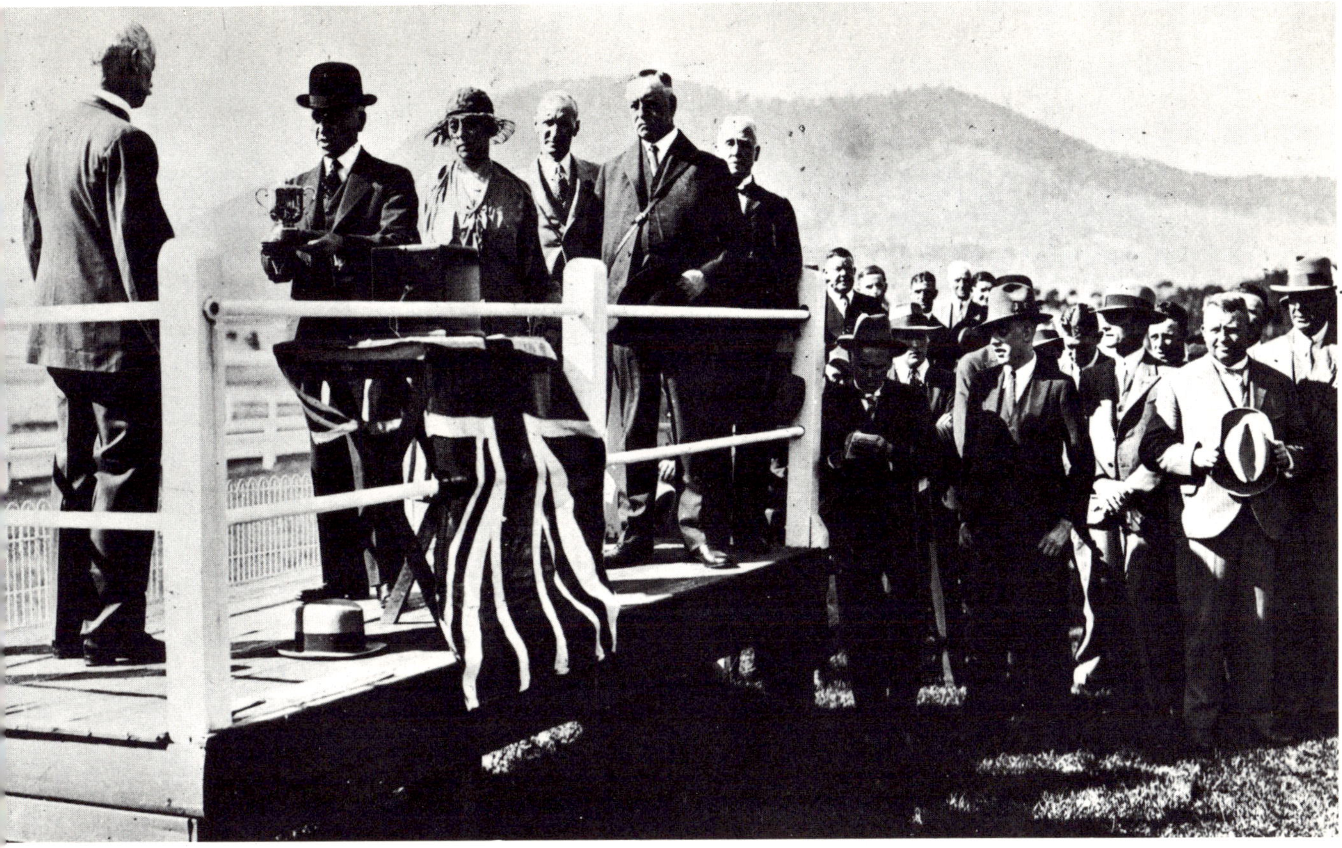

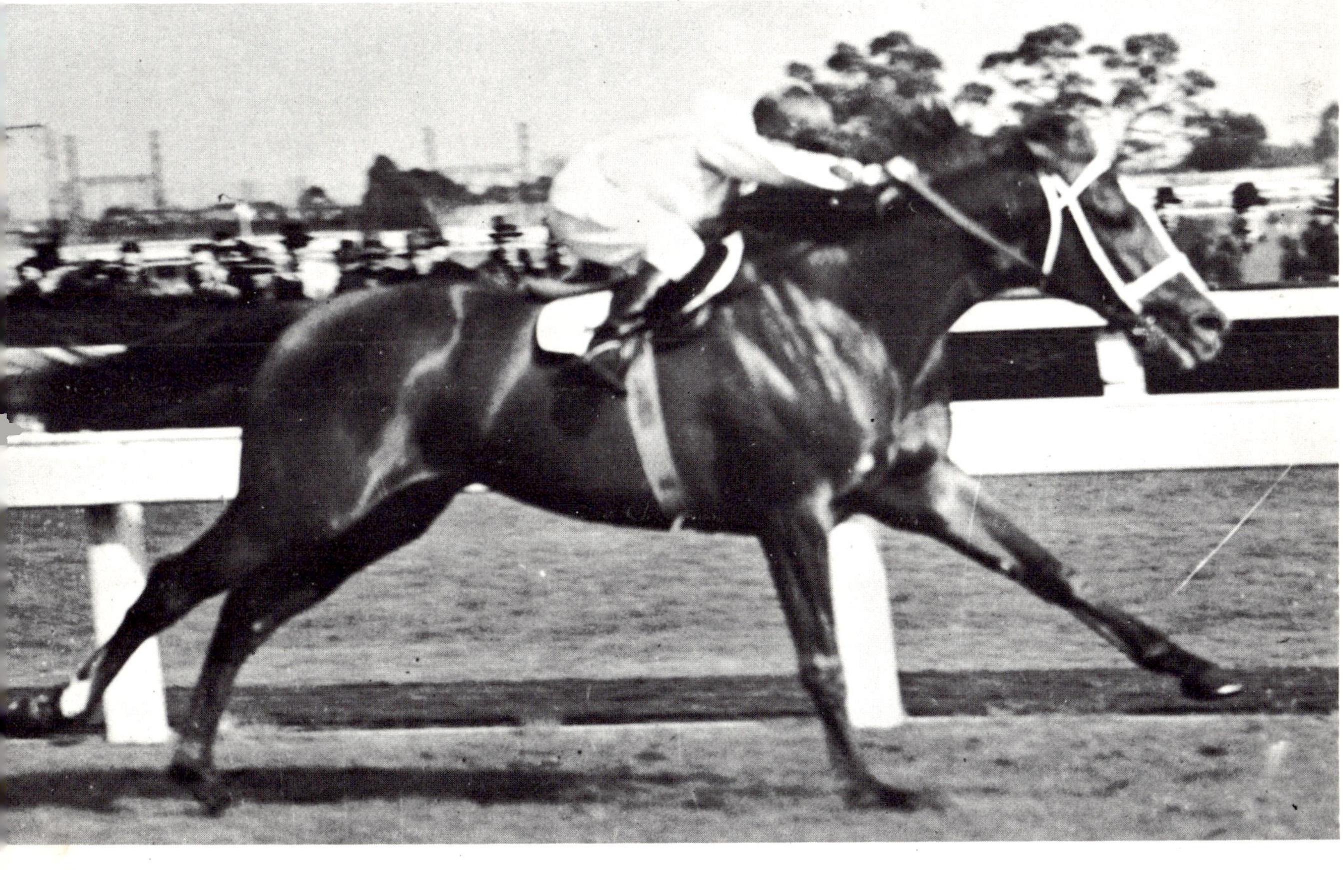

won the 1934 Melbourne Cup and developed into a magnificent chestnut standing more than sixteen hands. At stud he was a prolific sire of outstanding horses such as Civic Pride, Chaperone, Achilles and Magnificent. Americans thought so much of him that they paid $26,000 for him as a fourteen-year-old stallion. He is still the shortest-priced favourite to lose a race in Australia.

The 1930s also saw a great steeplechaser in action on the Australian turf—Redditch, which won the V.A.T.C. Australian Steeplechase twice and the V.R.C. Grand National Steeplechase. Redditch was a spectacular jumper, brimful of courage. Attempting to win the V.R.C. Grand National for the second time in 1935, he broke a leg and had to be destroyed. His death revived discussion about the cruel punishment horses suffered in jumping races. Steeplechases had been abolished in Sydney in 1931, but hurdle races continued for another eleven years.

Perhaps the best-loved horse of the thirties was Tranquil Star, which started in no less than 111 races. She was always a plucky trier and people knew they would get an honest run for their money from her. In all, Tranquil Star won twenty-three races, with twenty seconds and twelve thirds. Her best wins were in the Caulfield Cup, the V.R.C. St Leger, the L.K.S. McKinnon Stakes and the C.M. Lloyd Stakes. For a time Tranquil Star had won more stake money than any horse of her sex on the Australian turf, but then her great rival Flight passed her total of £21,690.

Over the years race club committees had been gradually tightening their rules. Geldings had been declared ineligible for classic races in 1932. In 1933 a conference of Australian race clubs ruled that only horses which qualified for the *Stud Book* could start in classic races. Once the effects of the Depression were shaken off it became a prosperous decade. In Brisbane the first Doomben Ten Thousand (then the Doomben Newmarket) was run.

Despite the diligence of stewards there were always people ready to make a shady dollar from racing. In December 1939, there was a sensation after the last race at Ascot, Melbourne, when it was discovered that the cables of all except one radio station had been cut.

top left : Redditch, the steeplechase champion of the 1930s taking a jump. This courageous horse won the V.A.T.C. Australian Steeplechase twice as well as carrying off the 1933 V.R.C. Grand National with 12 st. 5 lb. Herald and Weekly Times

left : Redditch sprints to the finish. His tragic death after a fall in the 1935 V.R.C. Grand National renewed heated public discussion on the dangers of steeplechasing and hurdling. Herald and Weekly Times

above : Jumping rider Graeme Walters, recently returned to New Zealand after riding in Europe. Jumping races in Australia are now confined to Tasmania, Victoria and South Australia. Windsor Photography

The only station that remained on the air had given a fake broadcast of the race several minutes *after* the race had been run. In the few minutes before that fake broadcast began, punters at key points all over Australia rushed to back the winner. It became clear later that they knew the result.

Two days after the fake broadcast the caller who made it was arrested and he later received a sentence. It was impossible to judge how many thousands had been won, but the coup was largely spoiled by a slight error in timing. One of the stations which went off the air when its cable was cut had been connected to the course announcer for a few seconds before the line went dead. Many bookmakers became suspicious when his voice went off the air.

The 1939-1940 season saw one of the great feats of Australian horsemanship when Billy Cook set an Australian record by riding 126 winners in the season. His tally included three dead-heats, and all of his winners were ridden on metropolitan courses. Cook's habit of booting home winners of the last race became legendary. Many times punters who had lost all their money got square by backing Billy Cook's mount in the last race before they went home. Cook later rode successfully in England, but he disliked the arduous travelling involved in race riding there, and returned home to become a successful trainer.

When Rivette won the 1939 Melbourne Cup for Harry Bamber, the blacksmith's son, she started hot favourite and bookies took a severe drubbing. The following year they had a killing when Old Rowley won the Cup and became the third horse to do so at odds of 100 to 1. The longest-priced winners in the history of the Cup were The Pearl in 1871, Wotan in 1936 and Old Rowley. Admittedly old Rowley did not have the form to recommend him but he was so well-bred that these odds were surprising.

On the Wednesday before Old Rowley's win an intruder sneaked along the lane that ran behind Cup favourite Beau Vite's stall. At what he thought was Beau Vite's stall he pushed a gun through a hole that had been previously cut in the rear wall and fired at the horse's legs. The badly-wounded victim was not Beau Vite, however, but El Golea, a horse of similar

above : Two great jockeys of different generations— Neville Sellwood (left) and Maurice McCarten. McCarten had taken off his silks to become a trainer by the time this photograph was taken. *McQuillan*

top right : Two champion combinations—*Jack* Thompson on Prince Morvi and Darby Munro on Carioca. Prince Morvi won both the A.J.C. and V.R.C. Derbies in 1953, many weight-for-age events, the Q.T.C. Sire's Produce Stakes and the S.T.C. Canterbury Guineas. *McQuillan*

right : Billy Cook on Carioca. Cook set an Australian record in the 1939-40 season, riding 126 winners. His mount in this photograph, Carioca, was bred in 1947, and after three relatively undistinguished seasons emerged as a champion. *McQuillan*

far right : Old Rowley, son of The Buzzard, was the third horse to win the Melbourne Cup at 100 to 1, giving bookmakers a field day. Old Rowley's jockey in that 1940 event was A. Knox. *Herald and Weekly Times*

colouring to Beau Vite. El Golea was at Alf Fryer's stables, Beau Vite at Fred Foulsham's stables next door. Only about twenty yards separated the horses.

Old Rowley was by The Buzzard, which later sired a second Cup winner, Rain Bird. The Buzzard, which stood at Lyndhurst Stud on the Darling Downs in Queensland, had an unmatched record as a sire of stayers. Bred by Lord Rosebery, he raced in England as The Bastard, but when he was sold to Australia racing authorities, apprehensive of the names that might be given his progeny, had him renamed. He sired winners of all the big Australian handicaps. His offspring included Buzalong, Basha Felika, L'Aiglon and Katanga, which was an extremely popular horse, winning many weight-for-age races.

The war years saw most Australian racecourses occupied by servicemen. Townsville was one course taken over by the Army, but the commanding officer rated racing as such an important entertainment for his men that the massive concentration of troops there moved out every Saturday morning so that the races could be held. In Darwin during the war years, a tradition that prisoners could be let out of Fanny Bay Gaol to attend the races began. The only condition was that they had to return after the last race.

At many points in the Pacific theatre between 1941 and 1946 Australian troops observed an unofficial cease-fire on the first Tuesday in each November to listen to Melbourne Cup broadcasts. Fighter pilots named their aircraft after Cup winners. Units without several sweeps going, even those in prison camps, were rare.

The war years also saw the emergence of the great stayer David, which had won the 1923 Sydney Cup and many other big races on the flat, as our most dominant sire of jumpers. David's sons and daughters won the Grand National Hurdle for three successive years, Saul in 1942, Claudette in 1943 and Zalmon in 1944. In 1945 David's progeny took the double, Bay David winning the Grand National Hurdle and Quixotic the Grand National Steeplechase.

By the time the war ended jumping events were confined to the southern states and had big followings only in South Australia and Victoria. Anpapejo had

*top left : Game horses and riders take a jump during a
V.R.C. Grand National Hurdlerace. La Trobe*

*left : Two horses take the water jump at the Ellerslie
course during the Great Northern Weekend in New
Zealand. Windsor Photography*

*above : The excitement of racing over the jumps is
caught in this photograph taken at the T.R.C. Grand
National Hurdle of 1967. Mercury*

won the last hurdle race in Sydney in 1942.

The rules of hurdling vary between states but the main rules are those adopted by V.R.C. These allow for hurdles 3 ft 3 in in height which are set up with a lean from the vertical. In steeplechases the obstacles are 3 ft 9 in high or more and have an 8 in lean from the vertical. Jumping races are over a minimum of two miles and the minimum weight is 9 st. Under these conditions perhaps the best performance has been by Lots of Time, which between March and June 1969, in Victoria, won nine successive races. Lots of Time thus beat by one win the previous record of eight straight wins by Air Fox in three years of hurdling in South Australia.

Towards the end of the war an important new race club, the Sydney Turf Club, held its first meeting in Sydney. This was the third club to use the name, but neither of the earlier organizations had any link with the modern S.T.C., which had its inaugural meeting at Randwick on 15 January 1944. The S.T.C. acquired both Rosehill and Canterbury racecourses and modernized them. Since then it has steadily grown in influence and today rivals the A.J.C. in the number of races it stages, with the prize money offered totalling more than $500,000 annually. The S.T.C's richest race, the Golden Slipper Stakes for two-year-olds, has become one of Australia's most important races. Conditions of entry involve both breeder and owner of the horses concerned and in some years the Golden Slipper could be Australia's richest horse race.

YES, MY HUSBAND'S A VERY KEEN SPORTSMAN — HE ALWAYS LEADS WITH THE BOO-ING!

far left : A cartoon which appeared in 1940.

top left : Sky High wins the S.T.C. Golden Slipper Stakes. The Golden Slipper is run over six furlongs, and is open to the two-year-old progeny of nominated mares. The race has become one of the most important Australian events, and may in the future take the place of the Melbourne Cup as the richest.

left : A dramatic moment as four horses prepare to take a jump together during a New Zealand event. Windsor Photography

above : An aerial photograph of Randwick racecourse. On 15 January 1944, Randwick saw the inaugural meeting of a new racing organization—the Sydney Turf Club. The new club was to take over and modernize the Rosehill and Canterbury Courses, and to gradually increase its influence in New South Wales. McQuillan

11. POST WAR
DEVELOPMENTS

11. POST WAR DEVELOPMENTS

Bernborough, the big bay from the bush, was six years old when he first came to the big tracks in Sydney, Melbourne and Brisbane. His racing career was short and spectacular, but it might never have begun without the shrewd judgment of a former Queensland buckjump riding champion and onetime professional horse-breaker, Harry Plant, who had become a top trainer in Queensland and then in Sydney.

Drama, excitement and controversy followed Bernborough, a son of Emborough, who first staggered uncertainly beside his mother Bern Maid at the late H. Winten's Rosalie Stud in the Darling Downs near Toowoomba, Queensland. Bernborough was taken to Brisbane to race as a two-year-old but the Queensland Turf Club rejected his nomination under a rule which allowed stewards to do this without giving a reason. Subsequently it developed that there was doubt over the horse's ownership. When he was sent to Sydney to run, the A.J.C. also refused to accept his nomination.

A steward of the Downs and South-West Racing Association in Toowoomba, George Kirk, held an enquiry into Bernborough's ownership. He announced that he was satisfied that A.E. Hawden was Bernborough's bonafide owner. Hawden said that he had bought the horse for £120 on 22 June 1940, from J.R. Bach whom he had asked to find him a good horse. Hawden produced a receipt to verify this. He said that Bach had bought Bern Maid with a foal at foot for £163 at the dispersal sale of the bloodstock of the late H. Winten. Hawden also said that he had leased Bernborough to a man named Roberts after Bernborough had won his first race in Toowoomba. This was to fulfil a promise he had made to Roberts.

Bernborough continued to race in Toowoomba where in four light seasons he won ten races in eighteen starts. No other race club would accept his nomination because of the Q.T.C. ban on him. Meanwhile word of the phenomenal speed of the horse had passed along the pipeline and several offers were made for him. Harry Plant solved the dilemma by taking Bernborough to Sydney and offering him for sale at an auction in his Sydney stables. Hawden had agreed to sell to the highest bidder. Bernborough was sold to the Sydney restauranteur A.O. Romano, who already had several horses trained by Plant, for £2,613, with only his provincial record to recommend him and his age of six heavily against him.

Between 8 December 1945 and 2 November 1946, Bernborough started eighteen times, won fifteen races, and lost three. The fifteen wins were consecutive. Not only did he win, but he won in a style which endeared him to the public, carrying big weights, getting in and out of trouble in his races, and repeatedly charging up the straight in breathtaking finishes.

As it had with Gloaming, Desert Gold, Ajax and other horses which had produced long winning sequences, the country watched Bernborough's continued success with growing excitement. He reached double figures and moved into the teens with the same jockey, Athol ('Call me George') Mulley, adding rare colour to the story.

Mulley was a classy jockey, but in his daily life he was unusually woolly-minded. He once sent a suit to the cleaner with £200 in banknotes in the pockets. The cleaner was not surprised when he learned who owned the suit. Another time Mulley set out in his swanky car for Richmond racetrack only to find that the races that day were at Kembla Grange. He had trouble at almost every race meeting through his habit of booking himself to ride several horses in the same race. He could never remember horses' names and referred to them for example, as 'that big grey colt' or 'that chestnut mare with the white foot'. Often he left his race colours at home or found several sets waiting for him to don for a race at the course.

The change of ownership lifted the Q.T.C. ban on Bernborough, who was free to race anywhere. He

right : Spam is the centre of attention as the 1946 Melbourne Cup field moves out of the mounting enclosure. Spam was brought to Australia from Ireland especially to run for the Cup, but the five months he was given to become acclimatized to the heat proved insufficient, and Russia took the big race. Herald and Weekly Times

248

looked as if he could, too, for he stood 17 hands 1 in, the same height as Phar Lap. His first section (top, between ears to top of wither) was 67 in. Phar Lap's was 66 in. His second section (top of wither along back to last point of the tail) was 67 in. So was Phar Lap's. The measurements for both first and second sections were regarded as perfect conformation.

In his first start for Romano on 8 December 1945, Bernborough did not win but he was so impressive that he was immediately made favourite for the Villiers Handicap a fortnight later. He carried 9 st 2 lb in the Villiers, which was over one mile and 19 yds, and he won by five lengths. He then went on to win one after another: The Carrington, the Australia Day Handicap, the V.A.T.C. Futurity, the V.R.C. Newmarket, the Rawson Stakes, the Chipping Norton Stakes, the All-Aged Stakes, the Doomben Ten Thousand, the Doomben Cup, the Warwick Stakes, the Chelmsford Stakes, the Hill Stakes, the Melbourne Stakes, the Caulfield Stakes.

His exciting sequence ended in the Caulfield Cup when he was fifth with 10 st 10 lb. He carried top weight in all these races. In the L.K.S. McKinnon Stakes a fortnight later at Flemington Bernborough trod on a loose piece of turf and badly damaged a sesamoid bone in his left foreleg. He did not race again. The vets patched up his leg and in December 1946, he was sold for £29,062 to the American film magnate Louis B. Mayer who sent him to stud in America, where Bernborough and his Caulfield Cup conqueror, Royal Gem, both became successful stallions.

While Bernborough was grabbing most of the racing headlines, a Sydney trainer was laying the foundations of a career which was to prove just as much a phenomenon of the Australian turf. This was Tommy Smith, the dapper little man with a taste for fashionable hats and bow ties who had overcome difficult beginnings to set himself up as a horse trainer. The first horse Smith started in a race finished last a furlong from the winner, but Tommy showed rare perseverance and eventually won thirteen races with that horse.

The Bragger, a former buckjumper, wore a buckjumper's saddle in barrier trials when Smith found

above : Athol Mulley on Sky High at the S.T.C. Golden Slipper Stakes. McQuillan

top right : Athol Mulley, the jockey who rode Bernborough for his fifteen wins in a row. A colourful figure, Mulley was notoriously absent-minded, once sending a suit to be dry-cleaned with £200 in notes in the pockets. McQuillan

right : Bernborough comes in for an easy win. His great heart and powerful muscles enabled him time after time to carry big weights to victory, to the delight and admiration of racegoers. Bernborough's regular jockey was Athol Mulley. Herald and Weekly Times

far right : Bernborough shows his paces on a training run. The big bay was the sensation of the Australian racing world in the 1940s. After fracturing a sesamoid bone he retired from racing to make a substantial contribution to racing as a sire in America. Herald and Weekly Times

him. He had a bad reputation for lawlessness and his feet were troublesome. Despite that dismal first start in January 1942, when The Bragger was so far back that other jockeys had dismounted when he finished, Smith still nurtured the ambition of one day training a winner and taking a photograph of it. 'I felt that if I could get a winner and display a picture of him I could show everybody I was a trainer', Smith said. He spent three years working on The Bragger before the horse won.

Since then Smith has trained hundreds of winners yearly and built an unprecedented record of success but he retains an affection for The Bragger which none of his champions can match. The Bragger was a family pet, part of the Smith family's daily routine and when at ten years old, he was fatally burned when his float caught alight, the Smith family grieved for the loss of a friend.

One of the greatest bargains on the Australian turf was Bernborough's contemporary Flight, which cost her owner Brian Crowley 60 guineas. She quickly became synonymous with courage, fighting back determinedly when headed in the straight. She had some pulsating struggles with Katanga, then rated the best weight-for-age horse in Australia. In one race Katanga, who apparently did not like the ladies, savaged Flight. Bernborough beat Flight by a head in another thriller in the Chipping Norton Stakes, but Flight won the L.K.S. McKinnon Stakes in which Bernborough broke down.

Flight finished her career in the Autumn Stakes at Randwick, running second to Russia, the Melbourne Cup winner. Her stake winnings of £30,627 from twenty-four wins gave Mr Crowley a handsome return for the modest sum he spent buying her, and laid the foundation for a highly profitable bloodline at stud. Before her death in 1953 Flight produced four sons and a daughter. Flight's daughter subsequently produced Skyline, winner of the A.J.C. Derby, the S.T.C. Hill Stakes and the S.T.C. Golden Slipper Stakes, and Sky High, winner of twenty-nine races and £77,055 in stakes. Sky High was sold to stud in America in 1967 for around $300,000. This is the highest sum ever paid for an Australian racehorse,

above: Flight, a bargain at 60 guineas in 1942, became the greatest stake-winning mare in Australasia, displacing Tranquil Star. At stud she produced four sons and a daughter. From the daughter came champion racehorses Sky High and Skyline. Herald and Weekly Times

right: Sky High, also from Flight's daughter, and another champion. Sky High was sold to stud in America for the then record sum of $300,000 — the same figure was later paid for the great Tobin Bronze. McQuillan

far right: Skyline, from the daughter of Flight, winner of the A.J.C. Derby, the S.T.C. Hill Stakes and the S.T.C. Golden Slipper Stakes streaks past the winning post. The jockey is Mel Schumacher. McQuillan

though the same figure was later paid for Tobin Bronze.

Despite her fine record, Flight was unfortunate in racing at the same time as several champion horses. Apart from Bernborough, Katanga and Royal Gem, she also had to contend with the brilliant Shannon.

Oddly enough, all Shannon's twenty-five starts in Australia were in Sydney. Shannon was bred at Kia-Ora Stud, Scone, and was owned and trained by Peter Riddle. He won the 1945 Epsom Handicap and was hot favourite for the same race the following year. Punters put a fortune on Shannon, but he was left at the start and did not move until the field had gone 100 yds. What followed ranks as one of the most astounding feats of riding ever produced on the Australian turf.

Jockey Darby Munro set out after the Epsom field and with thrilling horsemanship gathered in the stragglers. With the crowd stunned by Shannon's recovery, Munro swept right through the field only to lose by half a head to Blue Legend. A stride past the post Shannon was in front. Two days later Shannon whipped Flight and Magnificent in the A.J.C. George Main Stakes in the Australasian mile record time of 1 min 34.5 sec, and the following Saturday he beat Flight again in the King's Cup.

When his owner Peter Riddle died, Shannon was sold to Mr W.J. Smith for £27,300, but he raced only four times more in Australia, winning twice, Mr Smith then sold Shannon to America for $52,000. Shannon proved a bargain for his American owners, winning the Golden Gate Handicap and the Forty-niner Handicap, equalling the world record time in both events. He also won the Hollywood Gold Cup and the Argonaut Handicap. These wins, coupled with his Australian earnings gave Shannon a career total of £84,648, then the highest sum in stake money ever won by an Australian-bred horse. At stud in Kentucky Shannon's offspring brought high prices.

For half a century reports on the use of drugs—'stoppers' to make racehorses lose, or stimulants to make them win—had been common in Australian racing. Most of the early tests by race club vets proved negative, however, and there was a strong

*top left : Shannon, ridden by Darby Munro, the
jockey who piloted him to second place in the 1946
Epsom Handicap after he had been left at the post.
The rest of the field had gone 100 yds before Shannon
began, and yet he swept to the front in a brilliant run,
losing by only half a head. McQuillan*

*left : The old dining room for members at Randwick
racecourse in the 1950s. The new stand houses
dining rooms for members and the general public, but
'The Blue Room' as it was known still functions.
McQuillan*

*above : Somerset Fair, with New Zealand jockey
Grenville Hughes at Randwick. McQuillan*

feeling among racegoers that the clubs lacked the know-how to detect modern drugs. To counter this the A.J.C. opened its own laboratories in Sydney in 1947. Soon afterwards tests of specimens turned racehorse doping from an unproven scare into a reality.

On 8 May 1948, a swab taken from Frontal Attack was found to contain the drug caffeine. This was the first positive swab and the first disqualification of a Sydney race winner because of drugs. Caffeine had previously been found in several samples sent to the A.J.C. laboratory from Perth. Then Newborough and Mont Clair returned positive swabs after winning in Sydney and the battle against dope began in earnest.

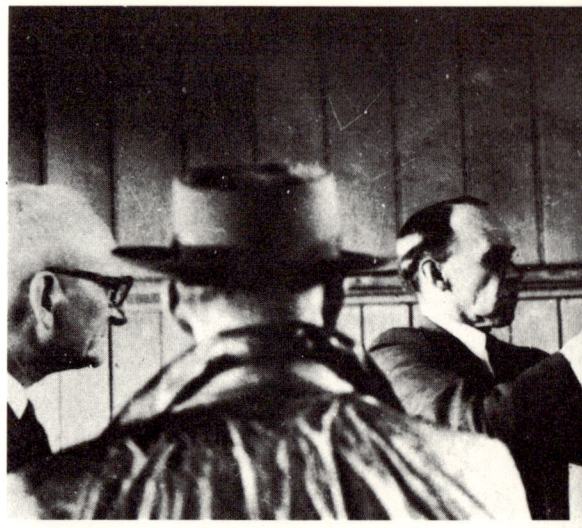

At the Sydney Easter carnival in 1953 four winners were disqualified after positive dope tests. Tarien, the English mare owned by former tennis champion R.O. Cummings and shirt manufacturer Dave Chrystal junior, had one of the easiest wins ever seen in the Doncaster Handicap, equalling the then race record of 1 min 35.2 sec. Tarien trained by Tommy Smith and ridden by George Moore, had been backed down to 7 to 4 and Sydney newspapers said stable followers had won £60,000 on the horse. A specimen taken from Tarien proved to contain the drug coramine (nikthethamide). The race and the winning stake of £5,073 was awarded to the second horse, Triclinium.

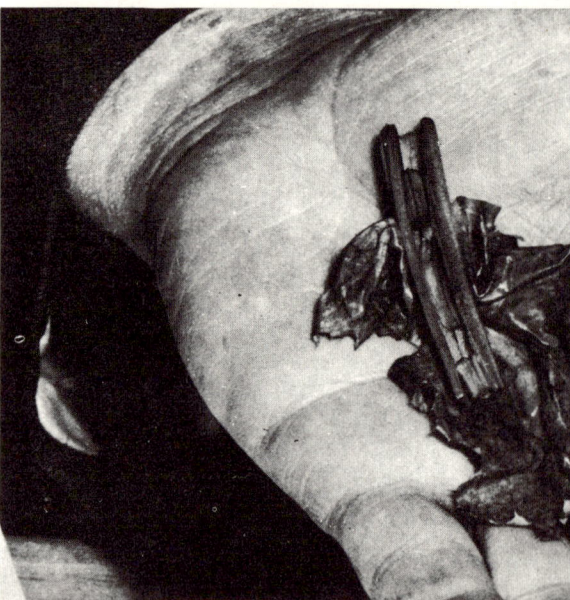

On the same day Cromis won the two-year-old classic, the Sires Produce Stakes, but a drug test for coramine proved positive and Cromis was disqualified. Cromis was owned in partnership by one of Australia's most notable racing personalities, Mr E.A. Underwood, vice-chairman of the V.R.C., and his sister-in-law Mrs J.W. Underwood. Two other winners at the same carnival, Culzean and Winged Glory, were also disqualified after positive tests for coramine. Culzean was owned in partnership by the Sydney businessman Douglas and K.G. (later Sir Kenneth) Luke, one of Melbourne's best-known sportsmen.

No action was taken against the owners or trainers of the four disqualified horses apart from the loss of stake money. The A.J.C. held that these people had met the requirements of the club in guarding their horses. It was never discovered who administered the drugs to the disqualified horses. The owners of

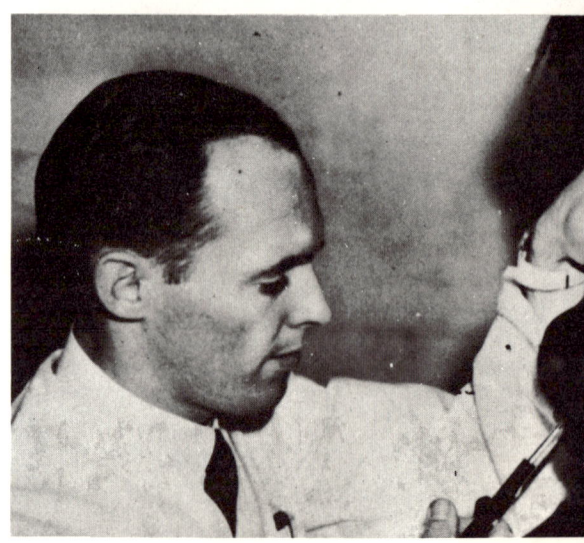

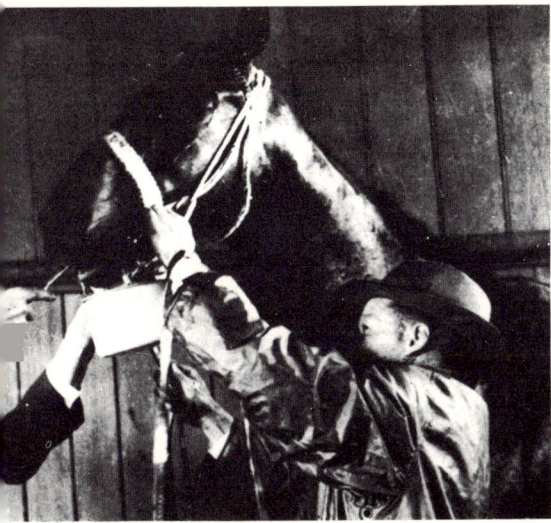

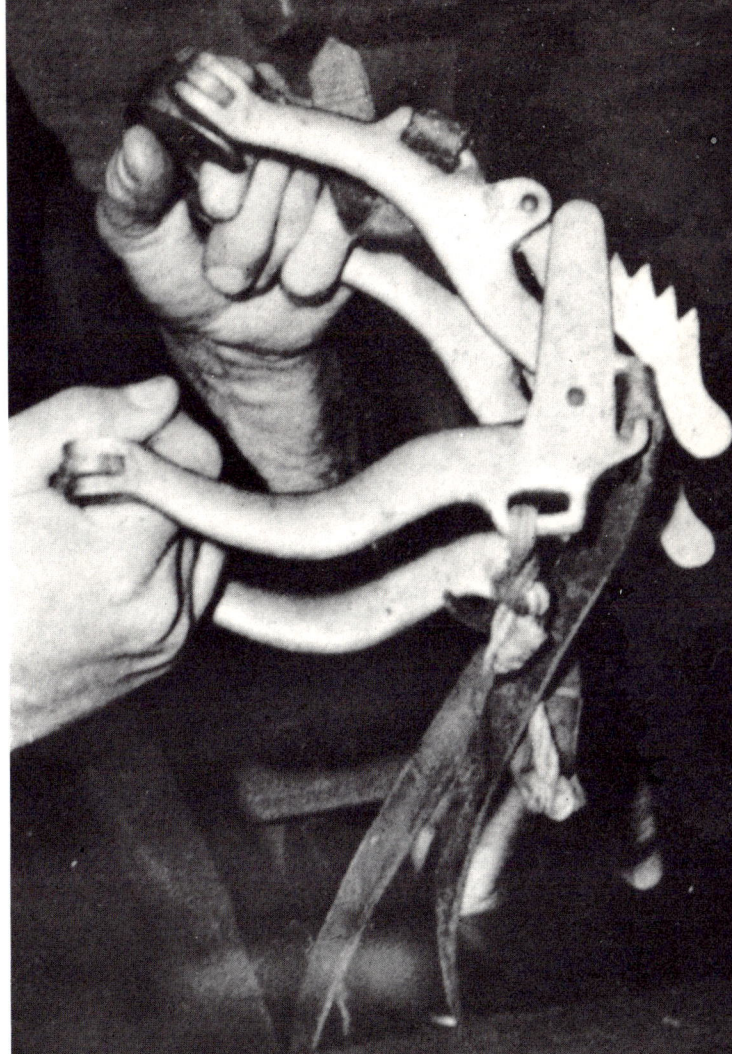

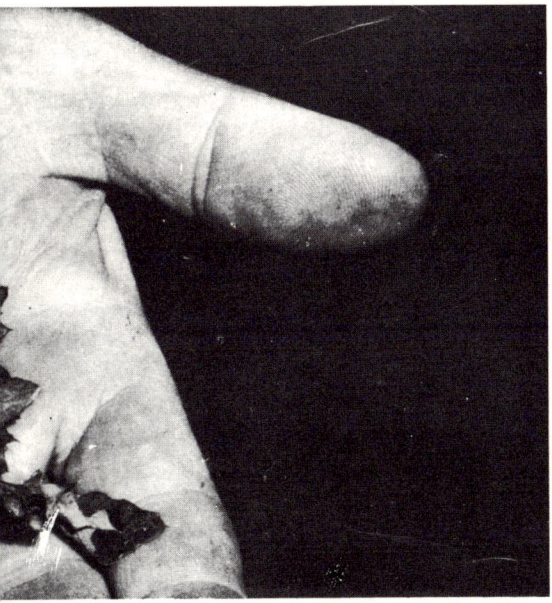

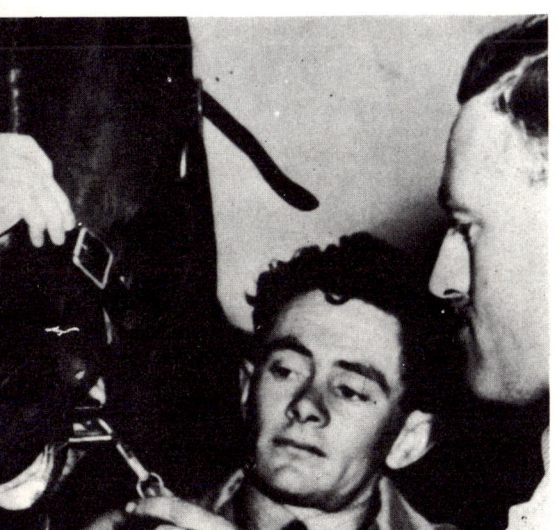

top left : Medulla is swabbed after a race. It is now standard practice to take samples from every winner and runner-up at capital city race meetings. Many trainers objected to this at first, but most have now accepted its necessity, and the accuracy of the drug tests. Herald and Weekly Times

centre left : A split thistle into which dope has been placed for a horse's consumption. Drugs are of two kinds—'stoppers' and stimulants : to make a horse lose, or give it a better chance of winning. Herald and Weekly Times

left : A closer view of a swabbling. The horse in this photograph is Comic Court, a great winner of the late 1940s and early 1950s. In the 1950-51 season, he had sixteen races for ten wins, including a record-breaking Melbourne Cup run carrying 9 st. 5 lb. Herald and Weekly Times

above : A 'gag'—an instrument used for forcing open horses' mouths. Herald and Weekly Times

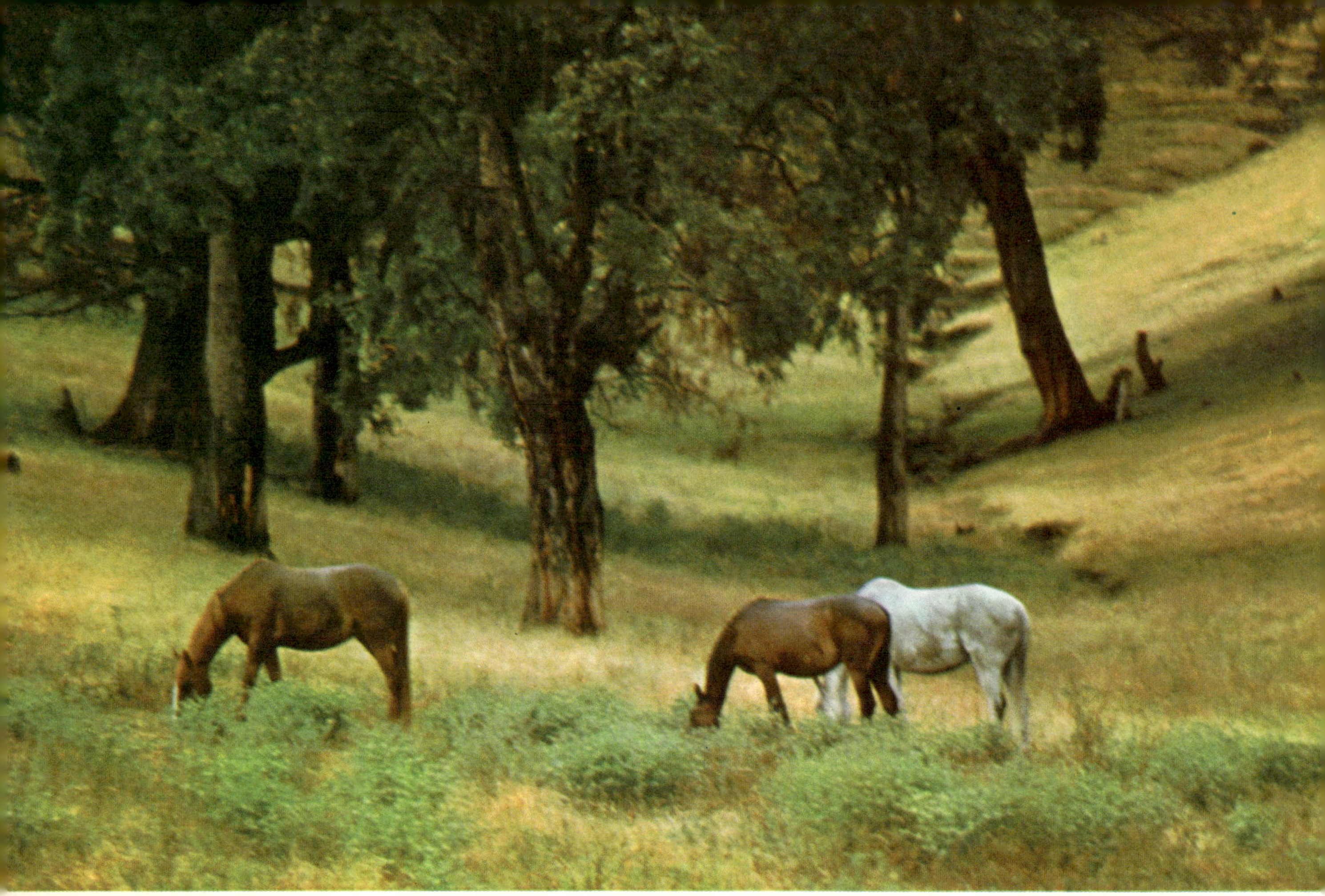

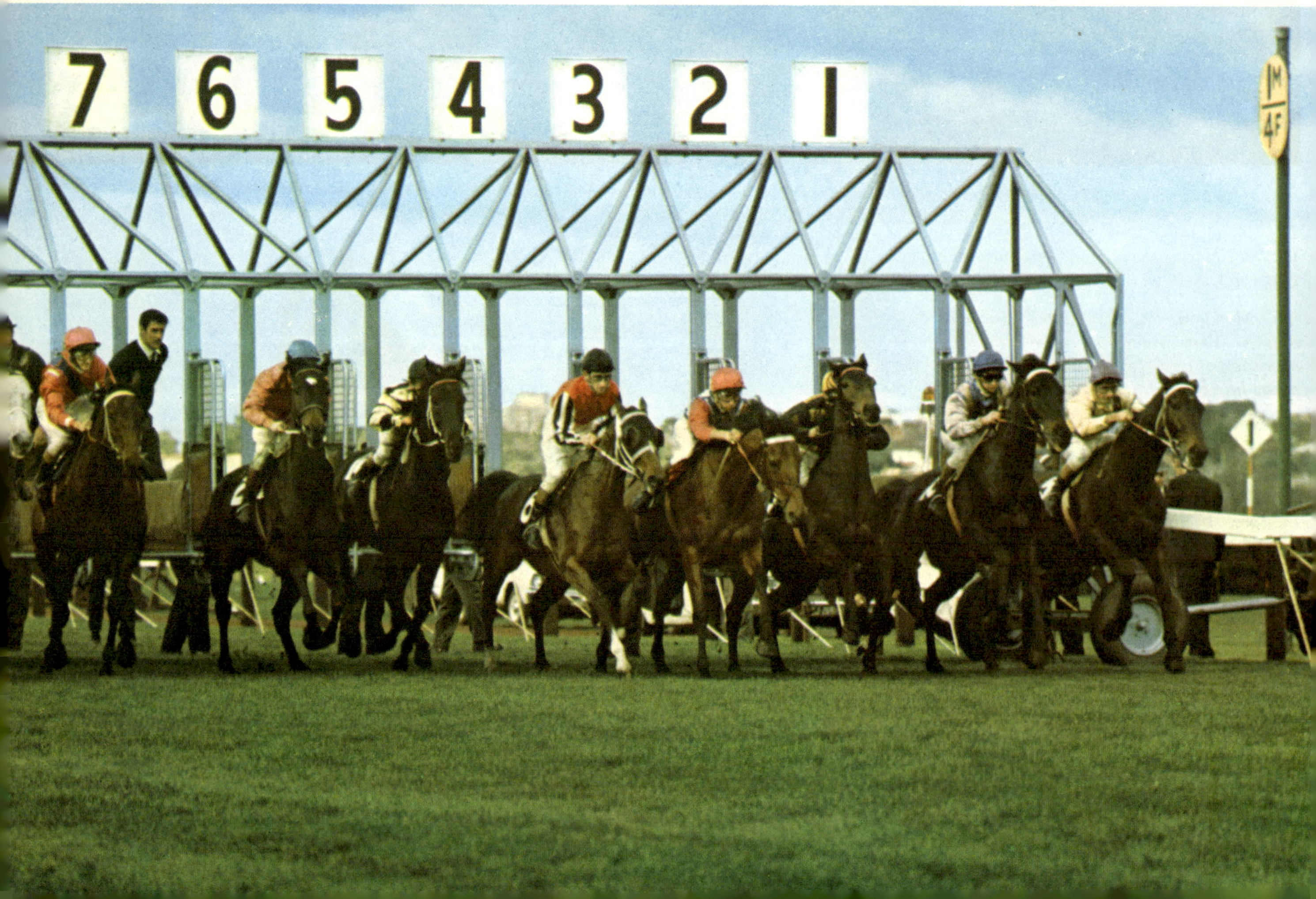
7
6
5
4
3
2
1
1M
4F
1

top left : Horses graze in lush pastures in eastern Australia.

left : Mobile starting stalls, now used on all big courses. They replace the rope barrier, raised on the operation of a trigger by the starter. Before this time, a flag had been used to signal the beginning of the race. The stalls release the horses at the flick of a switch, and can be moved quickly from the course. V.R.C.

above : The mounting yard at Flemington today. The crowd watches intently as the horses are prepared for the race. Victorian Tourist Authority

right : Galilee, with Miss World at the Caulfield Cup. Galilee is one of the most recent representatives of the New Zealand challenge which was becoming obvious in 1905 when a New Zealander became, for the first time, the leading owner in Australia. Galilee became, in 1966, one of the few horses to win the Caulfield and Melbourne Cups in the one year. The first was Poseidon. Victorian Tourist Authority

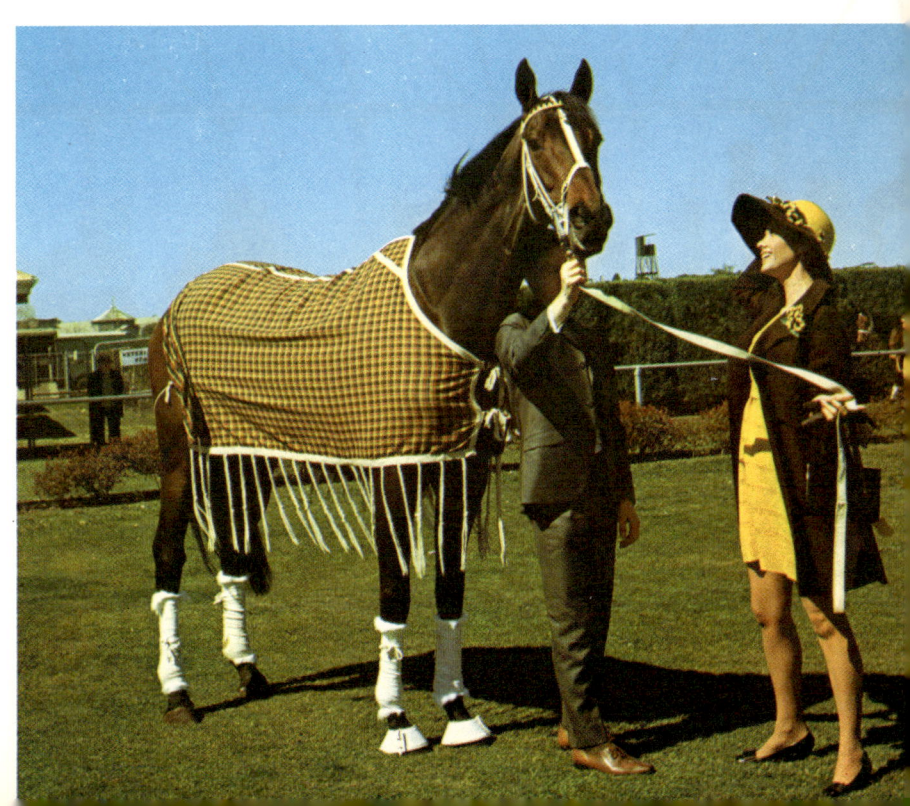

Cromis appealed to the A.J.C. committee against the decision and produced much technical evidence challenging the validity of the drug tests. The appeals were dismissed.

In 1948, the A.J.C. transferred its laboratory to Randwick racecourse and this is now by far the biggest in Australia. The staff analyses samples taken from horses in Victoria, Tasmania and Western Australia, but South Australian and Queensland race clubs conduct their own drugs tests. It is customary at all capital city race meetings to take samples from every winner and runner-up. The trainers were not happy about the laboratory tests when they were first introduced, claiming that horses given tonics to make them eat when they were off their food or other sickness cures could cause positive results in drug tests. The sensible conduct of the laboratory has largely won the trainers round, however, and most now accept that it is an essential part of our racing scene.

Regular drugs tests began in Australia at about the same time as the introduction of photo-finish cameras. The first photo-finish camera used in Sydney was installed at the S.T.C. course at Canterbury in March 1946. Several months later the A.J.C. installed photo-finish cameras at Randwick. They are now standard equipment at all major courses throughout the country, and photos are displayed soon after races for punters to study.

Dead-heats were fairly common until cameras were installed but now judges can tell to within a fraction of an inch if a horse won. Unquestionably many of the early dead-heats would have been avoided had the camera been used. It is fascinating to reflect, for example, on what would have happened at the Moorefield course in Sydney in 1903 when Lock Lockie, Barindi and High Flyer ran two dead-heats over twelve furlongs, had the camera taken both finishes. There is a record, too, of four horses running off for the six furlong Toowoomba Shorts Handicap in June 1897, after dead-heating when the race was first run.

Punters have found that the angles from which they watch race finishes can be deceptive—but the camera does not lie. There has been a notable decline in demonstrations over judges' verdicts since the photo-

A Dead-Heat : How Bets are Divided.

"**S**IMPLICITUS" (Tarana).—In the event of a division after a dead-heat bets are divided thus:—The amount put on by the backer is pooled with the amount the bookmaker is responsible for, and the money is equally divided between backer and layer. If you took £3 to £1 Graftnot, and staked your money, you would receive back £2. You, in fact, win £1. The rule is most equitable. The fact of Murat's backer receiving £9 10s for a booked bet of £20 to £1 does not entitle you to more than your proper share.

top left : A camera-graph for a win. The vertical white line, placed during the printing process, helps the judge to decide between two horses finishing close together, as in this photograph. The top part of the print shows the photograph of the race as seen in the mirror set into the winning post. A.J.C.

left : A camera-graph for the same race, this time showing third placing. The vertical line now drops past the nose of number 4, to show that he, not number 1, nearest the camera, deserves the judge's decision. A.J.C.

above : A newspaper correspondent discusses dead heats, which occurred quite frequently until photo-finish cameras were introduced in Australia. Judges' decisions were often challenged before this time, as everyone saw the race finish from a different angle.

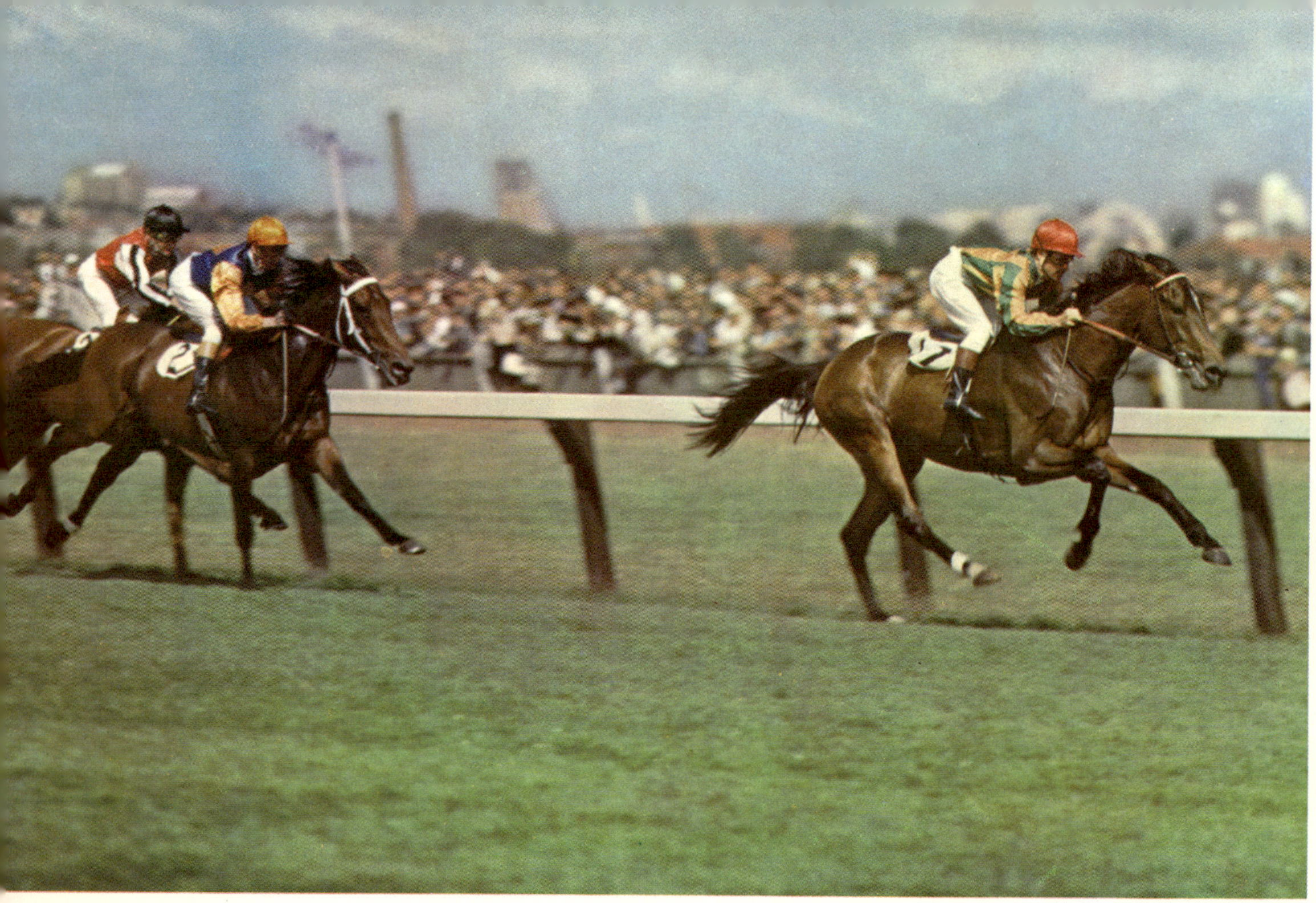

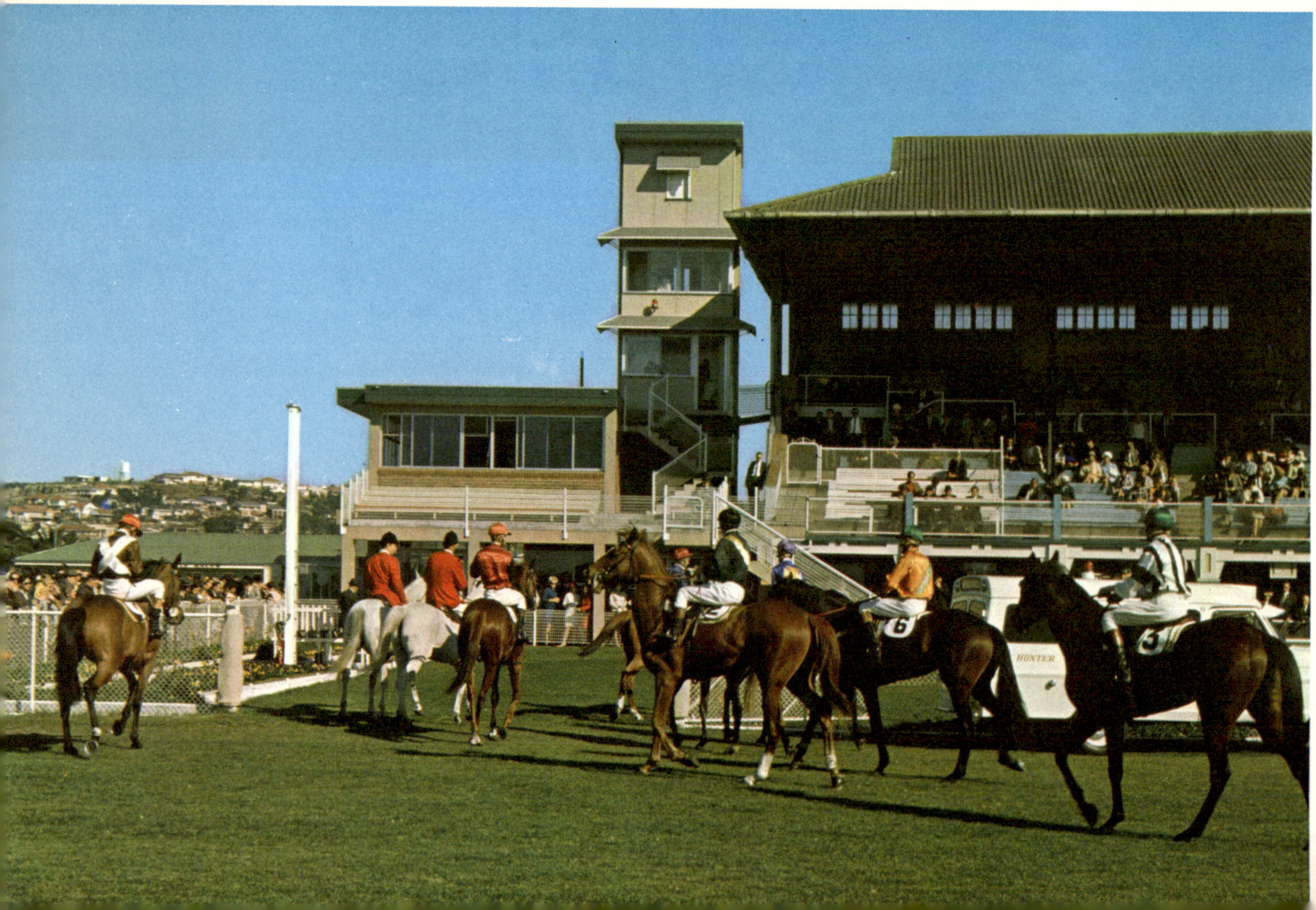

top far left : Lord Fury flies home to win the 101st Melbourne Cup in 1961. His tremendous run, which equalled the course record set by Comic Court over ten years before, gave a first Cup win to his trainer, Frank Lewis, and his jockey R. Selkrig. McQuillan

far left : Horses and jockeys file past the grandstand at the Newcastle course, opened in April 1907. The Newcastle Cup is run annually in September over 11 furlongs. Other important races are the Newmarket handicap, in May, and the Cameron Handicap, which is run in conjunction with the Cup during a two-day September meeting.

above, left : Two moments of excitement in a jockey's life—the triumphant parade before a cheering crowd (above) and left, the possession, even for a short time, of the Melbourne Cup, Australia's most sought-after racing trophy. V.R.C.

finish cameras were introduced. In the 1948 Melbourne Cup jockey Jack Thompson on Dark Marne was convinced he finished slightly ahead of the 66 to 1 winner, Rimfire. The judge gave the verdict to Rimfire after studying the photo. Four months later, after another hotly-disputed verdict on the same course in the Australian Cup, adjustments were made to the Flemington camera, reinforcing the conviction of some punters that Thompson and Dark Marne had been robbed.

There was no doubt, however, about the first triple dead-heat after the cameras were installed. The print showed that Pandie Son, Ark Royal and Fighting Force finished precisely in line at Flemington in 1956. Since then there have been at least six instances of horses dead-heating for first and third in the same race.

The early post-war years were a tribute to Australian bloodstock breeders and also saw the start of the formidable New Zealand challenges for rich Australian races. Between them Australian and New Zealand studs produced a marvellous array of champion horses. San Domenico, Delta, Dalray, Carioca, Hydrogen, Raconteur, Rising Fast, Prince Courtald, and Redcraze were all horses of exceptional ability. Between them they enabled Australian racing to recover from the wartime slump and set the stage for an exciting future.

San Domenic won £31,329 in stakes, a record for a sprinter to that time; Delta won the Metropolitan and Melbourne Cup and ended his career by setting an Australian record for nine furlongs in the Chelmsford Stakes; Dalray won the New Zealand Derby and St Leger and then the Metropolitan-Melbourne Cup double; Carioca won ten times and was placed three times in fourteen starts; Hydrogen surpassed Phar Lap's stake winnings with twenty-six wins and seventeen places; Raconteur proved one of the best horses ever seen in Perth, and won ten races in a row, including the Western Australian Breeders' Plate,

right: The P.J. Maloney Memorial Handicap, Tasmania, December 1964. Five horses race locked together—Arctic Beau (nearest camera: the eventual winner), Rethuh, Blue Neon, Port Erimus, and Sweet Chief. Bai Khabar and Silent Brook bring up the rear. Mercury

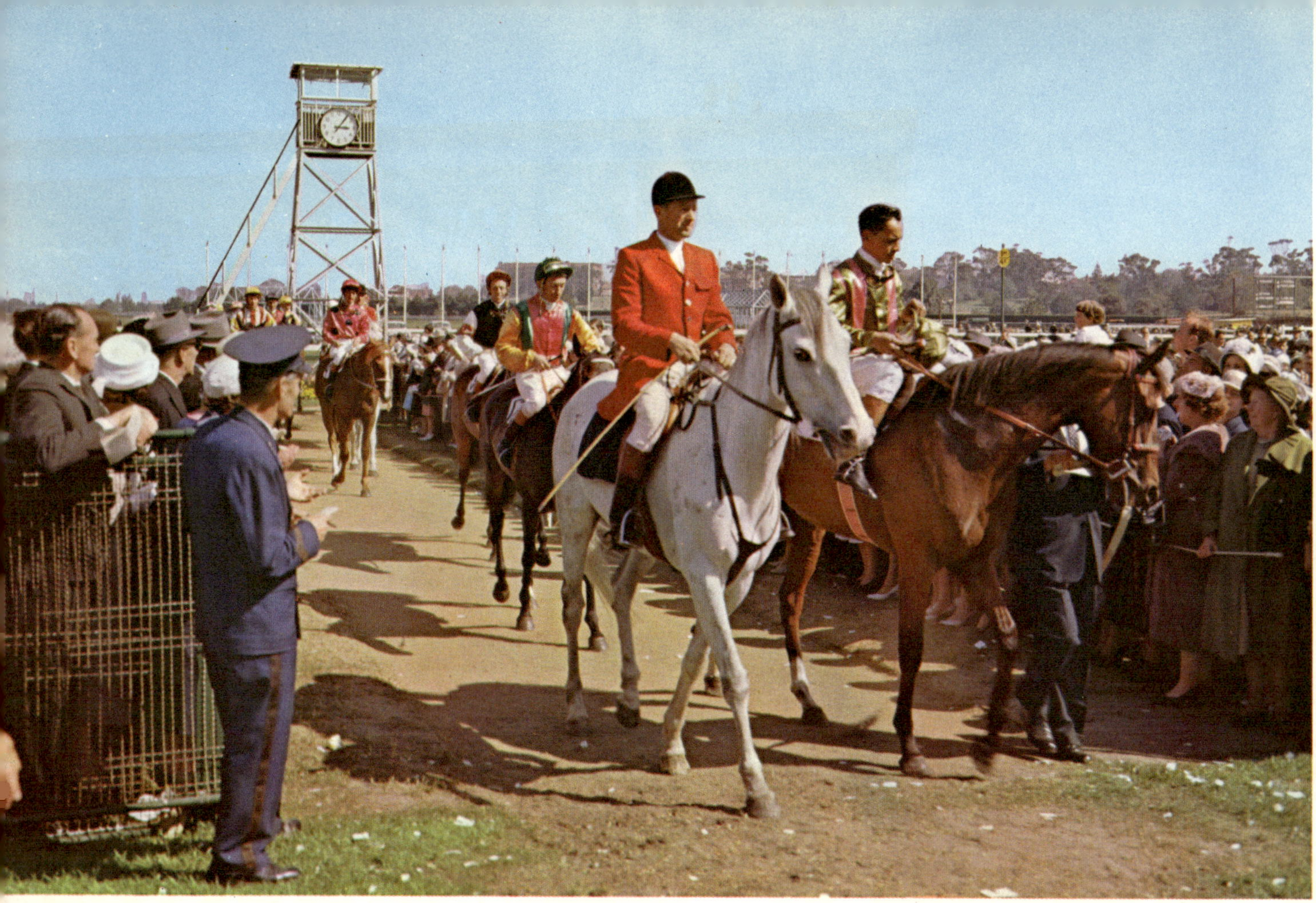
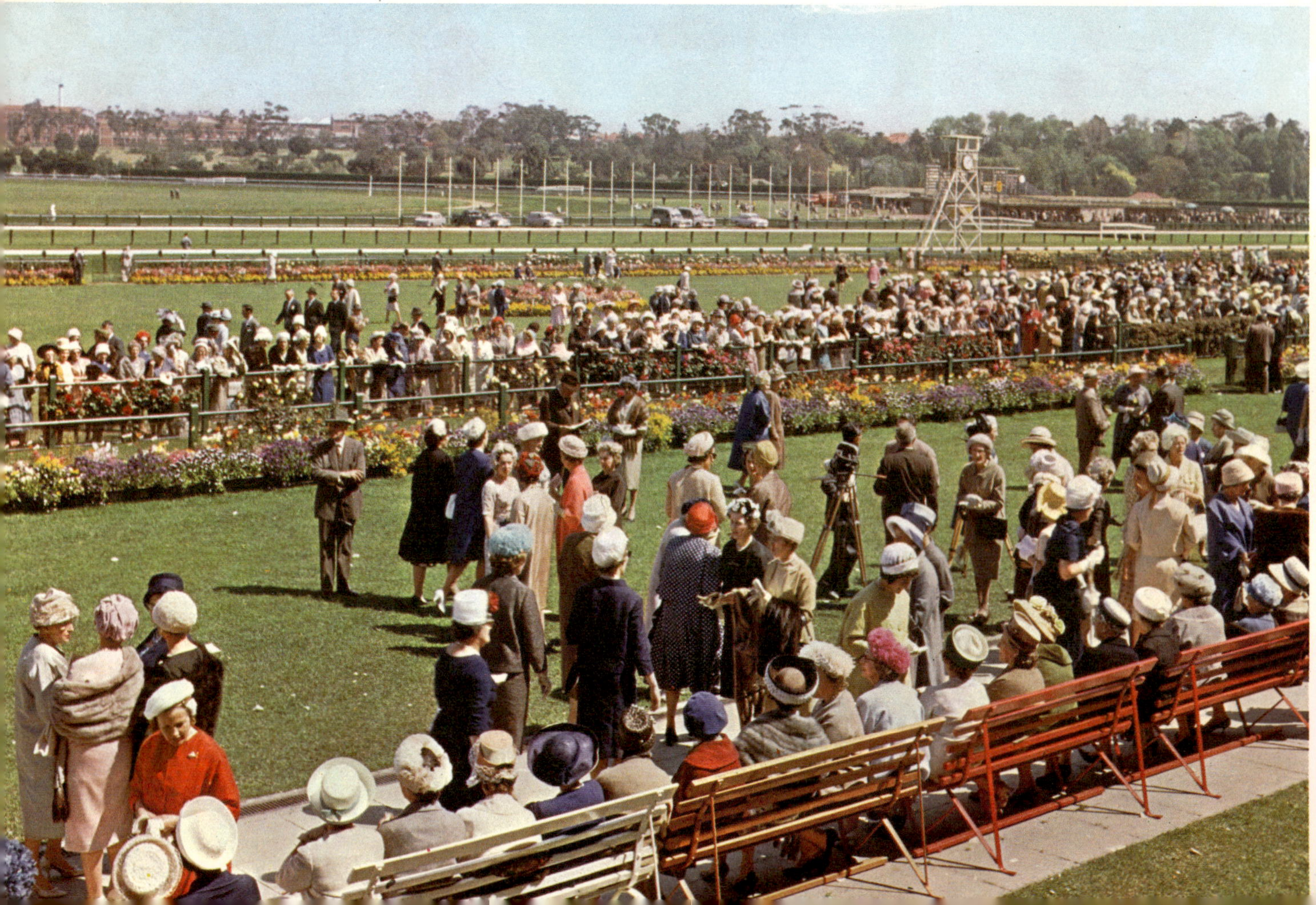

Scenes at beautiful Flemington racecourse. At top left, winning jockey F. Rays returns to scale on Carnival Day. V.R.C.

Guineas and Derby, and then had a great win in the A.J.C. Villiers; Rising Fast missed a place only twice in seventeen races and won the Caulfield and Melbourne Cups; Prince Cortauld topped the £50,000 mark in stakes wins, with a career total of twenty-five wins and £51,125; Redcraze dominated our big handicaps and weight-for-age races and won thirty-two races worth, with places, £71,481 in stakes.

New Zealand had introduced an off-course totalisator system of betting long before the idea was adopted in Australia and this brought rich yields to New Zealand race clubs, who were thus able to offer bigger prize money. When Australia finally copied the idea, a big heap of the winning stakes for our big races went back to New Zealand. Like Carbine, Phar Lap and Redcraze, many of our recent champions have been New Zealand bred.

far left: A painter puts the finishing touches on the winning post at Randwick. A long mirror is set into the post to provide a second image of the race to be used by the photo-finish camera in conjunction with the actual scene. The mirror picture helps the judge to decide the positions of horses which may be hidden from view by the rest of the field in the direct photograph. McQuillan

centre left: Ben Lomond, a great New Zealand racehorse, returns to scale. Windsor Photography

left: The New Zealand champion Il Tempo, photographed after his first Auckland Cup win. Windsor Photography

above: A photographer catches the finish of the 1948 Melbourne Cup—Darke Marne on the inside seems from this angle to be ahead of Rimfire, the 66 to 1 winner. The judge gave the race to Rimfire after studying the official photo, but many considered that the camera was defective, and the verdict was hotly disputed. Herald and Weekly Times

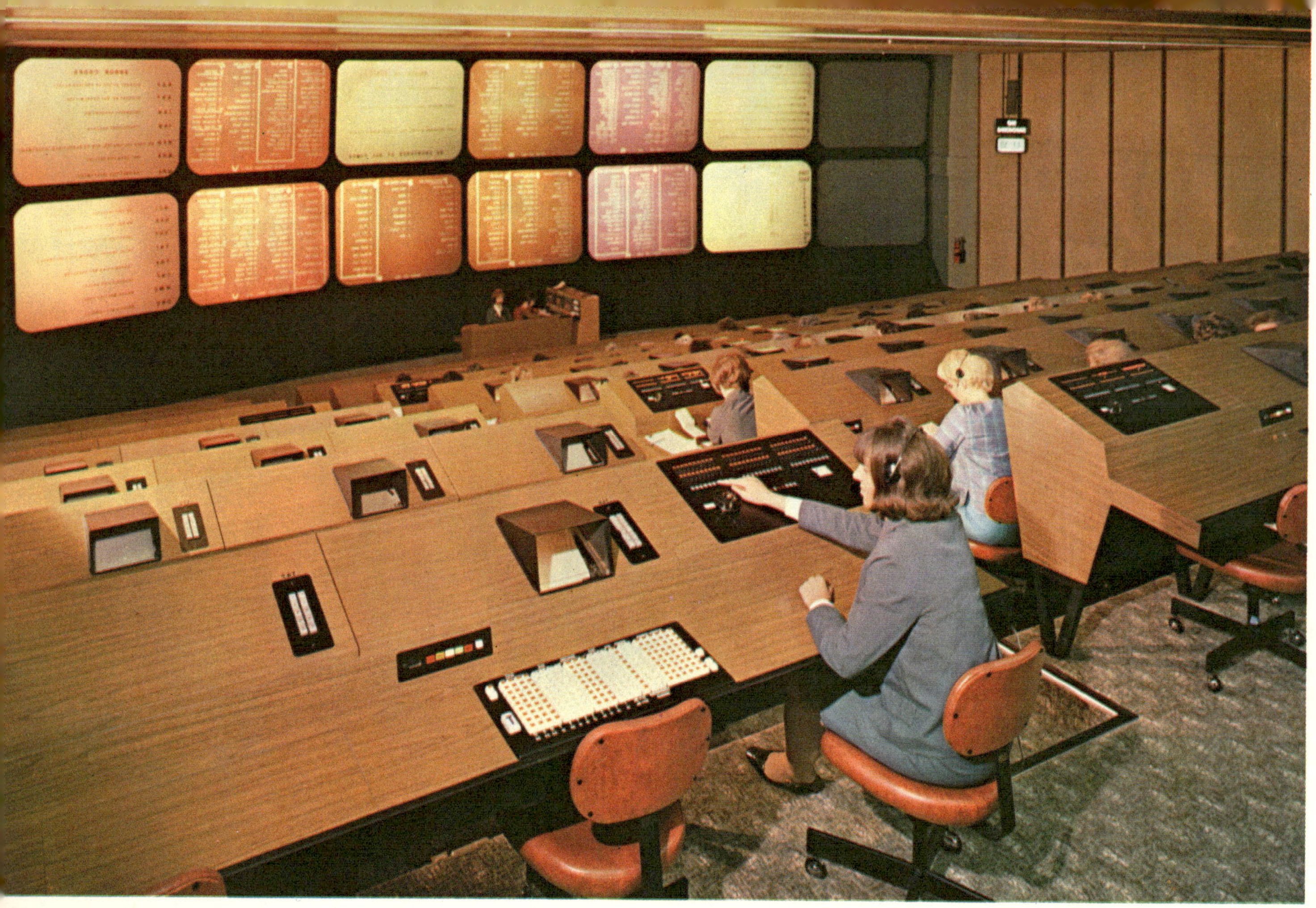

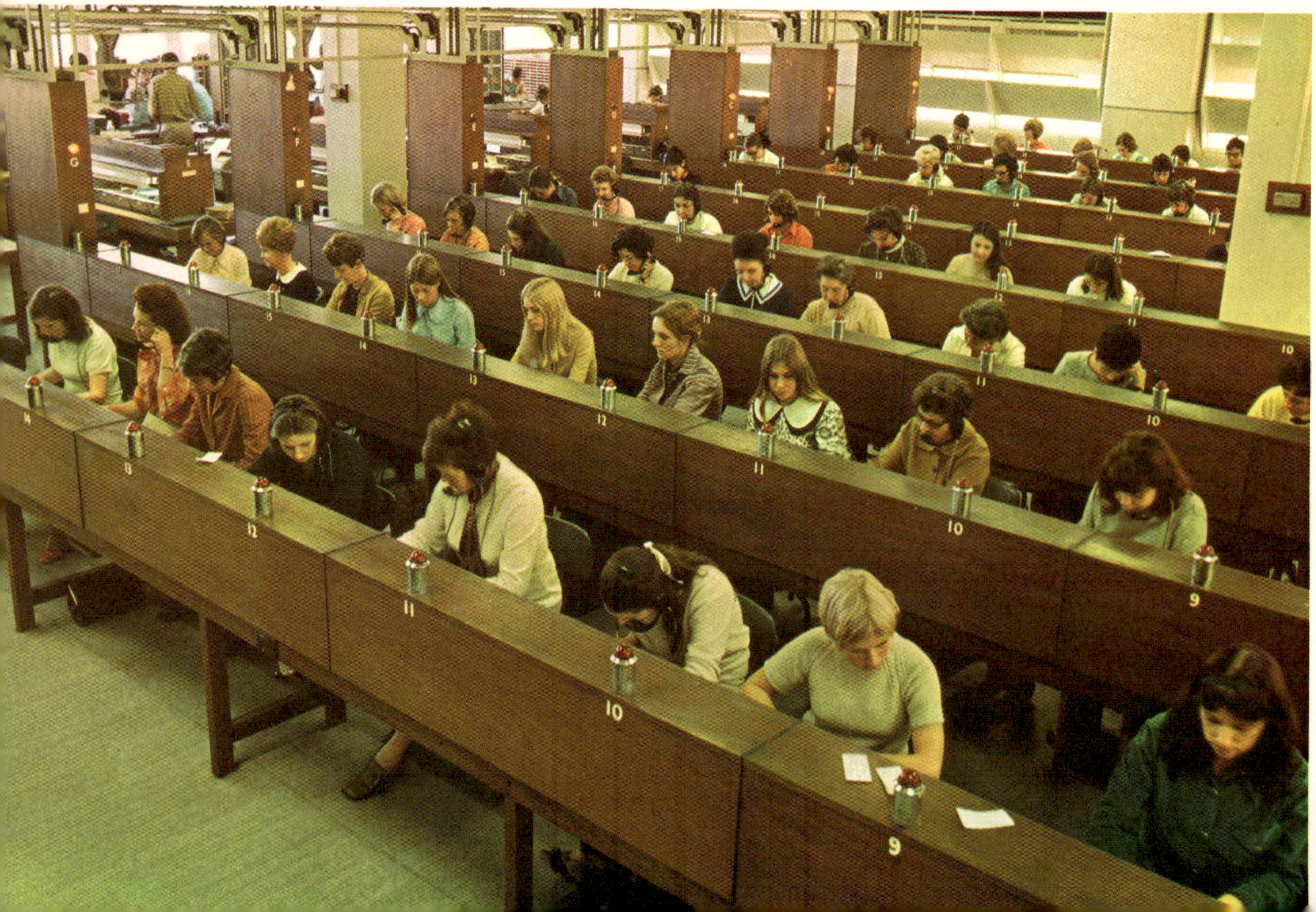

opposite page : Scenes inside the T.A.B. headquarters,
The T.A.B. has an enormous turnover, and its
establishment has benefited race clubs financially, in
that the Government returns a share of the profits to
them. The extra money has enabled the clubs to
improve course facilities and offer more prize money.

above : The new stand at Randwick—a symbol of the
progress made in racing since 1833, when the first
meeting was held on the course.

left : One of the many T.A.B. offices in Australia.
Here punters who do not wish to go to the racecourse
can lay bets at their convenience.

top left : Delta, winner of the Metropolitan and Melbourne Cup in 1951. Herald and Weekly Times

centre left : A great contemporary and rival of Delta —Hydrogen, in 1953 the greatest winner of stake money in Australia. Herald and Weekly Times

far left : Raconteur in the lead in the W.A. Breeders' Champion Stakes, 1952. West Australian

left : Prince Cortauld, bred in 1950, another New Zealand champion trained by Maurice McCarten. His winnings came to over £50,000 without a Melbourne Cup to boost the sum. McQuillan

above : The betting ring at Randwick in the 1950s— still crowded, still a place of ernest discussion and deep thought, still dominated by the flamboyant bookies. McQuillan

right : The grace of the champion Redcraze. His wins included the Caulfield Cup, carrying 9 st 13 lb, the A.J.C. Metropolitan, and the Brisbane Cup, all in 1956. McQuillan

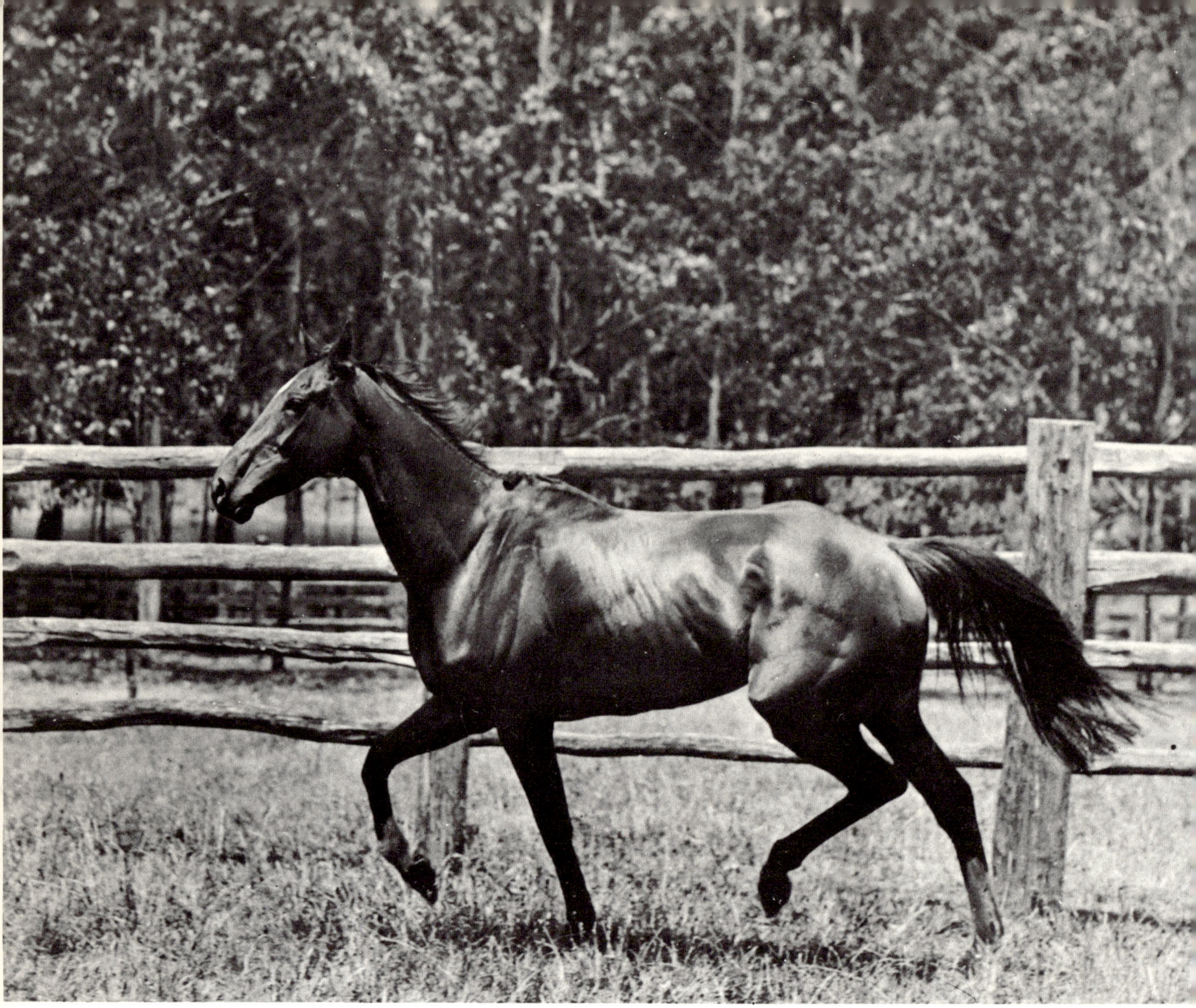

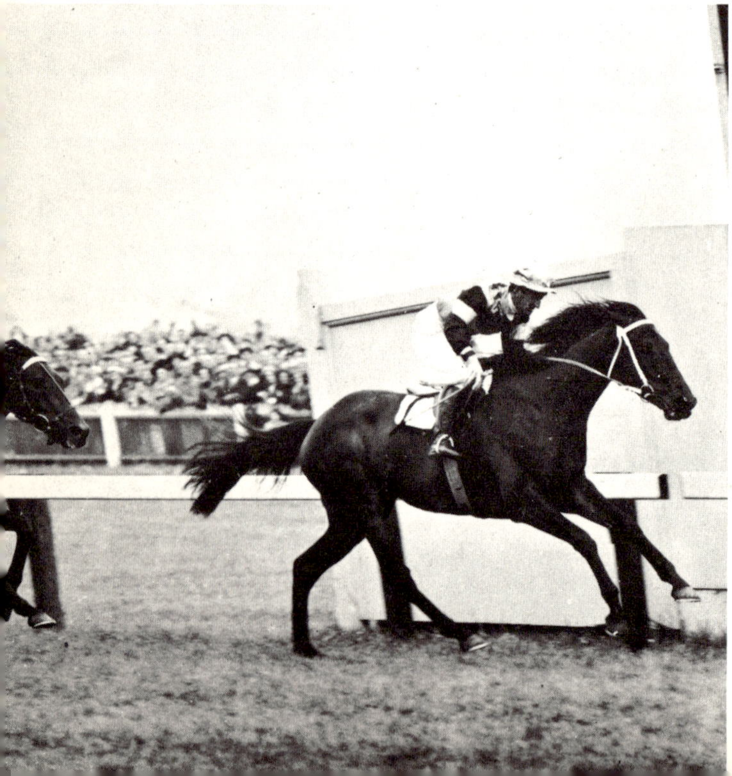

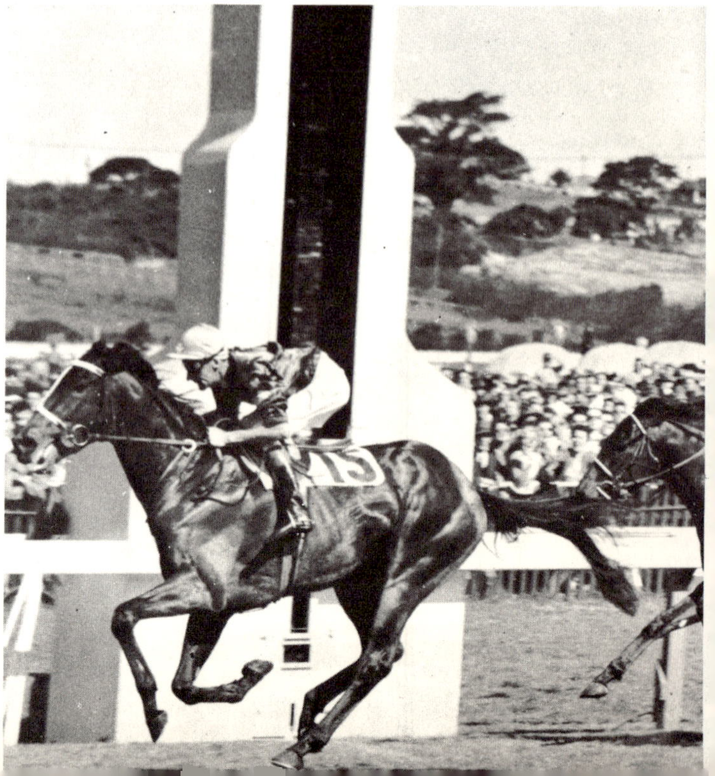
15

top left : Redcraze at spelling paddocks, resting after a strenuous season. He was to retire with £71,481 in stakes. *McQuillan*

far left : Rising Fast wins the 1954 Melbourne Cup, carrying Jack Purtell to his third Cup victory. *McQuillan*

centre left : Monte Carlo wins the A.J.C. Derby in 1956. He completed the one and a half miles in 2 min 31.3 sec, 2 sec faster than his winning run in the V.R.C. Derby of the same year. *McQuillan*

left : Redcraze, winner of thirty-two races, stands adorned with flowers after another triumph on an Australian course. This New Zealander was a force to be reckoned with in almost all our major handicaps and weight-for-age races in his prime, and lost the 1956 Melbourne Cup by only half a neck to Evening Peal, while carrying the great weight of 10 st. 3 lb. *McQuillan*

above : Caranna parades in the mounting yard before the 1955 A.J.C. Derby which he was to win in 2 min 33.2 sec. *McQuillan*

12. PROSPERITY

12. PROSPERITY

Tulloch, like Phar Lap, was a champion nobody wanted. Sydney trainer Tommy Smith bought him for £750 at the New Zealand yearling sales. When Smith tried to coax one of his patrons to take over the purchase, several turned him down before the veteran New South Wales owner-breeder E.A. Haley took Tulloch over. Tulloch became the first racehorse to win £100,000 in stakes in Australia and he did so despite a serious internal upset which took two years out of his racing career.

Although he was well-bred, by Khorassan from Florida, some experts criticised Tulloch's conformation as a yearling and this may have been the reason for the reluctance of Smith's well-heeled owners to buy him. Tulloch was second to Flying Kurana at his first start on 29 September 1956. He then won two races impressively but at his fourth start was beaten by the brilliant filly Concert Star in the Maribyrnong Plate at Flemington. Five days later Tulloch won the Byron Moore Stakes and was then sent for a three-month spell. He had two seconds after returning from the spell but in the third won the V.R.C. Sires' Produce Stakes.

Meanwhile Tulloch's rival, Todman, a Star Kingdom colt owned by Stanley Wootton and trained by Maurice McCarten, had started his career brilliantly, winning a Juvenile Handicap at Randwick in December 1956 by ten lengths in the Australian record time of 57.8 sec for five furlongs. Then Todman won the first Golden Slipper Stakes over six furlongs by eight lengths. The place-getters, Flying Kurana and Concert Star had already beaten Tulloch.

This set the stage for the first much-publicized clash between Tulloch and Todman, in the A.J.C. Sires' Produce Stakes at Randwick. Although Todman was favourite at 6 to 1 on, and led at the turn into the straight, Tulloch finished powerfully to win by two lengths. Only five days later Todman reversed this defeat, beating Tulloch by six lengths in the Champagne Stakes in the fastest six furlongs time ever run at Randwick by a two-year-old, 1 min 10 sec.

There was no doubting Tulloch's staying prowess, nor the breathtaking quality of Todman's sprinting, but over the Derby distance of a mile and a half which would prevail? The question was never answered as Todman broke down a month before the A.J.C. Derby and took two years to recover from a leg injury. Meanwhile Tulloch won the three Derbies, the A.J.C., V.R.C., and Q.T.C. When Straight Draw won the Metropolitan Handicap at Randwick his trainer Jack Mitchell said he would advise owner Ezra Norton against sending Straight Draw to the Melbourne Cup as Straight Draw would have no chance of beating Tulloch.

In October 1957, Tulloch won the Caulfield Cup in Australasian record time of 2 min 26.9 sec for the mile and a half, the third fastest time ever run for the distance anywhere in the world. At 6 to 4 on, he was the shortest-priced favourite to win the race, and with 7 st 8 lb he set a weight-carrying record for a three-year-old.

Tulloch's trainer Tommy Smith rated him a certainty for the Melbourne Cup, in which he would have carried 8 st 2 lb, 10 lbs over weight-for-age for a three-year-old. But to the consternation of Tulloch's thousands of fans, owner Haley scratched him two weeks before the Cup. 'I love horses too much to run a three-year-old in the Melbourne Cup,' said Haley. 'I will not risk breaking the colt's heart.'

Tulloch's scratching touched off a controversy which still rages. History was on Haley's side. No three-year-old had won the Cup with more than 7 st 8 lb in modern times, and in the previous thirty-five years only one three-year-old, Skipton, had won the race at all—and then from a weakened wartime field with 7 st 7 lb.

Tulloch's withdrawal left a mediocre field for the 1957 Cup, which was won by Straight Draw from Prince Darius, a horse Tulloch had beaten by six lengths in the A.J.C. Derby and by eight lengths in

right: Tulloch, Number 1, starts in the V.R.C. Derby, ridden by George Moore. The champion horse was to go on to win the race. McQuillan

the V.C.R. Derby. On the last day of the V.R.C. Cup carnival Tulloch won the C.B. Fisher Plate at 8 to 1 on and a week later won the Q.R.C. Derby by eight lengths.

At the end of his three-year-old season Tulloch had started twenty-one times for fifteen wins and six seconds and has earned £51,647, a record. Sent for a spell Tulloch grew into a magnificent racehorse, with a fine head like an expensive chess piece and intelligent demeanour. His curiosity was a constant stable talking point. Racing fans compared him with Carbine and Phar Lap. All three of these horses, which overshadowed all others of their period, were bred in New Zealand.

Tulloch lost at his first start in 1958 to Prince Darius in the St George Stakes at Caulfield. At his next start in the Queen Elizabeth Stakes at Flemington he was involved in a stirring struggle with Sailor's Guide and Prince Darius, with all three sprinting together over the last furlong. A photo of the finish put Sailor's Guide a half head in front of Prince Darius, with Tulloch a half head further back. Sailor's Guide later won $104,088 in America, for a career total of £66,044.

That race brought Tulloch to his peak and he then won six races in a row, including the St Legers at Randwick and Flemington, before he suffered the mysterious stomach ailment which many thought would end his career. Todman returned to racing in December 1959 and won a Flying Handicap with 9 st 7 lb in record time. He raced briefly and was then retired to stud. But when Tulloch returned to racing in March 1960, he was worked very hard indeed.

He reached a total of fifty-three starts and £110,123 in stakes. He had only one Melbourne Cup start, finishing seventh with 10 st 1 lb in 1960. Towards the end of his career, as he was dragged from one racetrack to another with all the appearance of a tired horse, racegoers could not help but wonder what had changed the horse-loving owner who in 1957 had scratched Tulloch from the Cup for fear of over-taxing him.

Todman was sired by Star Kingdom, a sprinter and champion sire of sprinters, which ranks as our best

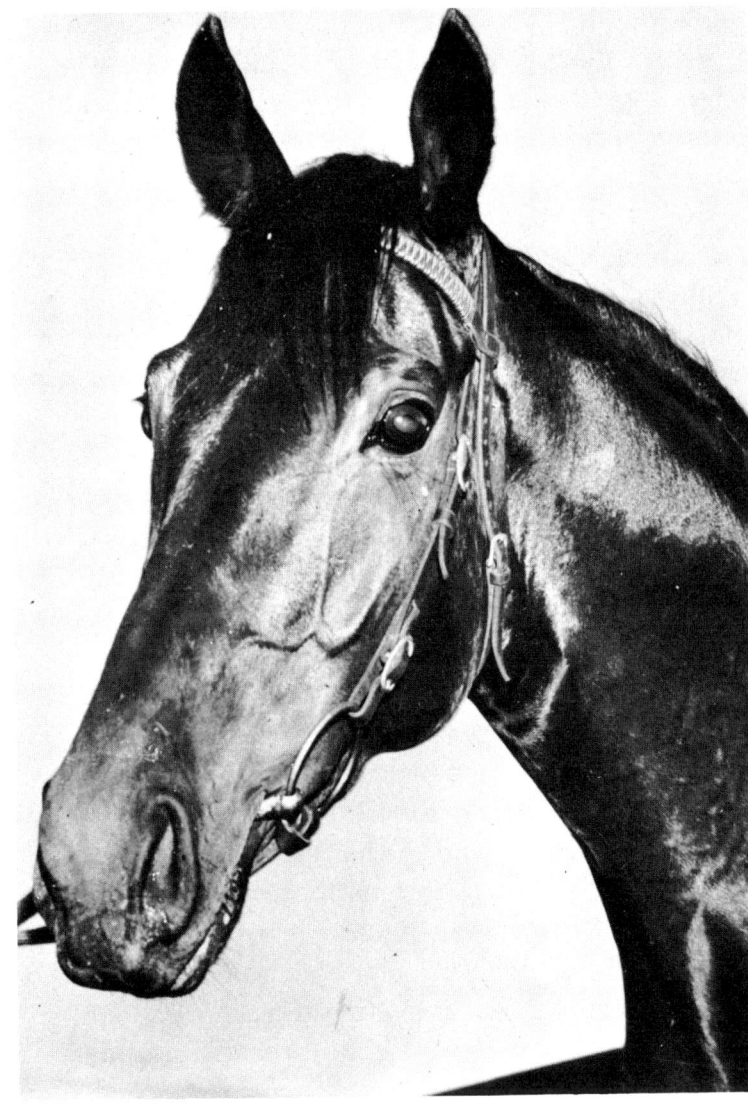

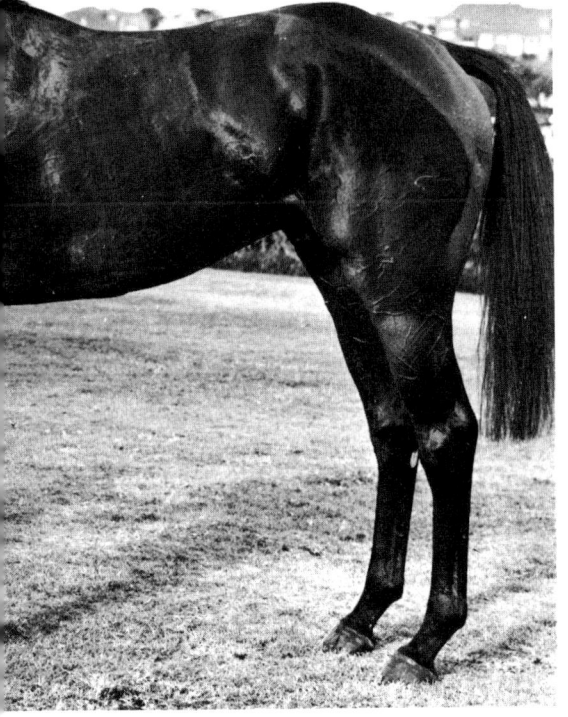

top left : The men who were partners in Tulloch's success. From left to right : T.J. Smith, (trainer), Mr Haley Snr. (owner). George Moore (jockey) and Mr Haley Jnr. McQuillan

left : Tulloch with his trainer T.J. Smith after winning the Queen Elizabeth Stakes. Like Phar Lap, Tulloch was unwanted as a yearling. He was bought by Tommy Smith at New Zealand yearling sales for only £750 and Smith found it hard to persuade any of his owners to take over the purchase. The ugly duckling was to go on to win fame for himself and fortune for his connections. McQuillan

above : Tulloch, a powerful, intelligent racehorse, the first in Australia to win £100,000 in stakes, despite an illness which took him away from racing for two years. McQuillan

stallion since the second war. Star Kingdom's two-year-olds topped the winning list for his first five seasons and again six years later. He was the leading sire for all ages for five seasons and second three times. He got two Derby winners, Sky High and Skyline, as well as Todman.

Todman's regular jockey and the man who rode Tulloch in his only Melbourne Cup start was 'Nifty' Neville Sellwood, one of the best Australian riders of all time. Sellwood had many engrossing clashes in the 1950s with another master horseman, George Moore, who rode Tulloch in most of his wins. Both Sellwood and Moore were 'battlers' when they began riding, and both made fortunes from race riding which enabled them to set up as country property owners. They were the best of a fine crop of Australian riders that included Jim Johnson, Jim Miller, Roy Higgins, and, earlier, Athol Mulley and Mel Schumacher.

Schumacher was disqualified for life after the 1961 A.J.C. Derby in which he rode Blue Era first past the post. After viewing a film of the race, stewards ruled that Schumacher had impeded the second horse, Summer Fair, by catching hold of the leg of its rider, Tommy Hill. On appeal Schumacher's sentence was reduced to ten years and after a determined campaign by racing men who claimed the sentence was too severe his license was renewed after five and a half years. Part of the argument in having Schumacher reinstated was that the same leg-pull trick had been used many times over the years but had not been detected until films of entire races were introduced.

Sellwood had the distinction of riding four winners at one meeting twenty-four times. He rode five winners in one day at Randwick in 1954. By contrast Moore rode five winners at one meeting five times and rode four winners on a programme eighteen times. Sellwood was killed on 7 November 1962, when a filly named Lucky Seven fell and rolled over him at Maison Lafitte, near Paris. He had remained in France in preference to taking a Melbourne Cup ride because he wanted to clinch the French jockeys' premiership, which he was leading with 102 winners at the time of his death. Yves St Martin also rode 102 winners and shared the premiership with Sellwood. St Martin

top : Neville Sellwood, regular jockey of the champion sprinter Todman. A skilful horseman, he rode four winners in one meeting twenty-four times during his career. Like George Moore, he also rode successfully in Europe. McQuillan

above : Star Kingdom, a champion sprinter and sire of many great racehorses including Todman, Sky High and Skyline. Star Kingdom is considered to be the best Australian stallion since the second world war. McQuillan

top right : Todman was raced only briefly after his return to the track in December 1959 following two years' absence. He was then retired to stud. During his career he was trained by Maurice McCarten and ridden regularly by Neville Sellwood. McQuillan

right : Two champions : Prince Darius (left) and Tulloch (right) Prince Darius ran second to Straight Draw in the 1957 Melbourne Cup, the Cup in which Tulloch's owner refused to let the three-year-old start. McQuillan

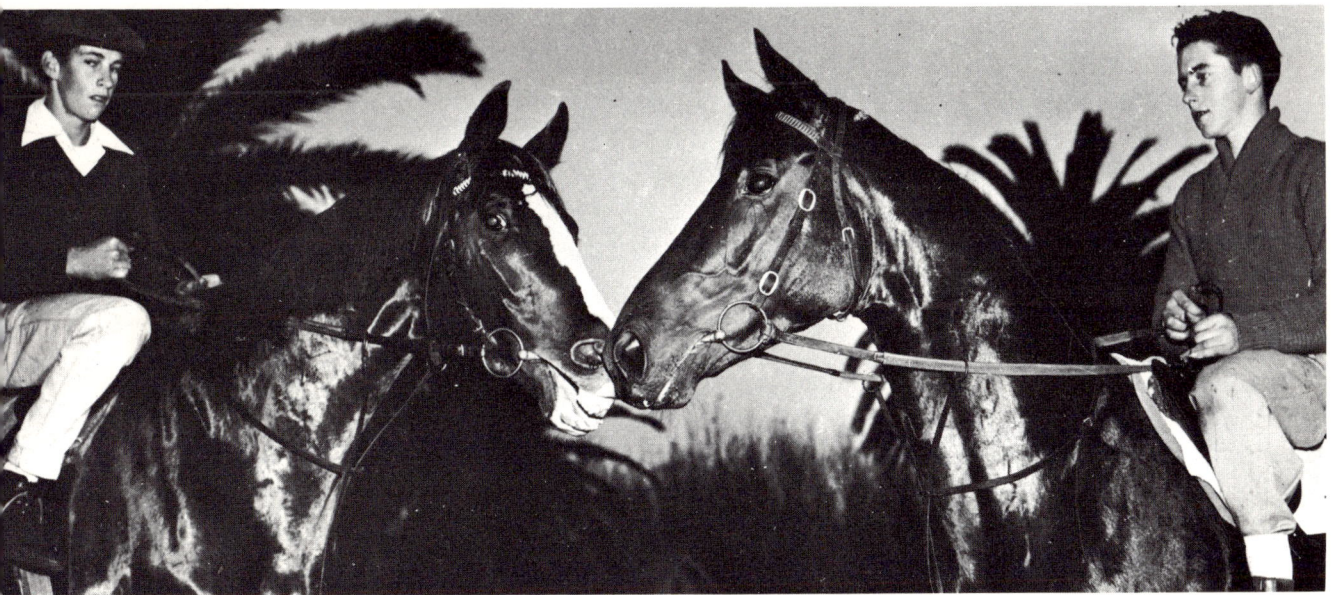

285

gave the prize, a gold whip, to Sellwood's widow.

In England Moore won the Ascot Gold Cup on Cheshire, the Gimcrack Stakes on Paddy's Sister, the Champagne Stakes on Paddy's Sister, the Two Thousand Guineas on Taboun and Royal Palace, the One Thousand Guineas on Fleet, The Derby on Royal Palace, the Coronation Cup on Fleet, and the King George VI and Queen Elizabeth Stakes on Busted. In America he won the $25,000 San Diego Handicap on Manyunk. In France he won the French Derby on Charlottsville and the Prix de l'Arc de Triomphe on Saint Crespin. But he never won a Melbourne Cup. At the 1969 Sydney Easter Carnival there were twenty-nine races in four days and Moore won fifteen of them. He rode the last two on Doncaster Day and the first four on Sydney Cup day for six wins in a row, and his Sydney Cup day tally was five wins. He retired on 4 April 1970.

Moore's immense popularity with punters was understandable—he won on an amazing percentage of heavily-backed horses. From the time he returned to race riding in 1956 after a suspension of almost three years Moore had 3,403 mounts in Sydney, from which he gained 1,040 wins, 620 seconds and 447 thirds. An investment of $10 on each of his mounts would have returned a profit of $1,831.

Sellwood won two Melbourne Cups, on Delta (1951) and Toparoa (1955), an English Derby on Larkspur, the Sydney Cup on Gold Scheme, Sailor's Guide and Grand Garry, the Caulfield Cup on Tulloch and Basha Felika, the A.J.C. Derby on Deep River, Prince Morvi, the Victoria Derby on Delta, Prince Morvi, Sailor's Guide and Sky High, the Epsom Handicap on Titanic, Silver Phantom, Knave, Noholme, the Doncaster on Bernbrook, the Metropolitan on Delta, the Brisbane Cup on Cambridge, the Doomben Cup on Tossing and Prince Delville, the Doomben Ten Thousand on El Khobar and In Love, and the Australian Cup on Gaybao. He was six times premier jockey in Sydney and rode a total of 1860 winners. On his first ride in England he won the Two Thousand Guineas and on first ride in the United States he won on the French horse Valor II.

The success of Sellwood and Moore in Europe

top left : Straight Draw flies home to win the 1957
Melbourne Cup from Prince Darius by a neck.
Straight Draw, ridden by Noel McGrowdie, won the
big race at 13 to 1 carrying 8 st 5 lb. This was the Cup
from which Tulloch was scratched, and many experts
believe that he would have won had he been allowed to
run. McQuillan

left : The race which cost Mel Schumacher five and a
half years of his racing career, the 1961 A.J.C. Derby.
Schumacher's mount Blue Era (on the rails) which
won the race, was disqualified after a protest in which
it was claimed that Schumacher impeded the second
horse, Summer Fair (outside) by catching hold of the
leg of its rider. Schumacher was disqualified for life,
but after an appeal his sentence was reduced.
McQuillan

above : George Moore, one of the many Australian
jockeys to succeed overseas. His record in England
includes wins in the Ascot Gold Cup, the Derby and
the Coronation Cup. He also rode in France and
America. McQuillan

enchanced Australians' outstanding record there since the war. Rae 'Togo' Johnstone began it by winning the English Derby on My Love (1948), Galcador (1950) and Lavandin (1956). His 1950 feat of winning four classics, the One Thousand Guineas, Derby, Oaks and St Leger has never been matched by an Australian. But Scobie Breasley has the best record of Australian jockeys in England. From 1955 until his retirement to become a trainer in 1969 he rode more than 100 winners a year. He won the 1957 Prix de l'Arc de Triomphe, Europe's richest race, the 1964 English Derby on Santa Claus and the 1966 English Derby on Charlottown. He won the English jockeys' premiership four times, in 1957 (173 wins), 1961 (171 wins), 1962 (179 wins) and 1963 (176 wins).

The only Australian apart from Breasley to win four English jockeys' premierships was Frank Wootton. Edgar Britt, Frank Dempsey, Frank Bullock, Jim Munro, Jim Pike, Bill Evans, Eddie Cracknell, Garnet Bourgoure, Ron Hutchinson, Bill Pyers, Bill Williamson, Tommy Burns, Billy Cook, Jack Thompson, Jack Purtell and Noel McGrowdie are among other Australian jockeys to ride successfully in England. Britt rode more than 1,200 winners in fourteen years in England, including seven classics. In 1948 he finished second in the jockeys' premiership to Sir Gordon Richards.

Moore formed a dominant partnership with trainer Tommy Smith, who in 1968-1969 headed the Sydney trainers' premiership for the seventeenth successive season. Five times Smith has trained more than 100 winners in a Sydney season. His best season was in 1967-1968, when he created an Australasian record with 143 wins and $500,959 in stakes. In England in 1967 horses trained by Noel Murless won £321,123 Commonwealth record. Moore was Murless's stable jockey and rode many of his winners. Returning to Sydney he then rode many of the winners in Smith's record total. In the 1968-1969 season, when Sydney races carried $2,500,000 in stakes, Smith's horses won $390,980 of it, and with inter-state winnings added, gained a total of $448,790.

These figures are all the more impressive when it is considered that Smith was suspended for a month in

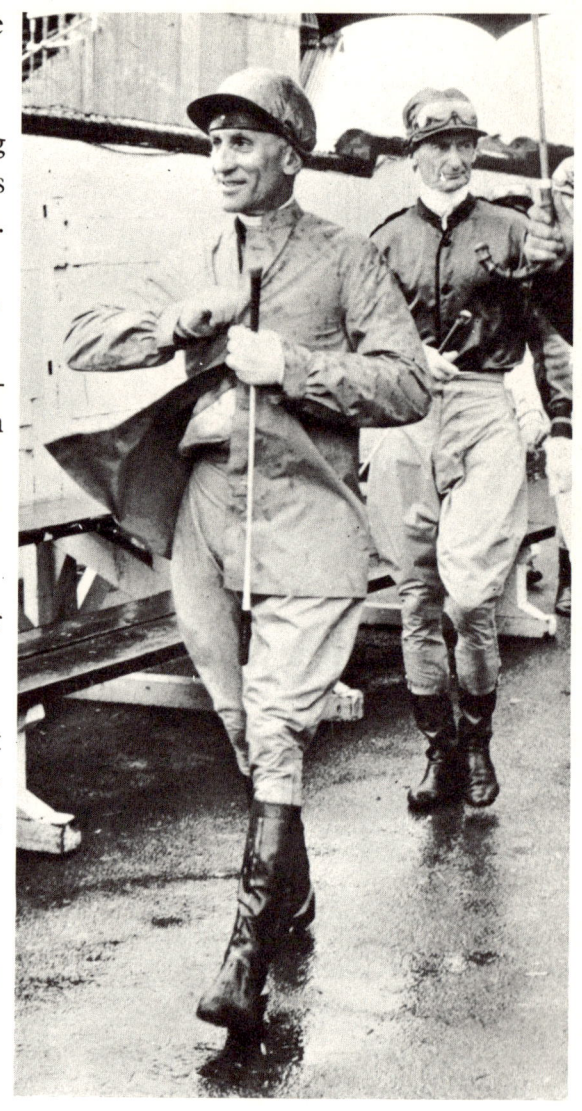

above : Scobie Breasley (left) had an outstanding record in England, riding more than 100 winners a year there from 1955 until his retirement to become a trainer in 1969. During this time he won the English jockey's premiership four times, in 1957, 1961, 1962, and 1963. Age

top right : Monte Carlo, ridden by Jack Thompson. McQuillan

right : Ron Hutchinson, another Australian jockey to ride successfully in England. McQuillan

far right : Bill Williamson, regular jockey of champion Rising Fast. Unfortunately Williamson missed the winning ride on Rising Fast in the 1954 Melbourne Cup because of an injury. His place was taken by Jack Purtell who was carried to his second consecutive Cup victory, and his third Cup win overall. In 1955 Williamson did ride Rising Fast in the big race, but the 2 to 1 favourite was beaten by Toparoa, ridden by Neville Sellwood. Williamson was another Australian jockey to ride winners in Europe. McQuillan

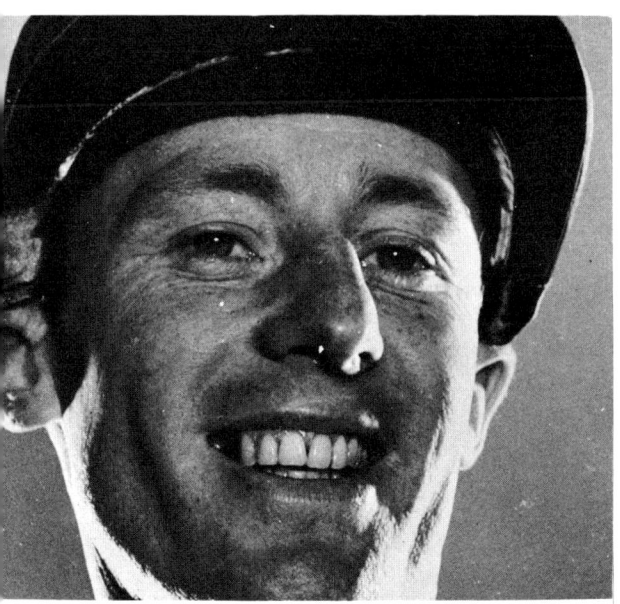

December 1968, by A.J.C. stewards because Jupiter, a horse he trained, had blood on his nostrils after a race and Smith failed to report it. In New South Wales horses which bleed while racing are automatically barred from racing for three months. The numerous owners with horses in Smith's stables all decided to leave them there so they were, in effect, suspended, too, except for a few who temporarily placed horses with other trainers. Three months after the suspension ended Smith made his greatest training coup when his stable won fourteen of the twenty-nine races at the 1969 Randwick Easter carnival. Over the four days Smith reported three of his horses as bleeders.

Most racegoers, awed by Smith's training feats, became fascinated in the late 1960s by a potential challenge to Smith's dominance from Adelaide trainer Bart Cummings. James Batholomew Cummings, born in Adelaide on 14 November 1928, was the devoutly religious son of horse trainer Jim Cummings. He worked first for his father and at twenty-five went out on his own. His father died in 1960 before Bart's big successes. Bart records in a card index system every track gallop, every race start, and spell of all his horses, together with conditions, times, jockeys. He also has a priest bless his stables periodically.

In 1965 Cummings trained Light Fingers and Ziemma, first and second horses in the Melbourne Cup. In 1966 he had first and second again, with Galilee and Light Fingers. And in 1967 he trained his third Cup winner in succession, Red Handed, a training record. Tommy Smith at that time had had only one Cup winner, Toparoa, a poorly-performed gelding on whom he had performed a minor miracle. But Smith had been badly disappointed when Tulloch's owner refused to let him start in the Cup in 1957. In the 1968-1969 season Cummings was premier trainer in both South Australia and Victoria. Compared with Smith's 102 winners in Sydney, Cummings trained fifty-eight winners in Adelaide and thirty-seven and a half in Melbourne.

The introduction early in 1960 of the Totalisator Agency Board—T.A.B.—virtually eliminated illegal S.P. bookmakers in the eastern states. T.A.B. offices were set up in all major centres where the public could

above: A winning team—jockey Roy Higgins and trainer Bart Cummings. Cummings rose to prominence in the racing world late in the 1960s. He was premier trainer for the 1968-69 season in both South Australia and Victoria. His horses won the Melbourne Cup three years in succession in 1965, 1966 and 1967. Age

top right: Light Fingers fights to the last to carry off the 1965 Melbourne Cup from stable mate Ziemma. Bart Cummings trained both horses. Light Fingers was an extremely popular Cup winner. She carried 8 st 4 lb, the highest weight ever carried to victory by a mare in the gruelling race. Herald and Weekly Times

centre right: Red Handed, first past the post in the Melbourne Cup of 1967—a third Cup winner for Bart Cummings, and another victory for jockey Roy Higgins. Herald and Weekly Times

right: Galilee comes in for Bart Cummings in the 1966 Melbourne Cup, with the game little mare, Light Fingers, second. Galilee another New Zealand champion, started favourite, after having won the Caulfield Cup. Herald and Weekly Times

RED WILLIAM · TOBIN BRONZE · PRINCE CAMILLO · PRINCE GRANT · YANGTZE · MIDLANDER · ZIEMA · LIGHT FINGERS

PRINCE CAMILLO · PADTHEWAY · FLOODBIRD · RED HANDED · RED CREST

ROYAL CORAL · TEA BISCUIT · GALA CREST · GATUM GATUM · AVENIAM · DUO · LIGHT FINGERS · GALILEE

bet until a short time before each race. Punters accustomed to betting right up to the start of races were irritated at first by the T.A.B. deadlines but this soon cooled when they realized how much they benefited from the collection of money for the tote pool from outlying centres.

The T.A.B. had a huge turnover almost from the start and state governments returned a percentage to race clubs, greyhound and trotting clubs. This money strengthened all the country's major gambling sports, enabled them to offer more prize money for races and to start planning for the erection of new grandstands and other course amenities. In the year ended 30 June 1970, the New South Wales T.A.B. had a turnover of $242,135,344, an increase of $43,207,842 on the 1969 turnover. T.A.B. officials said that their 'win' tote dividends over 8,633 races held in the year bettered bookmakers' odds by two to one. The breakdown between sport was: horse racing $148,764,788, trotting $37,586,632 and greyhound racing $54,520,408. These figures were typical of those returned in other states.

The T.A.B. payments to race clubs have produced a big increase in the total prize money offered each season, but an enormous proportion of the big stakes has gone to New Zealand-bred horses. In the eighteen years from 1952 to 1969 New Zealand-bred horses won eleven Melbourne Cups, eleven Caulfield Cups, ten Brisbane Cups and seven Sydney Cups. A New Zealand sire, Alcimedes, topped the list in Australia in 1966-1967, largely because his son Galilee won the Sydney, Caulfield and Melbourne Cups. So bigger stakes have not stimulated our breeding industry as expected, but have led to heavier Australian buying of New Zealand horses.

Classy horses have always increased crowds and betting on the Australian turf and this was certainly so in the prosperous 1960s despite the loss overseas of horses like Wiggle, a mare which won $104,994 in the United States. Polo Prince, (1964 Cup winner), Light Fingers (1965), Galilee (1966), and Rain Lover (1968 and 1969) were all splendidly-bred and performed that way. The great Tobin Bronze emerged to run up stake earnings only Tulloch has sur-

above: Betting at Flemington. Ministry of Tourism, Victoria

top right: Money changes hands at Flemington in November 1968. Ministry of Tourism, Victoria.

right: The New Zealand sire Alcimedes, leading sire for the 1966-67 season in Australia. His son Galilee had won the Sydney, Caulfield and Melbourne Cups. Alcimedes, by the great English stayer Alycidon, has got many other good horses, including winners of the A.J.C. Derby and the Queen Elizabeth Stakes. Windsor Photography

far right: Bart Cummings, (right) and jockey Roy Higgins with Red Handed and his proud owner after the 1967 Melbourne Cup. Ministry of Tourism, Victoria.

passed in Australian horse racing history.

Tobin Bronze won $179,171 in Australia, plus $56,199 in America, for a grand total of $235,360, from twenty-eight wins, ten seconds and six thirds in sixty starts. Pago Pago won the 1963 Golden Slipper Stakes with a superlative show of speed, and not long afterwards was sold to America for $178,490. Winfreux won twenty-seven races and $144,566.

Vain, the Victorian two-year-old champion of the 1968-1969 season, in seven starts won $84,495, more than twice as much as any colt of his age had won before in Australia and a notable example of how T.A.B. kickbacks to race clubs had helped rewrite the record books. Vain was by Wilkes, who took over from Star Kingdom as our top sprint sire. When Vain went to stud in 1970 he was given forty-one mares in his first season at an Australian record fee of $2,500 a time.

Outstanding horses provided ideal betting mediums for Australians and Asians who had become rich in the Far East business boom and for Australians who had prospered from local mining deals. The lure of owning a champion also proved strong and three buying teams rewrote the record books. Mr and Mrs Stan Fox, of Sydney, the Asian syndicate headed by Filipino Filipe Ysmael, and the 'Fabulous Foysters', J.B., J.A. and Lloyd Foyster, New South Wales farmers who had sold their beach sand mining interests for $13,000,000, bid against each other to set new price standards. The Foysters paid $39,000 for the Wilkes colt High Sierra and $38,000 for the Agricola colt Right Make Up.

In the four-day 1966 Melbourne Cup carnival bookmaker Bill Waterhouse had a total of $1,300,000 bet with him, only $500,000 less than the total bet on the course tote. On Oaks day in that meeting Frank Duval, an Australian known as the 'Hong Kong Tiger' because he drew his wealth from Hong Kong business successes, had these bets with Waterhouse: $100,000 to $20,000, $90,000 to $20,000 and $100,000 to $25,000 What Fun in the Oaks Stakes. It was second to Farmer's Daughter; $70,000 to $40,000 and $65,000 to $40,000 Bastille in the Raymond Stakes—it was second to Lord Palford in a photo-finish: $10,000 to

top : Amarco, the dam of the great Tobin Bronze, another New Zealand-bred champion to carry off huge stakes in Australia before being sold to America. Windsor Photography

above : E.J. Didham, top New Zealand jockey for the 1969-70 season, and rider of Baghdad Note, winner of the 1970 Melbourne Cup. Windsor Photography

top right : Champion mare Wiggle has a preliminary canter with jockey W. Camer. Wiggle was to be sold to owners in the United States of America where she won $104,994. McQuillan

right : The mighty Tobin Bronze, whose stake earnings were exceeded only by Tulloch's in Australia. He also raced in America, adding $56,199 to his Australian $179,171. From sixty starts, Tobin Bronze gained twenty-eight wins, ten seconds and six third. Age

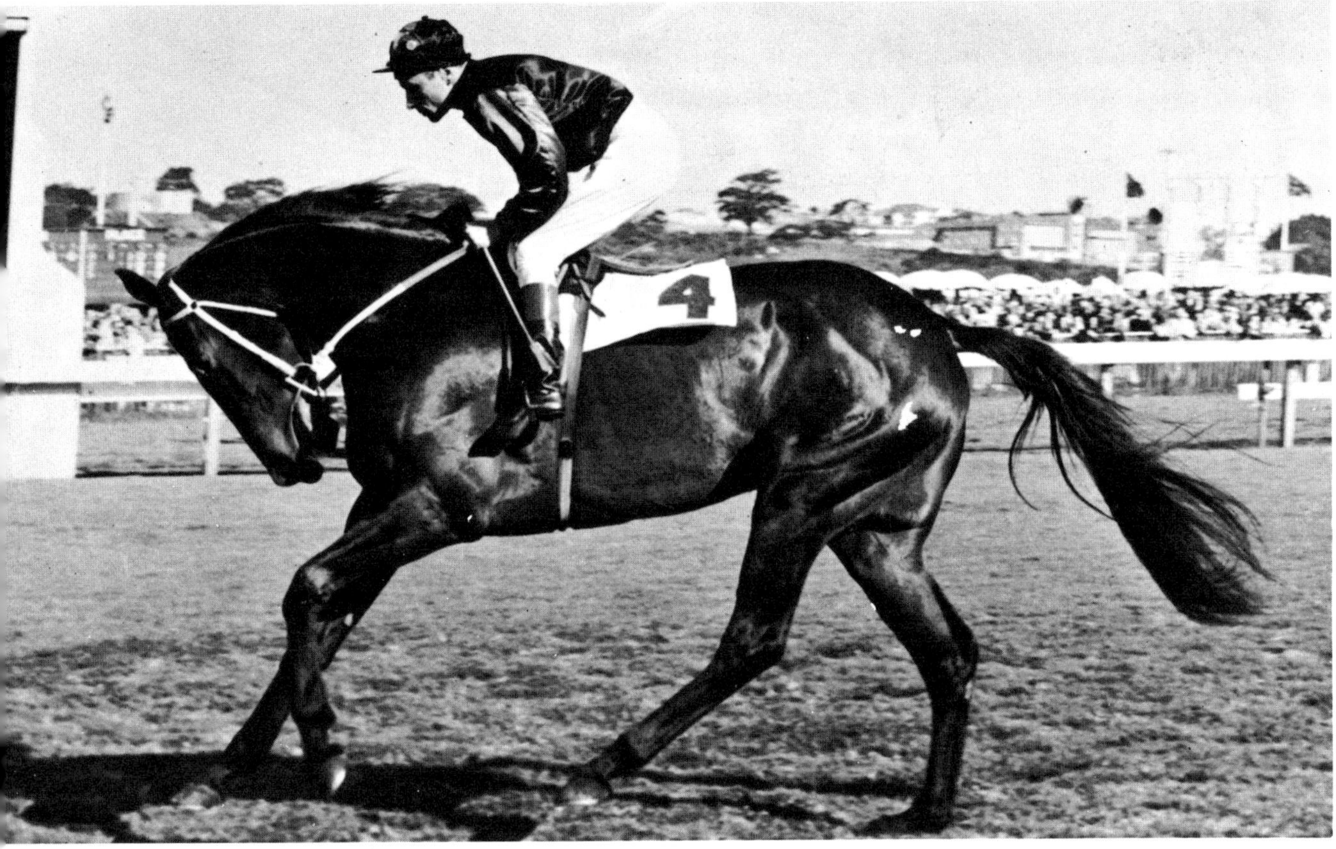

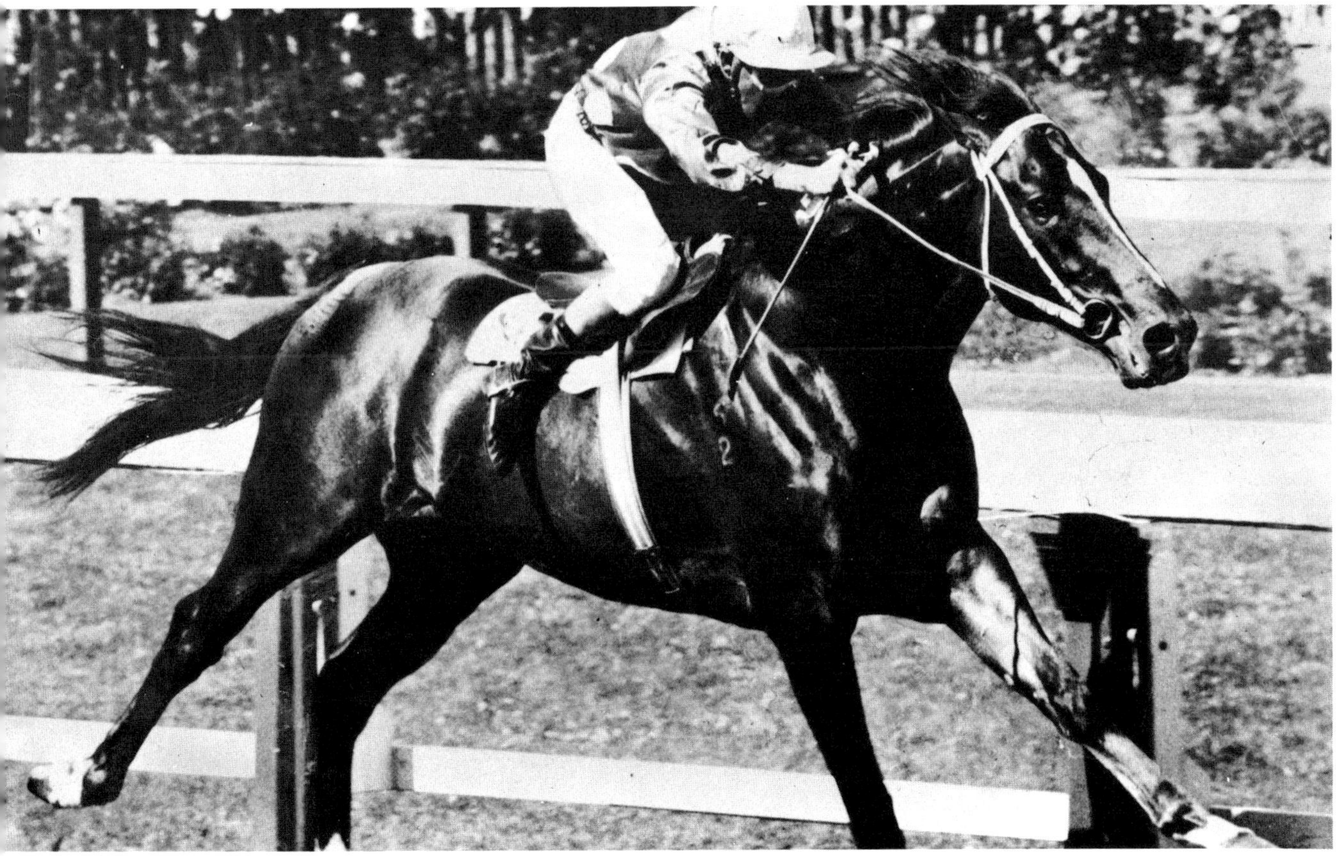

$4,000 on Pharaon in the Batman Stakes—second in a photo-finish. (In this case he had meant to call $100,000 to $40,000 on, and was very relieved after the race to learn of his mistake.)

Waterhouse's willingness to take big bets brought him national notoriety. Even at a country meeting in Wagga his duels with Duval were headline news. On Caulfield Guineas day, 1967, Waterhouse held $500,000 in bets to then the biggest sum for a single day taken by an Australian bookmaker. One of Waterhouse's bets that day was $100,000 to $90,000 on Tobin Bronze, which won, with Filipe Ysmael.

Ysmael invested a fortune buying horses to race in Australia and he backed them with big money. But in December 1968, it all ended when the V.R.C. stewards disqualified Ysmael, his trainer Charlie Waymouth and jockey George Hope after Ysmael's horse Follow Me had been beaten in the Hollymount Handicap for two-year-olds at Moonee Valley. Follow Me had opened at odds-on in the betting but drifted to 6 to 4 against. Follow Me finished eleventh in a race won by High Calibre, also owned by the Asian Syndicate with which Ysmael was associated.

All the disqualified parties appealed but after a long hearing on 13 February 1969, the appeals were dismissed. Evidence was given at the hearing that a commissioner who usually acted for the Ysmael string had put $21,600 on Dalthing, which had brought the price of this horse in from 9 to 4 to evens. The commissioner said he was acting for a Sydney trainer. Ysmael subsequently offered his horses at auction but despite some very high bids all were refused. The biggest bid ever made at auction for a horse in Australia —$250,000 for Derby winner Always There—was turned down, as the reserve price was $400,000.

A further example of the strict control of our racing by clubs and their stipendary stewards came in September 1969, when the A.J.C. disqualified jockey Sammy Mezzasalma, the cousins Joe and Len Pegano and Spero Arris for life. Their disqualifications

*right: A thrilling close-up of a race at Randwick.
A.J.C.*

296

followed the impounding of a battery saddle at Rosehill when Mezzasalma rode Smashing Blonde in a training workout. The battery was of the type that could be remote-controlled by someone off the course.

Two months after these disqualifications Big Philou, backed for a fortune in the Melbourne Cup, had to be withdrawn thirty-eight minutes before the race. He was found in his stall scouring excessively. His trainer Bart Cummings sent for a vet and when he arrived Big Philou could not hold up his head. Stewards said Big Philou had been given a purgative by persons who had apparently intended the 'dope' concerned to work during the race. The mayhem that has characterized Australian racing history was not over, it seemed.

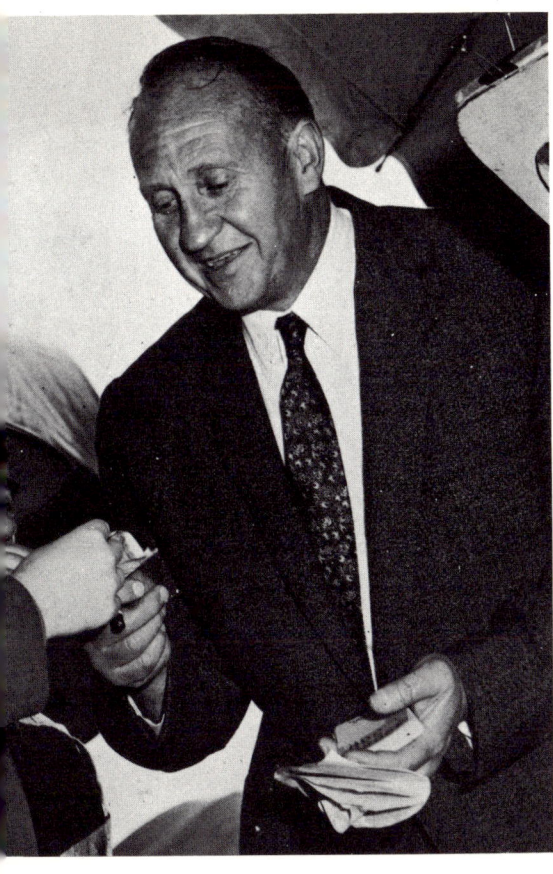

far right : *A muddy Noel McCrowdie is weighed on the jockey scale after a hard race.* McQuillan

top left, above : *Bookmakers take bets, from big and small punters alike. Australia is still a country of gamblers, and the introduction of the T.A.B. in early 1960 enabled many to enjoy themselves without having to visit the course or take their chances with illegal off-the-course bookmakers.* McQuillan

left : *Mr Filipe Ysmael and family enjoy the races at Caulfield during the 1960s. Mr Ysmael invested huge amounts of money in Australian horse racing—buying horses to race and betting on them substantially—but in 1968 he was disqualified from operating on Australian courses.* Age

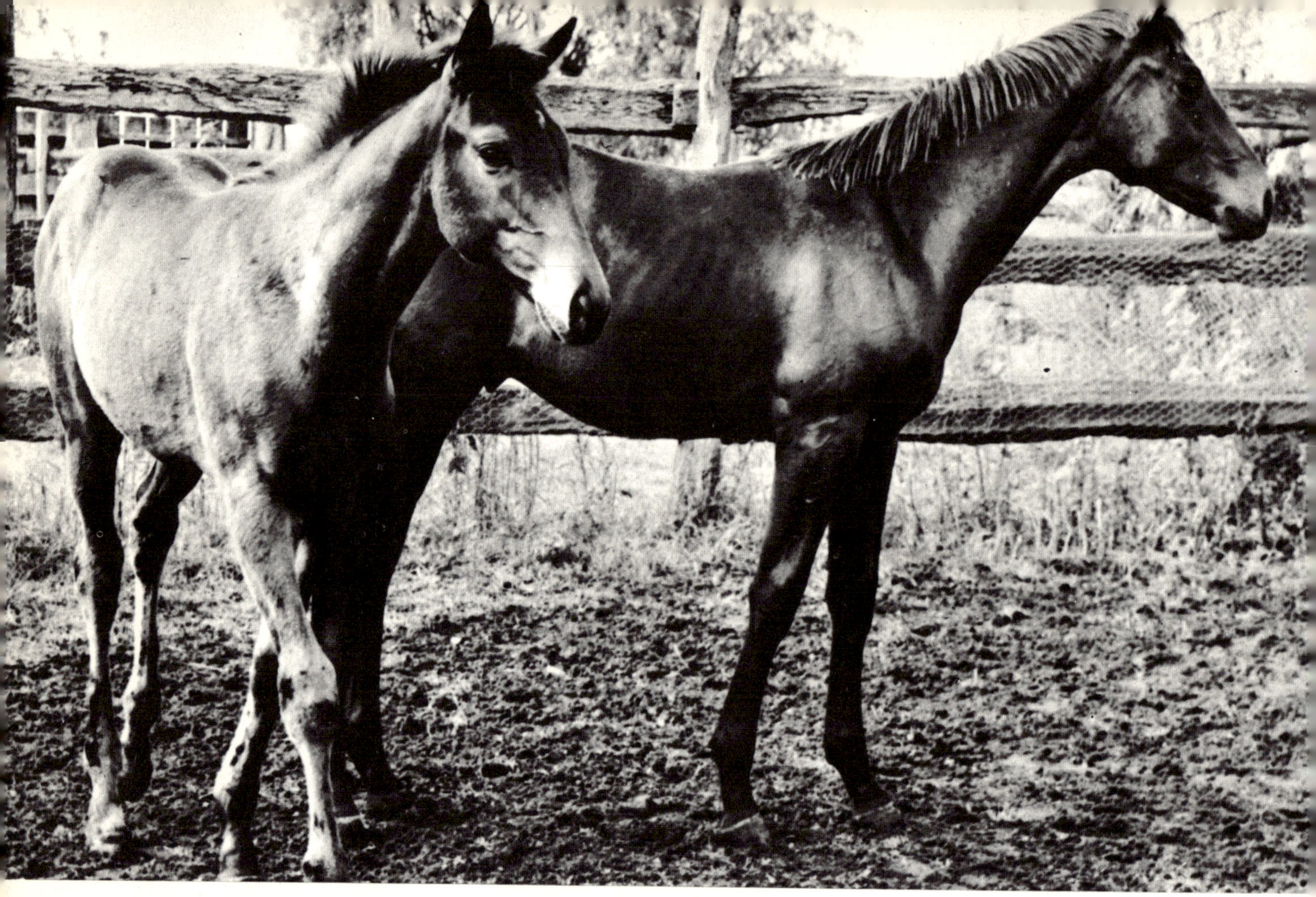

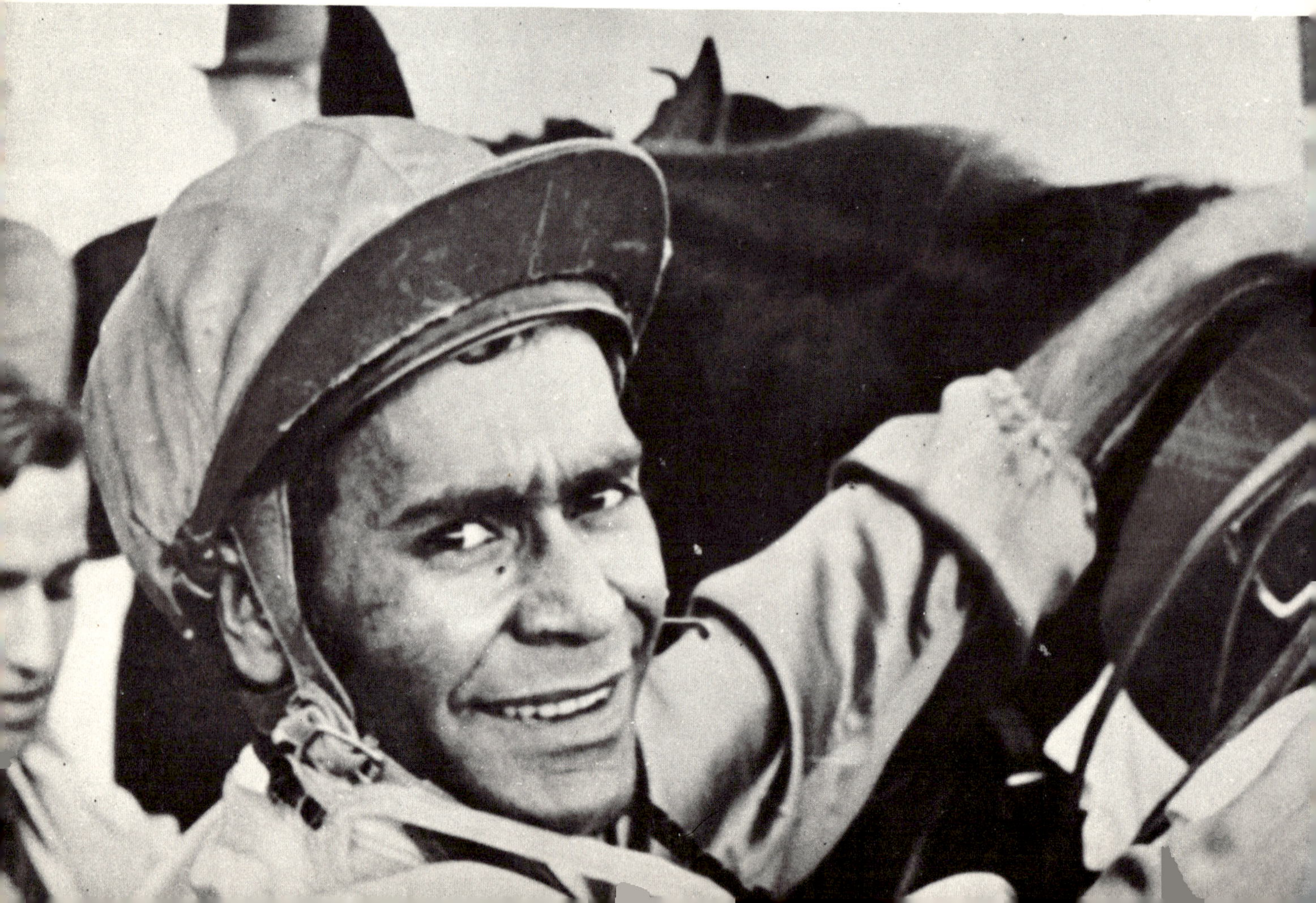

top left : Tulloch's first colts at Scone, New South Wales. Before his retirement to stud, Tulloch ran in fifty-three races, winning thirty-six. He also gained twelve seconds and four thirds, being unplaced only once—in the 1960 Melbourne Cup carrying 10 st 1 lb. McQuillan

left : Australia's first Aboriginal jockey, Darby McCarthy, has been riding successfully for several years.

top right : Darby McCarthy wins at Randwick on Broker's Tip, a horse with which he formed a successful partnership.

right : Rain Lover enjoys a drink of water at his stables. In 1968 he showed himself to be a true champion, winning the Melbourne Cup by eight lengths, setting a new record of 3 min 19·1 sec, and in 1969 he became the first horse since Archer to take two successive Cups.

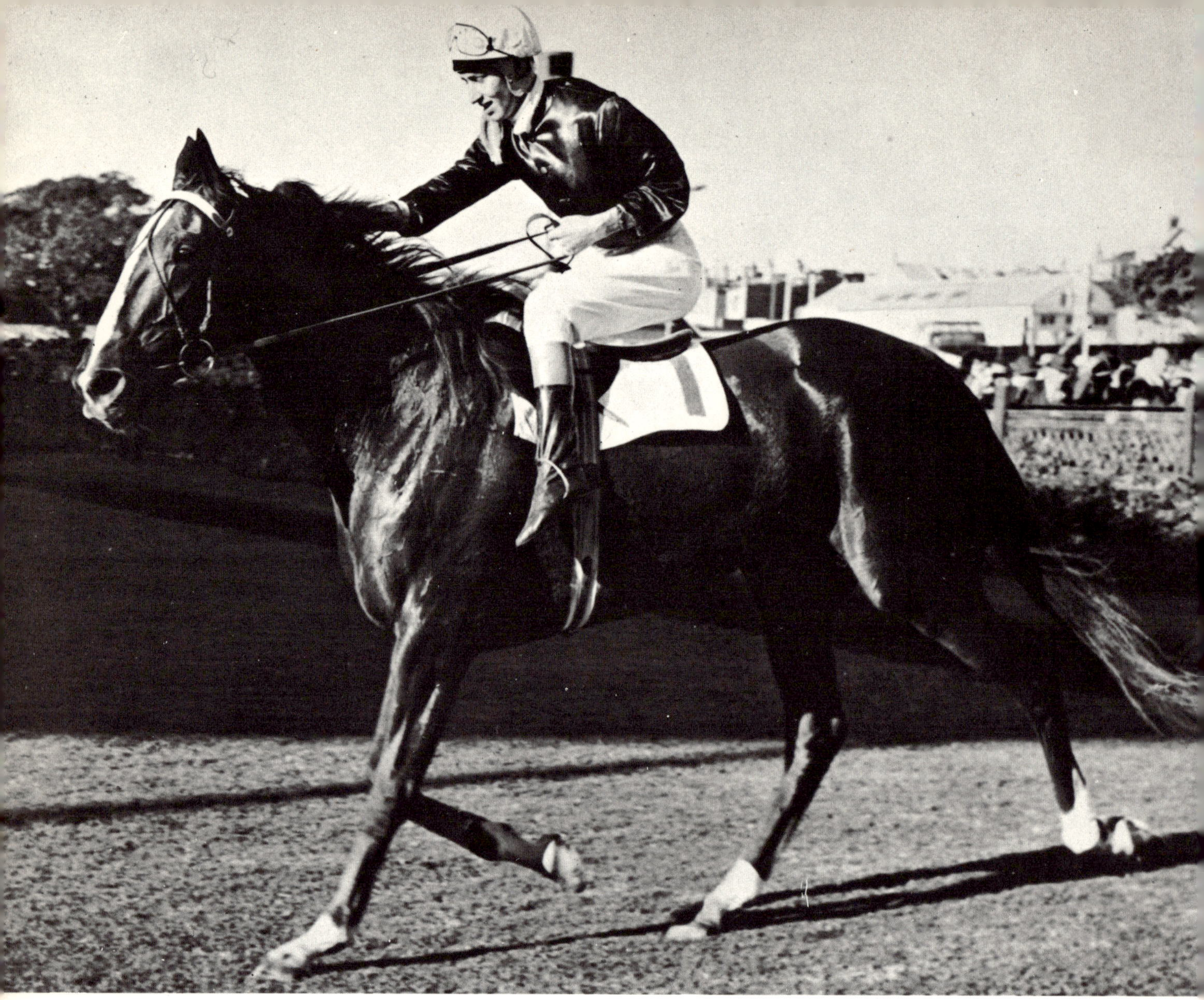

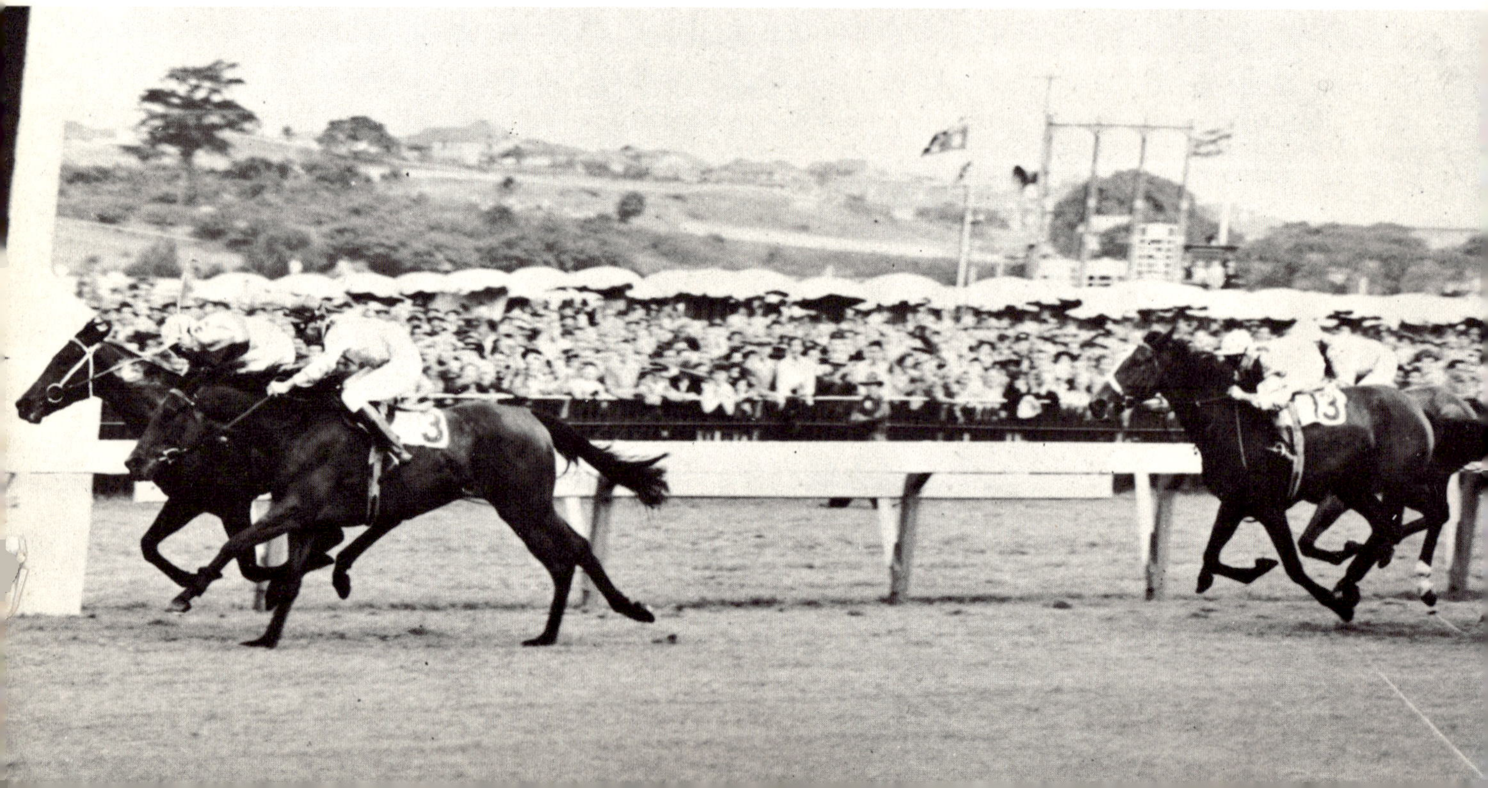

3
13

top left : Roy Higgins on Indian Summer. Higgins is perhaps best known for his association with trainer Bart Cummings. He rode Cummings' mare Light Fingers to victory in the 1965 Melbourne Cup and to second place in the following year, and in the 1967 Cup race, he again scored first place with Cummings' Handed. *McQuillan*

left : Sailor's Guide wins the Sydney Cup in 1956, carrying 8 st 2 lb. He ran the one and a half miles in 3 min 30·6 sec. This champion horse was later sent to America where he won $104,088, giving him a total of £66,044 in stake winnings. *McQuillan*

above : George Moore returns to scale after another win at Randwick. His success in riding heavily-backed horses to victory has earned him the confidence of punters. *McQuillan*

right : The trophy for the first Queen Elizabeth Stakes, held in 1954 during a royal visit. This weight-for-age race is run annually over one and three-quarter miles at Randwick. Famous winners include Prince Cortauld, Sailor's Guide and Tulloch. *A.J.C.*

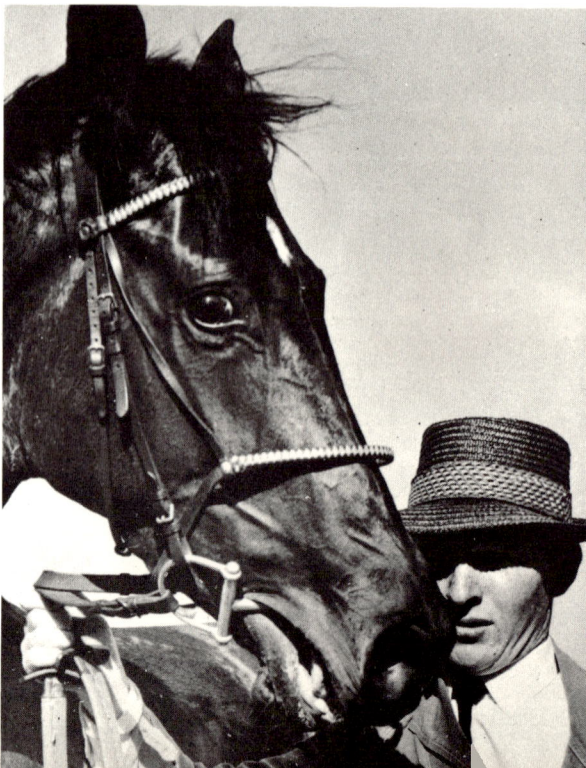

top left: Blue Era, at the A.J.C. Derby. McQuillan

far left: Noel McGrowdie proudly displays the Melbourne Cup won by Straight Draw. McQuillan

left: Summer Fair, the horse which won on protest after the 1961 A.J.C. Derby in which Blue Era, ridden by Mel Schumacher, had been first past the post. McQuillan

above: Neville Sellwood on Knave, winner of the 1956 A.J.C. Epsom Handicap. The great jcokey was killed on 7 November 1962 in a fall while attempting to clinch the French Jockey's premiership which he was leading with 102 winners. McQuillan

right: Wenona Girl, another champion mare to thrill Melbourne racegoers, carrying on the tradition of great heart demonstrated by winning mares such as Wakeful, Gladsome, Flight, Tranquil Star and Light Fingers. McQuillan

top left : Lunch in the car park on Melbourne Cup day 1967. *Ministry of Tourism, Victoria*

left : Melbourne Cup Day, 1968, and a pipe band adds to the excitement. Ministry of Tourism, Victoria

above : People stream from the special Melbourne Cup train on the first Tuesday in November 1968. *Ministry of Tourism, Victoria*

307

THE MELBOURNE CUP—1861 to 1970

Year	Winner	Age	Rider	Weight	S/P	Strs	Time	Won by	Second Horse	Third Horse
1861	Archer	5	J. Cutts	9.7	6/1	17	3.52	6 lth	Mormon	Prince
1862	Archer	6	J. Cutts	10.2	2/1	20	3.47	10 lth	Mormon	Camden
1863	Banker	3	H. Chigney	5.4	10/1	23	3.44	2 lth	Musidora	Rose of Denmark
1864	Lantern	3	S. Davis	6.3	10/1	23	3.55	½ lth	Poet	Rose of Denmark
1865	Tory Boy	a	E. Kavanagh	7.0	20/1	28	3.44	4 lth	Panic	Riverina
1866	The Barb	3	W. Davis	6.11	6/1	28	3.43	Head	Exile	Falcon
1867	Tim Whiffler	5	I. Driscoll	8.11	5/2	25	3.39	2 lth	Queen of Hearts	Exile
1868	Glencoe	4	C. Stanley	9.1	10/1	24	3.42	lth	Strop	Shenandoah
1869	Warrior	6	J. Morrison	8.10	10/1	26	3.40	2 lth	The Monk	Phoebe
1870	Nimblefoot	a	J. Day	6.3	12/1	28	3.37	½ hd.	Lapdog	Valentine
1871	The Pearl	5	J. T. Kavanagh	7.3	100/1	22	3.39	2 lth	Romula	Irish King
1872	The Quack	6	W. Enderson	7.10	5/1	24	3.39	4 lth	The Ace	Dagworth
1873	Don Juan	4	W. Wilson	6.12	3/1	24	3.36½	2 lth	Dagworth	Horatio
1874	Haricot	4	P. Piggott	6.7	16/1	20	3.37	½ hd	Protos	The Diver
1875	Wollomai	6	R. Batty	7.8	16/1	20	3.38	2½ lth	Richmond	Goldsbrough
1876	Briseis	3	P. St Albans	6.4	7/1	33	3.36	2 lth	Sybil	Timothy
1877	Chester	3	P. Piggott	6.12	5/1	33	3.33½	Head	Savanake	The Vagabond
1878	Calamia	5	T. Brown	8.2	10/1	27	3.35¾	¾ lth	Tom Kirk	Waxy
1879	Darriwell	5	S. Cracknell	7.4	33/1	27	3.30¾	½ lth	Sweetmeat	Suwarrow
1880	Grand Flaneur	3	T. Hales	6.10	4/1	22	3.34¾	lth	Progress	Lord Burghley
1881	Zulu	4	J. Gough	5.10	50/1	33	3.32½	½ lth	The Czar	Sweetmeat
1882	The Assyrian	5	C. Hutchins	7.13	33/1	25	3.40	½ lth	Stockwell	Gudarz
1883	Martini Henri	3	J. Williamson	7.5	5/1	29	3.30½	1½ lth	First Water	Commotion
1884	Malua	5	A. Robertson	9.9	7/1	24	3.31¾	½ lth	Commotion	Plausible
1885	Sheet Anchor	a	M. O'Brien	7.11	20/1	35	3.29½	Head	Grace Darling	Trenton
1886	Arsenal	4	W. English	7.5	5/1	28	3.31	Neck	Trenton	Silvermine
1887	Dunlop	5	T. Sanders	8.3	20/1	18	3.28½	lth	Silvermine	The Australian Peer
1888	Mentor	4	M. O'Brien	8.3	7/1	28	3.30¾	1½ lth	Tradition	The Yeoman
1889	Bravo	6	J. Anwin	8.7	8/1	20	3.32½	lth	Carbine	Melos
1890	Carbine	5	R. Ramage	10.5	4/1	39	3.28¼	2½ lth	Highborn	Correze
1891	Malvolio	4	G. Redfearn	8.4	16/1	34	3.29¼	¾ lth	Sir William	Strathmore
1892	Glenloth	5	G. Robson	7.13	50/1	35	3.36¼	3 lth	Ronda	Penance
1893	Tarcoola	a	H. Cripps	8.4	40/1	30	3.30½	½ lth	Carnage	Jeweller
1894	Patron	4	H. G. Dawes	9.3	33/1	28	3.31	¾ lth	Devon	Nada
1895	Auraria	3	J. Stevenson	7.4	33/1	36	3.29	Neck	Hova	Burrabari
1896	Newhaven	3	H. Gardiner	7.13	4/1	25	3.28½	6 lth	Bloodshot	The Skipper
1897	Gaulus	6	S. Callinan	7.8	14/1	29	3.31	½ hd	The Grafter	Aurum
1898	The Grafter	5	John Gough	9.2	8/1	28	3.29¾	½ neck	Wait-a-Bit	Cocos
1899	Meriwee	3	V. Turner	7.6	7/1	28	3.36¼	lth	Voyou	Dewey
1900	Clean Sweep	3	R. Richardson	7.0	20/1	29	3.29	1½ lth	Malster	Alix
1901	Revenue	5	F. Dunn	7.10	7/4	19	3.30½	½ lth	San Fran	Khaki
1902	The Victory	4	R. Lewis	8.12	25/1	22	3.29	Neck	Vanity Fair	Abundance
1903	Lord Cardigan	3	N. Godby	6.8	5/1	24	3.29¼	¾ lth	Wakeful	Seaport
1904	Acrasia	a	T. Clayton	7.6	14/1	34	3.28¼	¾ lth	Lord Cardigan	Blinker
1905	Blue Spec	6	F. Bullock	8.0	10/1	27	3.27¼	¾ lth	Scot Free	Tartan
1906	Poseidon	3	T. Clayton	7.6	4/1	21	3.31½	1½ lth	Antonius	Proceed
1907	Apologue	5	W. Evans	7.9	3/1	19	3.27½	¾ lth	Mooltan	Mountain King
1908	Lord Nolan	3	J. R. Flynn	6.10	16/1	22	3.28¾	½ hd	Tulkeroo	Delaware
1909	Prince Foote	3	W. H. McLachlan	7.8	4/1	26	3.27½	3 lth	Alawa	Aberdeen
1910	Comedy King	4	W. H. McLachlan	7.11	10/1	30	3.27¾	½ neck	Trafalgar	Apple Pie
1911	The Parisian	6	R. Cameron	8.9	5/1	33	3.27¾	2 lth	Flavian	Didus
1912	Piastre	4	A. Shanahan	7.9	7/1	23	3.27½	1½ lth	Hallowmas	Uncle Sam
1913	Posinatus	5	A. Shanahan	7.10	15/1	20	3.31	¾ lth	Belove	Ulva's Isle
1914	Kingsburgh	4	G. Meddick	6.12	20/1	28	3.26	Neck	Sir Alwynton	Moonbria
1915	Patrobus	3	R. Lewis	7.6	8/1	24	3.28½	½ neck	Westcourt	Carlita
1916	Sasanof	3	F. Foley	6.12	12/1	28	3.27¾	2½ lth	Shepherd King	St Spasa
1917	Westcourt	5	W. H. McLachlan	8.5	4/1	20	3.26¾	sht ½ hd	Lingle	Wallace Isinglass

THE MELBOURNE CUP—1861 to 1970

Year	Winner	Age	Rider	Weight	S/P	Strs	Time	Won by	Second Horse	Third Horse
1918	Nightwatch	5	W. Duncan	6.9	12/1	27	$3.25\frac{3}{4}$	$\frac{1}{2}$ lth	Kennaquair	Gadabout
1919	Artilleryman	3	R. Lewis	7.6	10/1	20	$3.24\frac{1}{4}$	6 lth	Richmond Main	Two Blues
1920	Poitrel	6	K. Bracken	10.0	8/1	23	$3.25\frac{3}{4}$	$\frac{1}{2}$ lth	Erasmus	Queen Comedy
1921	Sister Olive	3	E. O'Sullivan	6.9	16/1	25	$3.27\frac{3}{4}$	$\frac{3}{4}$ lth	The Rover	Amazonia
1922	King Ingoda	4	A. Wilson	7.1	8/1	32	$3.28\frac{1}{4}$	$\frac{1}{2}$ lth	The Cypher	Mufti
1923	Bitalli	5	A. Wilson	7.0	4/1	26	$3.24\frac{1}{4}$	$\frac{3}{4}$ lth	Rivoli	Accarak
1924	Blackwood	6	P. Brown	8.2	8/1	18	$3.26\frac{1}{2}$	Head	Manfred	Spearfelt
1925	Windbag	4	J. Munro	9.2	5/1	28	$3.22\frac{3}{4}$	$\frac{1}{2}$ lth	Naos	Pilliewinkie
1926	Spearfelt	5	H. Cains	9.3	10/1	21	$3.22\frac{3}{4}$	$\frac{1}{2}$ lth	Stand By	Pantheon
1927	Trivalve	3	R. Lewis	7.6	6/1	26	3.24	lth	Silvius	Son o' Mine
1928	Statesman	4	J. Munro	8.0	7/2	17	$3.23\frac{1}{2}$	4 lth	Strephon	Demost
1929	Nightmarch	4	R. Reed	9.2	6/1	14	$3.26\frac{1}{2}$	3 lth	Paquito	Phar Lap
1930	Phar Lap	4	J. E. Pike	9.12	8/11	15	$3.27\frac{3}{4}$	3 lth	Second Wind	Shadow King
1931	White Nose	5	N. Percival	6.12	8/1	14	3.26	2 lth	Shadow King	Concentrate
1932	Peter Pan	3	W. Duncan	7.6	4/1	27	$3.23\frac{1}{4}$	Neck	Yarramba	Shadow King
1933	Hall Mark	3	J. O'Sullivan	7.8	4/1	18	$3.27\frac{1}{4}$	Head	Shadow King	Topical & Gaine Carrington
1934	Peter Pan	5	D. Munro	9.10	14/1	22	$3.40\frac{1}{2}$	3 lth	Sarcherie	La Trobe
1935	Marabou	4	K. Voitre	7.11	9/2	22	$3.23\frac{3}{4}$	$2\frac{1}{2}$ lth	Sarcherie	Sylvandale
1936	Wotan	4	O. Philips	7.11	100/1	20	$3.21\frac{1}{4}$	Neck	Silver Standard	Balkan Prince
1937	The Trump	5	A. Reed	8.5	11/2	28	$3.21\frac{1}{2}$	$\frac{1}{2}$ lth	Willie Win	Sarcherie
1938	Catalogue	a	F. Shean	8.4	25/1	22	$3.26\frac{1}{4}$	3 lth	Bourbon	Ortelle's Star
1939	Rivette	6	E. Preston	7.9	5/1	26	3.27	$\frac{1}{2}$ lth	Maikai	Pantler
1940	Old Rowley	a	A. Knox	7.12	100/1	20	3.26	$\frac{3}{4}$ lth	Maikai	Tidal Wave
1941	Skipton	3	W. Cook	7.7	8/1	23	$3.23\frac{3}{4}$	$2\frac{1}{2}$ lth	Son of Auros	Beau Vite
1942	Colonus	4	H. McCloud	7.2	33/1	24	$3.33\frac{1}{4}$	7 lth	Phocion	Heart's Desire
1943	Dark Felt	6	V. Hartney	8.4	7/2	24	$3.23\frac{1}{4}$	3 lth	Counsel	Claudette
1944	Sirius	4	D. Munro	8.5	3/1	23	$3.24\frac{1}{2}$	$\frac{1}{2}$ lth	Peter	Cellini
1945	Rainbird	4	W. Cook	7.7	12/1	26	$3.24\frac{1}{4}$	$2\frac{1}{2}$ lth	Silver Link	Leonard
1946	Russia	6	D. Munro	9.0	16/1	35	$3.21\frac{1}{4}$	5 lth	On Target	Carey
1947	Hiraji	4	J. Purtell	7.11	12/1	30	3.28	$\frac{1}{2}$ lth	Fresh Boy	Red Fury
1948	Rimfire	6	R. Neville	7.2	66/1	30	3.21	$\frac{1}{2}$ hd.	Dark Marne	Saxony
1949	Foxzami	4	W. Fellows	8.8	16/1	31	$3.28\frac{1}{2}$	$1\frac{1}{2}$ lth	Hoyle	Benvolo
1950	Comic Court	5	P. Glennon	9.5	25/1	26	$3.19\frac{1}{2}$	3 lth	Chicquita	Morse Code
1951	Delta	5	N. Sellwood	9.5	10/1	28	$3.24\frac{1}{4}$	$\frac{3}{4}$ lth	Akbar	Double Blank
1952	Dalray	4	W. Williamson	9.8	5/1f	30	$3.23\frac{3}{4}$	$\frac{1}{2}$ lth	Welkin Sun	Reformed
1953	Wodalla	4	J. Purtell	8.4	14/1	21	$3.23\frac{3}{4}$	$\frac{1}{2}$ lth	Most Regal	My Hero
1954	Rising Fast	5	J. Purtell	9.5	5/2f	25	3.23	$1\frac{1}{4}$ lth	Hellion	Gay Helios
1955	Toparoa	a	N. Sellwood	7.8	6/1	24	$3.28\frac{1}{4}$	$\frac{3}{4}$ lth	Rising Fast	Sir William
1956	Evening Peal	4	G. Podmore	8.0	15/1	22	$3.19\frac{1}{2}$	$\frac{1}{2}$ nk	Redcraze	Caranna
1957	Straight Draw	5	N. McGrowdie	8.5	13/1	19	$3.24\frac{1}{2}$	Neck	Prince Darius	Pandie Sun
1958	Baystone	6	M. Schumacher	8.9	10/1	29	$3.21\frac{1}{4}$	$1\frac{1}{2}$ lth	Monte Carlo	Red Pine
1959	Macdougal	6	P. Glennon	8.11	8/1	28	3.23	3 lth	Nethergold	White Hills
1960	Hi Jinx	5	W. A. Smith	7.10	50/1	32	$3.23\frac{3}{4}$	$\frac{1}{2}$ nk	Howsie	Ilumquh
1961	Lord Fury	4	N. Selkrig	7.8	20/1	25	$3.19\frac{1}{2}$	$1\frac{1}{2}$ lth	Grand Print	Dhaulagiri
1962	Even Stevens	5	L. Coles	8.5	3/1f	26	$3.21\frac{2}{3}$	4 lth	Comicquita	Aquanita
1963	Gatum Gatum	5	L. Johnson	7.12	25/1	26	$3.21\frac{1}{10}$	1 lth	Ilumquh	Grand Print
1964	Polo Prince	6	R. Taylor	8.3	12/1	26	$3.19\frac{3}{4}$	$1\frac{1}{4}$ lth	Elkayel	Welltown
1965	Light Fingers	4	R. Higgins	8.4	15/1	26	$3.21\frac{1}{10}$	$\frac{1}{2}$ hd	Ziema	Midlander
1966	Galilee	4	J. Miller	8.13	11/2	22	3.21.9	2 lth	Light Fingers	Duo
1967	Red Handed	5	R. Higgins	8.9	4/1	22	3.20.4	Neck	Red Crest	Floodbird
1968	Rain Lover	4	J. Johnson	8.2	7/1	26	3.19.1*	8 lth	Fileur	Fans
1969	Rain Lover	5	J. Johnson	9.7	8/1	23	3.21.5	Head	Alsop	Ben Lomond
1970	Baghdad Note	5	E. Didham	8.7	25/1	23	3.19.7	$\frac{3}{4}$ lth	Vansittart	Clear Prince

SYDNEY CUP, (2 M.)
(Run at Randwick, Easter Carnival)

Year	Winner	Wgt.	Rider	Trainer	Sire	Second Horse	Third Horse	Time
1916	Prince Bardolph	7.3	G. Meddick	—	Bardolph	Green Cap	Scoutmaster	3.24¾
1917	The Fortune Hunter	8.6	A. Wood	—	Flavus	Harriet Graham	Court Jester	3.26
1918	Rebus	7.12	C. O. Davies	—	Radium	Shadowland	Lanius	3.26¼
1919	Ian 'Or	6.10	T. F. McNamara	—	Martagon	Night Watch	Arch Marella	3.31½
1920	Kennaquhair	9.5	A. Wood	—	Kenilworth	Poitrel	Millienne	3.22¾
1921	Eurythmic	9.8	F. Dempsey	J. Holt	Eudorus	Arch Marella	Amazonia	3.24¾
1922	Prince Charles	7.11	J. Munro	S. R. Lamond	Prince Foote	Kashmir	Stare	3.26¼
1923	David	9.7	A. Wood	W. Booth	Baverstock	Heir Apparent	Shillinglee	3.26½
1924	Scarlet	7.6	J. Crowe	—	Bright Steel	Stony	King of the Forest	3.28¼
1925	Lilypond	9.0	W. Duncan	—	Lilyveil	Windbag	Solidify	3.26¾
1926	Murray King	7.2	S. McNamara	G. Price	Comedy King	Caserta	Naos	3.26
1927	Plastoon	7.12	S. Davidson	E. Fisher	Piastre	Limerick	Tibble	3.33¾
1928	Winalot	8.2	J. Toohey	J. W. Cook	Rossendale	Tangible	Strongbow	3.32¼
1929	Crucis	7.5	W. Cook	D. Lewis	Satelles	Paddi Eve	Kidaldes	3.23¼
1930	Gwillian G.	7.0	J. Simpson	W. A. Ross	Colugo	Royal Smile	Soulton	3.23½
1931	The Dimmer	7.12	E. Bartle	C. P. Barden	Spearhead	Alcman	Donald	3.35¼
1932	Johnnie Jason	8.4	R. Wilson	C. Unwin	Treclare	Admiral Drake	Vellmond	3.32
1933	Rogilla	8.10	G. Robinson	L. Haigh	Roger de Busli	Nord	Gippsland	3.23
1934	Broad Arrow	7.1	E. Britt	W. McGee	Treclare	Gippsland	Limarch	3.28
1935	Akuna	7.0	H. Hanley	D. Lewis	Archery	Dark Chief	Sylvandale	3.27¾
1936	Contact	8.4	M. McCarten	D. Lewis	Marconigram	Egmont	Spear Prince	3.24¾
1937	Mestoravon	7.13	J. Duncan	R. L. Cashman	Polymestor	Sir Ross	Oro	3.21¾
1938	L'Aiglon	6.8	A. Harvey	D. Lewis	The Buzzard	Apollo	Young Crusader	3.23
1939	Mosaic	8.2	E. Bartle	J. H. Abbs	Posterity	L'Aiglon	Malagigi	3.21½
1940	Mosaic	9.1	D. Munro	J. H. Abbs	Posterity	Royal Chief	Maikai	3.25½
1941	Lucrative	8.2	M. McCarten	P. H. Fr'dm'n	Gay Lothario	Hope	Pandect	3.20¾
1942	Veiled Threat	8.1	R. Parsons	J. M. Mitchell	Veilmond	Velocity	Beau Vite	3.25½
1943	Abspear	8.9	D. Munro	E. Hush	Spearfelt	Wellesley	Moondarewa	3.26
1944	Veiled Threat	8.13	D. Munro	J. M. Mitchell	Veilmond	Mayfowl	Grand Fils	3.27
1945	Craigie	8.4	J. Duncan	G. Douch	Chatham	Russia	Flight	3.25½
1946	Cordale	7.7	G. Moore	G. Ray	Conspirator	Swan River	Russia	3.28½
1947	Proctor	7.10	W. Briscoe	D. Lewis	Actor	Rainbird	Spam	3.27½
1948	Dark Marne	8.3	J. Thompson	D. L. Burke	The Marne	Columnist	Lungi	3.26¼
1949	Carbon Copy	8.5	A. Breasley	D.S. McCormick	Helios	Vagabond	Benvolo	3.23½
1950	Sir Falcon	7.13	J. Thompson	J. Mitchell	The Buzzard	Hurry Up	Hoyle	3.26¾
1951	Bankstream	7.0	N. McGrowdie	V. Thompson	Midstream	Freedom	Comic Count	3.22
1952	Opulent	7.1	N. McGrowdie	J. L. Munro	Beau Son	Dalray	Taressa	3.37¼
1953	Carioca	8.9	W. Cook	P. C. Hoysted	Felt Yet	Advocate	Friendly	3.22½
1954	Gold Scheme	8.7	N. Sellwood	L. J. Ellis	Golden Souvenir	Double Blank	Priory	3.21¾
1955	Talisman	7.4	S. Cassidy	C. B. Hasler	Midstream	Finito	Beaupa	3.29½
1956	Sailor's Guide	8.2	N. Sellwood	G. Daniel	Lighthouse II	Beaupa	Miss High Caste	3.30.4
1957	Electro	8.8	D. Weir	J. A. Haigh	Delville Wood	Aqua Boy	Sombrero	3.22.4
1958	Straight Draw	8.13	N. McGrowdie	J. M. Mitchell	Faux Tirage	Caranna	Rushover	3.22
1959	On Line	7.13	B. Howlett	F. McGrath	Chateau Roussel	Foxmara	Bardshar	* 3.10.9
1960	Grand Garry	8.8	N. Sellwood	T. J. Smith	Dairay	Valerius	Melray	3.20.7
1961	Sharply	7.9	B. Howlett	W. J. Elliott	Edwards II	Tulloch	Rimyll	3.24.9
1962	Grand Print	8.8	R. Higgins	J. Besanko	Carbon Copy	River Seine	Dhaulagiri	3.35.7
1963	Maidenhead	7.4	W. A. Smith	K. G. Cantrell	Edwards II	The Dip	Kamikaze	3.33.1
1964	Zinga Lee	8.7	D. Royle	W. J. McNabb	High Peak	Summer Regent	River Seine	3.23.3
1965	River Seine	8.7	G. Podmore	N. Prendergast	Tsaoko	Blue Shaun	Bon Filou	3.25.1
1966	Prince Grant	8.2	G. Moore	T. J. Smith	Alcimedes	High Principle	Gin and Bitters	3.24
1967	Galilee	9.7	J. Miller	J. B. Cummings	Alcimedes	Prince Grant	Striking Force	3.21.1
1968	General Command	9.3	G. Moore	W. Wilson	Agricola	Prominence	Padtheway	3.26.4
1969	Lowland	8.8	R. Higgins	J. B. Cummings	Agricola	Rain Lover	Rocket Fuel	3.24.4
1970	Arctic Symbol	7.9	N. Voigt	J. Moloney	Arctic Explorer	Lochcourt	Te Kura	3.35.8

* Race Record

DONCASTER HANDICAP, (1M.)
(Run at Randwick, Easter Carnival)

Year	Winner	Age	Rider	Wgt.	Trainer	Sire	Second Horse	Third Horse	Time
1916	Eurobin	4	W. Foulsham	8.13	—	Andria	Woorak	Brattle	1.39¼
1917	Wedding Day	4	M. Connell	8.0	—	Antonio	Polycrates	Whitefield	1.39
1918	Dame Acre	4	P. Maher	8.0	—	Linacre	Panacre	Cetigne	1.38
1919	Hem	5	T. F. McNamara	6.7	—	Featherstitch	Greenstead	King's Word	1.45¼
1920	Sydney Damsel	6	J. Killorn	8.4	—	King William	Chrysolaus	Mt. Frisco	1.37¾
1921	Specialty	3	J. Toohey	7.9	D. Lewis	Persian Knight	Wish Wynne	Beauford	1.37½
1922	Julia Grey	5	J. Toohey	8.12	A. E. Thompson	Paddington	Sir Maitland	Tressady Queen	1.38
1923	The Epicure	5	J. Toohey	8.2	—	The Sybarite	Duke Isinglass	Etive	1.38½
1924	Whittier	4	F. Dempsey	9.5	H. McCalman	Woorak	Trimacre	The Monk	1.36½
1925	Fujisan	3	G. Harrison	8.1	—	Valais	King Cyliene	All Sunshine	1.38¾
1926	Valicare	3	J. Munro	8.9	—	Valais	Valiant	Irish Prince	1.37¾
1927	Don Moon	4	K. Daniels	7.12	—	Don Reynaldo	Horoscope	Garrula	1.42¾
1928	Simeon's Fort	5	W. Duncan	8.5	M. T. McGrath	Hainault	Aorangi	Don Moon	1.45¼
1929	Karuma	4	J. Toohey	8.4	J. Carey	Magpie	Sion	Loquacious	1.38½
1930	Venetian Lady	5	D. Munro	8.5	E. F. Walker	Wolaroi	High Disdain	Raisin	1.37
1931	Sir Christopher	5	J. Munro	8.5	R. L. Cashman	Chysolaus	Mollison	Casque d'Or	1.37
1932	Jacko	3	D. Lightfoot	6.10	S. R. Lamond	Magpie	Legislator	Tom Pinch	1.37¼
1933	Winooka	4	J. Pike	9.13	M. Polson	Windbag	Jacko	Parkwood	1.35¾
1934	Chatham	5	J. Pike	10.4	F. Williams	Windbag	Golden Wings	Whittingham	1.40½
1935	Hall Mark	4	K. Voitre	9.8	J. Holt	Heroic	High	Silver King	1.37½
1936	Cuddle	5	M. McCarten	9.4	G. Price	Psychology	Cabalist	Barak	1.38
1937	Sarcherie	6	R. Maxwell	8.10	M. Webster	Archery	Silver Rose	Evening Mist	1.35½
1938	Hamurah	4	P. Hickey	7.9	W. Henderson	Salmagundi	King's Head	Buzalong	1.37½
1939	Gold Rod	5	M. McCarten	9.2	G. Price	Chief Ruler	Korimako	St. Constant	1.37
1940	Mildura	4	D. Munro	8.8	G. Price	Manfred	Beaulivre	El Golea	1.36¾
1941	Mildura	5	E. McMenamin	9.3	W. Gander	Manfred	Rimveil	Evergreen	1.35¼
1942	Tuhitarata	6	H. Badger	7.10	W. Gander	Simeon's Fort	Arahura	Evergreen	1.45¼
1943	Kingsdale	4	E. McMenamin	8.9	L. J. O'Sullivan	Andrea	Magi	Merrimba	1.36½
1944	Goose Boy	a	F. Shean	8.2	N. Dewsbury	Wee Warrah	Flight	Easter Time	1.36
1945	Abbeville	6	G. Bougoure	8.5	T. M. McGrath	Palfresco	Enthuse	Barnsley	1.40¼
1946	Blue Legend	3	J. Duncan	7.5	R. H. Abbott	Waikare	Abbeville	Sajakeda	1.40
1947	Blue Legend	4	H. Badger	8.11	R. H. Abbott	Waikare	Crusader	Wellington	1.41¾
1948	The Diver	5	G. Moore	7.12	T. J. Brosnan	The Buzzard	Fine Fettle	Murray Stream	1.38¾
1949	Bernbrook	3	N. Sellwood	8.4	H. T. Plant	Midstream	Vagabond	Mortar	1.36¼
1950	Grey Boots	4	R. Selkrig	7.7	H. V. Cooper	Nizami	Achilles	Buzmark	1.38¼
1951	Oversight	3	J. Thompson	7.13	F. Dalton	Beau Son	Davey Jones	Great World	1.36¼
1952	Prelate	4	R. Reed	7.0	J. Donohoe	School Tie	Iron Duke	Desert Warrior	1.39
1953	*Triclinium	4	H. Welch	7.4	D. Lewis	Genetout	Iroquois	Mardi Tout	1.35¼
1954	Karendi	4	W. Camer	8.4	Jack Green	Wayside Inn	Triclinium	Carioca	1.36
1955	Fire Dust	4	N. McGrowdie	7.10	G. Brown	Precept	Count Roussel	Prince Morvi	1.39
1956	Slogan II	4	J. Thompson	7.8	F. Dalton	Lucky Bag	King's Fair	Decisive	1.38.2
1957	Slogan II	5	J. Thompson	7.12	F. Dalton	Lucky Bag	Mac's Amber	Fire Dust	1.37.3
1958	Grenable	5	N. McGrowdie	8.5	F. B. Lewis	Bois De Rose	Teranyan	Theodric	1.35.2
1959	Tudor Hill	5	G. Howard	8.11	N. A. Francis	Ottoman	On Guard	Book Link	1.36.3
1960	Tudor Hill	6	G. Howard	9.0	N. A. Francis	Ottoman	In Love	Prince Lea	1.35
1961	Fine and Dandy	4	K. Smith	8.10	H. T. Plant	Star Kingdom	Friar's Peak	Sky High	† 1.34.2
1962	Te Poi	4	J. Thompson	7.5	R. A. Dickerson	Dogger Bank	Prince Regoli	Emboss	1.40.5
1963	Fine and Dandy	6	W. Pyers	8.12	H. T. Plant	Star Kingdom	Our Cobber	Merthyr	1.35
1964	Persian Puzzle	6	H. Molloy	8.7	S. W. Haydon	Persia	Papilio	Florida Keys	1.35.1
1965	Time and Tide	6	D. Lake	9.4	H. T. Plant	Star Kingdom	Our Fun	Ripa	1.37
1966	Citius	3	G. Moore	8.8	W. J. Murrell	Star Kingdom	Castanea	Bowl King	1.34.8
1967	Tobin Bronze	4	J. Miller	9.5	H. G. Heagney	Arctic Explorer	Cabochon	Redcap	1.35.4
1968	Unpainted	4	S. Spinks	8.10	T. J. Smith	The Cobber	Cabochon	Shakedown	1.34.7
1969	Bye Bye	4	N. Voigt	8.4	T. J. Smith	Wilkes	Foresight	Sandy's Hope	1.35.9
1970	Broker's Tip	4	H. Cope	8.11	H. H. Riley	Summertime	Alrello	Black Onyx	1.36.4

* Tarien finished first but was disqualified by order of the Stewards following a swab

† Race Record

311

HORSE INDEX

313

GENERAL INDEX